POTHOLES AND PAVEMENTS

POTHOLES AND PAVEMENTS

A Bumpy Ride on Britain's National
Cycle Network

LAURA LAKER

BLOOMSBURY SPORT
LONDON • OXFORD • NEW YORK • NEW DELHI • SYDNEY

BLOOMSBURY SPORT
Bloomsbury Publishing Plc
50 Bedford Square, London, WC1B 3DP, UK
29 Earlsfort Terrace, Dublin 2, Ireland

BLOOMSBURY, BLOOMSBURY SPORT and the Diana logo are trademarks
of Bloomsbury Publishing Plc

First published in Great Britain 2024

A catalogue record for this book is available from the British Library

Library of Congress Cataloguing-in-Publication data has been applied for

ISBN: PB: 978-1-3994-0646-8; eBook: 978-1-3994-0645-1;
ePdf: 978-1-3994-0644-4

2 4 6 8 10 9 7 5 3 1

Typeset in Minion Pro by Deanta Global Publishing Services, Chennai, India
Printed and bound in Great Britain by CPI Group (UK) Ltd., Croydon, CR0 4YY

For anyone who dreamed big, against the odds.

CONTENTS

FOREWORD

Potholes and Pavements is a little gem of a book. Here you will find travelogue, history and autobiography all entwined, plus a deep understanding of policy – and a fair dose of polemic to boot.

By the end, the reader comes to understand not merely the energy and enthusiasm which cycling often inspires, but the reasons for that enthusiasm, including its astonishing but still widely under-appreciated social, medical, economic and environmental benefits. And still more important, what we can do to realise them.

As every page makes clear, Laura Laker is not merely a brilliant writer about cycling; she has made it part of her life. The book charts her journeys around the UK, nominally along and in pursuit of the National Cycle Network, but also down a thousand smaller highways and byways, amid myriad local stories and personal experiences.

But Laura also introduces us to many of the key people and organisations that have made our nascent British active travel revolution possible. These include national figures such as John Grimshaw, Andrew Gilligan and Chris Boardman, but also a cast of dozens of other people moved by the simple desire to transform and reinvigorate their neighbourhoods. The picture is complex, and active travel is not, and should never be, a party-political matter. But as the book shows, it is a matter of political, public and private choice.

Rightly, Laura is especially alert to people who do not fit the standard caricature of middle-aged men in Lycra®: mothers with children, kids walking or biking to school, the elderly, people with disabilities, and those from poorer backgrounds and diverse heritage, but who are often left out of – sometimes inadvertently designed out of – the wider picture.

As other countries such as the Netherlands and Denmark demonstrate, cycling and active travel generally must be made universally accessible and available in this country.

And they can be so. But that requires central and devolved governments, local authorities, town and city leaders, companies large and small, cycling and walking organisations, enthusiasts and others to work together to create a sustaining culture and an array of new and consistently high-quality infrastructure.

That in turn means long-term investment, effective urban design, training for young people, and leaders at all levels willing to address often ungrounded public worries about such things as '15-minute cities' and the so-called 'war on drivers'.

The Department of Transport has done what it can over the past ten years, as I can testify from two tours of ministerial duty there. But the unwillingness of British government as a whole to recognise and support the health benefits of cycling in particular remains inexplicable.

As is often pointed out, if the effects of cycling in strengthening our physical and mental health, boosting our cardiovascular fitness and reducing our vulnerability to infection and dementia and a host of other conditions were more widely understood, it would be acclaimed as a miracle cure. Yet both funding and rhetoric remain patchy, inconsistent and low.

The Department of Health and Social Care has a crucial role to play here, both as regards social prescribing and support for cycling and active travel to boost the health of its own vast workforce. But this is a whole-of-government responsibility, and it demands as its counterpart a parallel process of investment by enlightened companies seeking to enhance the wellbeing of their employees.

Over the next decade, accelerating changes in technology will open up cycling and powered transport of all kinds to more and more users. But if we are to take full advantage of them, we need a significantly more serious, vigorous, joined-up and long-term strategy, which draws together public and private energies at all levels of British society. Let's do it.

Jesse Norman MP
Former Minister of State in the
Department for Transport

INTRODUCTION: FLIGHT

I'm flying. There's a railway bridge over a gorge, it's early spring, and me and my pink electric bicycle are on a 99-mile weekend adventure. Below us, huge dusky-coloured trees hold their bare branches to the sky and a wind, puffing down the valley like a steam train, briefly takes my breath away. I'm cycling the Devon coast-to-coast route on the National Cycle Network (NCN) and it has, as if by magic, conjured me across an otherwise hilly part of the UK, substantially on flat, traffic-free, ludicrously beautiful paths, following a former railway line. It has whooshed me alongside birds flitting busily down country lanes, past a churchyard bursting with flowers and a ruined Norman prison, from the English Channel to the Bristol Channel.

Momentarily the spell is broken. A liminal space appears between two farm gates plonked right across the path, where a rocky track meanders through a small wilderness. I take a short voyage beyond the looking glass, bumping along between saplings and scrub to a place where the railway never existed, and then, just as suddenly, I'm back, waddling through a farm gate, once more on a railway trail crossing Devon.

By this point, a year into my on/off exploration of around 1200 miles of the UK's approximately 13,000-mile network of signed cycling (and walking) paths, I'm perplexed, but not necessarily surprised that one of the UK's most famous and popular cycle routes is summarily barred by a landowner who whimsically reserves the right to close the path to users if the mood takes them.

I experienced wonderful things in my year exploring the NCN, cycling through landscapes that left me with little else to say but 'wow', from southern river estuaries to highland mountain passes, traversing cross-city cycle routes that each year make millions of

1

unremarkable, everyday cycling (and walking) trips possible. Along the way I met amazing people and had my mind totally changed about something I thought I knew everything about.

A decade ago, I discovered the NCN for the first time, cycling from Newcastle to Edinburgh along the route romantically dubbed Coast and Castles or, more prosaically, NCN1. Despite leading my friend and me over grassy clifftops, through muddy, rutted fields, along glass-strewn pavements that intermittently crossed busy roads, and more than once describing three sides of a square for no apparent reason, my fascination and frustration with the NCN began there, and has continued ever since. It's a feeling familiar to many who have tried to use the NCN to get somewhere. Somehow you can find yourself five miles from your destination with seven miles of cycling left to do – seven miles that could plausibly involve any of the above scenarios.

Over the years I've witnessed the NCN doing wonderful things for people, like reuniting communities after more than a century with a hugely ambitious walking and cycling bridge. I've looked at plans for an inter-city route that could perhaps replace motorway trips with cycling, walking and public transport. I've met people who have dedicated up to 40 years of their lives to achieving, against all odds, the impossible. I've seen lives unexpectedly transformed by cycling.

The UK is possibly one of the greatest places in the world to cycle. Our tiny island nation is wonderfully compact, with a diverse people, fascinating history and extraordinary natural and industrial wonders all squished together. You don't have to ride far to reach something of practical use or inspiration. Most of our trips are short: the 2022 National Travel Survey found that in England 71% of all trips we made were less than five miles. You or I could cycle that in less than 30 minutes, saving money, and fitting in a bit of exercise and, dare I say it, joy, into our day.

As things stand, we use a motor vehicle for 67% of trips of less than five miles. This is not always out of choice. Between half and three quarters of Brits want to cycle more, both for everyday trips and for fun, and polls say we support investment in everyday routes and leisure routes, even if it means taking road space from cars. The main reason we don't cycle more is an understandable fear of sharing space with motor traffic. Where cycling does exist in the UK, it does so in spite of the conditions. Funding, leadership and strategic planning have rarely come together at the same time, and yet when they do the results are transformative. As a journalist and cyclist I'm interested in what we could achieve if we let the bicycle, and pedal power in all its forms, reach its full potential.

While we'd expect a national highway system or rail network to follow consistent standards, with cycling in the UK anything goes. The NCN is, uniquely for a piece of national infrastructure, run by a charity, Sustrans, and its thousands of volunteers. They lack the powers to insist on certain standards and get by without reliable, long-term funding. You could think of the NCN as a strategic network, a series of spines across the UK with other connecting cycle routes delivered by councils, National Highways (the trunk roads body) and sometimes even local residents. What these routes have in common, other than a lack of consistent funds, is a historically spooky design approach, involving phantom bike lanes that disappear and reappear seemingly at random, just when you need them, say at busy junctions, or the poltergeists that shove cyclists on and off pavements with little warning. If you've ever wondered why cyclists don't use bike lanes, it's because of decades' worth of routes like this that are sometimes worse than nothing. Adding to its ghostlike appeal, only 26% of us have ever heard of the NCN.

None of this is deliberate. It's more a function of prevailing conditions. All Britain's cycle routes, NCN or not, are subject to the caprices of whether current politicians understand cycling or not (and they often don't), whether local authorities are willing to reallocate road space from motor traffic (many aren't) and whether a patchwork of landowners object to cyclists rambling through their estate.

In 2019 I attended Sustrans' opening of a mind-blowingly beautiful, off-road, loch-side NCN path outside Oban whose construction a caravan park owner had hampered for a decade because of concerns about passing path users' potential impact on holidaymakers. In the meantime, local children attempting to cycle to school had to choose between a muddy, unlit and overgrown path that became impassable in winter or a busy main road. This also happened to form part of the iconic 234-mile Caledonia Way, a jewel in the NCN's crown, a gorgeous adventure route crossing Scotland from Campbelltown to Inverness, which I then rode north-east over three days. It was frankly so ridiculously beautiful its memory almost brings a tear to my eye even now.

Despite my griping, what stayed with me most about my first NCN journey north to Edinburgh was its beauty, its wildness, and the way, with its tiny blue and red signs, it ushered me and my friend to some truly gorgeous parts of the UK. Over three days we struggled through windswept sand dunes and pedalled in wonder along a still-damp causeway to Lindisfarne Island at low tide as three swans flew low overhead, honking gently. We camped in high winds, passed epic castles and ended the ride, delighted, on Edinburgh's Royal Mile.

Along the way, long-distance cycle routes like these connect villages and homes, towns and even cities. In some countries, such routes have melded with fine-grained networks for cycling and walking, spreading, like fingers, into towns via a grid of safe, protected cycle routes and low traffic streets – just like roads. You can (and I did) cycle around the Netherlands predominantly on such separate cycle paths. In France, Germany and Denmark people enjoy such networks, from school age to old age – it's just another part of the transport network; the part that actively improves people's health and wellbeing every day.

While this book is about my journeys on the NCN, it is about cycle routes of every stripe: those built by councils in towns and cities, and by volunteers in rural areas. It is also about people. The NCN matters because it's emblematic of cycling routes up and down the UK. And even if you don't cycle, how we get about every day matters. When the traffic snarls up on our local roads because driving is the only option available, whether we're travelling for one mile or 50, it can make our daily lives needlessly frustrating and stressful.

Millions of Britons are trapped into car ownership, because of a lack of alternative transport options. We spend, on average, 13% of our gross income on them, according to research, rising to 19% with finance deals. Taxpayers have forked out roughly £80 billion since 2010 in fuel duty subsidies, which, research has found, has increased our carbon emissions by 7% by making driving cheaper than other options. Transport is the single biggest contributor to our carbon emissions – 34% of our total with road transport most of that – and it has remained stubbornly high, largely because we've failed to adequately fund the alternatives.

More cycling, walking and wheeling – which includes mobility aids like wheelchairs and handcycles – is always a positive; 'active travel' could improve a litany of societal woes. That includes our finances, but also our health: physical inactivity is responsible for one in six deaths in the UK, a toll equal to smoking. Aside from the heart-breaking emotional cost of losing loved ones early – something I've experienced first-hand – this costs the UK £7.4 billion annually and the NHS almost £1 billion.

Getting active can help prevent colon cancer by 30%, heart disease by up to 35%, type 2 diabetes by up to 40%, depression and dementia by up to 30%, and hip fractures by up to 68%. If we make exercise part of our everyday lives, we don't even notice we're doing it and we're much more likely to stick at it – not least because it's plain fun. There is barely a thing that couldn't be made better if cycling and walking were a viable part of our everyday lives – and that's just one of the things that makes it so great. It also makes the places we live and travel to fairer and far more pleasant.

Even if we cycled just once a week, one study found, we could cut our carbon footprint by a quarter, as well as reducing congestion. Because even electric cars produce harmful particulates from their brakes and tyres, we would improve air quality, no matter which car we drove.

The year I sat down to write this book marked a little over 10 years since I started writing full-time about cycling. After various unfinished courses, firings from jobs I didn't like and changes of direction, journalism, and writing about cycling, and transport more broadly, was the only thing that I found I could stick at. The more I learned about it, the more I saw its potentially transformative impact on our lives. The more I did it, the more I loved it.

As a child, I disliked sports lessons with a passion. If another kid or a teacher yelled at me to run for a ball, I would stubbornly walk. This meant that formal exercise wasn't part of my life until almost adulthood. I fell into riding a bike while at university, as a means of getting about London. I'd moved from Cardiff to London to complete a degree in health and nutrition. I noticed one day my course mate, Szilvia, had arrived damp and gleaming from the rain. When I realised she'd cycled in, I was perplexed. I couldn't understand why anyone would voluntarily get on a bike in wet weather, let alone why they would look so happy about it.

I had a lovely new blue Trek bike, thanks to an insurance claim, and Szilvia persuaded me to cycle in with her one day. We lived near one another in north London and as I struggled to keep up with her alongside Regent's Park on the way home that afternoon my mind was entirely changed. Suddenly London was available on my schedule and in a far more vivid way than I'd ever experienced it. I can still remember the distinct smell of a coffee roastery I passed on the way to uni. I was hooked. Soon I was cycling in all weathers. You couldn't stop me, and my blogs from those early days speak of a newfound zeal for London, life and cycling that others who have rediscovered cycling in adulthood will recognise.

I slowly built myself a career as a freelance journalist while working at various temping assignments across London. I now spend most of my working life writing for a variety of specialist and national titles on transport and active travel, as well as co-hosting a well-loved podcast on active travel, *Streets Ahead*. Despite being an eternal amateur in the act of cycling, I clock up thousands of incidental miles in London each year, occasionally heading off, ill-equipped, on poorly thought-out cycling adventures.

The COVID-19 pandemic saw a cycling renaissance, as roads suddenly emptied of motor vehicles were reclaimed by people on foot and on bikes. During the first months of lockdowns, cycling grew by 100% on weekdays in England and 200% on weekends, and visitor numbers on the NCN rose by 19%. Around the world, governments' interest in two-wheeled transport accelerated, including in the UK. Acknowledging cycling's value in keeping people healthy and moving, at the behest of the UK governments, councils rolled out emergency cycling and walking infrastructure, from pop-up bike lanes to widened pavements to low traffic neighbourhoods (LTNs), some of which were made permanent.

In Leicester, one of the many cities to embrace the challenge, a mile per week of new main-road bike lanes were rolled out at their peak, at just over £29,000 per mile – a bargain basement price when you consider a trunk road comes in somewhere at around £1 billion per mile. England and the transport-devolved governments of Wales, Scotland and Northern Ireland all increased their cycling spend and ambitions. What followed was a time of change for the NCN too.

While our national road and rail networks enjoy dedicated government-backed bodies, with regular funding for maintenance and improvement, the NCN enjoys the loving support of a charity and its dedicated staff and volunteers, with a ragbag of stop-start funding from government, donations and private funds. The NCN is a network connecting a slightly random selection of towns, cities, places of beauty, hilltops and villages across the country, where conditions allow, and it is incredibly patchy in nature, with a correspondingly patchy reputation.

In 2020 I broke the news that Sustrans, the charity in charge of the NCN, would cut 25% of the network, or de-designate it, while improving 55 sections, because it was no longer up to a safe standard. This was long overdue: in the network's 40-odd years the once-quiet roads cyclists had shared with motor traffic had become busier and, in a rush for network miles, some thoroughly unsuitable sections had been added – along with more than 16,000 barriers on its traffic-free routes.

Chicane fences and odd-shaped bits of metal, added with good intentions to prevent motorbike riders using the network, inadvertently locked out wheelchair users and those with non-standard cycles, like cargo bikes or tricycles. If you can't lift your bike, these barriers can be a struggle to navigate even with a standard cycle. A pledge to cut those miles and remove those barriers was an honest recognition of the flaws, and an attempt to ensure novice cyclists who started a journey on the NCN would be able to finish it. Two years earlier, in an article I wrote for the *Times*, Sustrans' CEO, Xavier Brice, admitted to me many of the NCN's paths were 'crap' – an acknowledgement something urgently needed to change.

These issues didn't dampen the network's popularity, however: by 2020 4.9 million people took 765 million trips on it. While more than half of trips on the network, per traffic-free mile, are cycling ones, the rest are made on foot. That's right: while it's called the 'National Cycle Network', it actually carries more walking trips – 410 million in 2018 to 377 million cycling trips – and most of the time those users share a single path, which brings its own issues.

The enormous growth in cycling, both on and off the UK's NCN and indeed around the world, was a change in wind direction made possible only when we put our cars away for a few months. It swept away the noise, danger and pollution on ordinary streets, revealing just how much space had become dominated by motor traffic. The sight of all kinds of people pedalling tentatively around their neighbourhoods, and then slowly further afield, reminded us that with safe, quiet roads, people will choose to cycle. New pop-up lanes into town and city centres expanded the bicycle's potential further, demonstrating that not only would we ride in our free time, but we would cycle to work, to the shops and to school.

The trouble was, once the traffic started returning, and some of the pop-up routes were dismantled the wind shifted once more and we got back into our cars. Bikes, momentarily liberated, were relegated back to their sheds and garages. The window that briefly blew open, though, offered a beguiling whiff of clean air and birdsong; an alternate reality in which we could perhaps do things differently or even – dare we say it – better. However, would we remember this time once the bustle of life had returned? And would we have the collective courage to keep that window open?

1

FALLING OUT

In early 2022, emerging from lockdown and having barely left London in two years, I was longing for adventure. I desperately needed to reconnect with the things I loved – not least cycling. I was stressed and in debt from some major emergency work on my roof, and each time I got a whiff of the open road or a view of some countryside I would sigh pathetically. I perhaps didn't fully realise it at the time, but I desperately needed a break. I'd witnessed a pandemic transformation of my home streets in east London into a Low Traffic Neighbourhood (LTN), and a lot had changed in the wider city for walking and cycling. It felt like a good time to get out on the road.

In fact, since May 2021 the huge growth in cycling had been subsiding amid resurgent motor traffic levels. There was a sense that active travel gains, and all the benefits they brought, were slipping away as pop-up cycle routes, introduced by councils in 2020 by government edict and with government funding, were removed by local politicians fearful of a growing backlash from small but vocal parts of their electorate. Some residents were concerned road changes would stop them going about their lives, while business owners worried replacing parking with cycle lanes and expanded pavements would harm footfall.

While understandable, many of these fears were unfounded – no-one would be prevented from reaching their homes in LTNs, for example, and where businesses are concerned, research shows people on foot and bikes spend more in shops than those who arrive by car. However, fuelled by hyperbole and misinformation on social media, local campaigns and messaging groups, the flames of worry were fanned into mild panic. Budget cuts meant councils lacked the staff and expertise to hold the public conversations needed to allay those fears, and cries that the changes, albeit experimental, were an undemocratic assault on freedoms took hold. At the time, representative polls found more than three quarters of people supported reducing traffic in their local area, and more than two thirds the reallocation of road space for walking and cycling, but those who opposed them shouted loudest and those were the voices we heard. Meanwhile, the cracks in the UK's transport system were about to be revealed by a summer of rail strikes and the looming threat of funding cuts to already decimated bus services.

It was 45 years since the first NCN route was built and, while it is a broad network, crisscrossing the country, it is not the entirety of the UK's cycle routes. However, if the NCN is emblematic of cycling in the UK, exploring it by bike seemed a good way to take the temperature of our nation's cycle provision as a whole. Looking at the map of the NCN, available as a layer of the digital Ordnance Survey map, I realised it was possible to follow it roughly around the outside of the country, tracing the coastline. I both love the sea and have an incredibly poor sense of direction, so keeping the water on my left seemed, if not foolproof, then at least helpful.

The vague idea was to travel from my home in London via the Thames Path and keep going around the outside of the country. I wouldn't attempt to ride it all – I didn't need to be completist and anyway at the time the NCN totalled more than 12,000 miles – so I'd pick up some sections where I left off over multiple days and other parts I'd skip, depending where the wind blew me. I wanted to use my pink electric bike – it has a motor that gives you a boost when you pedal – for some of it and my 'gravel' bike – basically a road bike with slightly chunkier tyres for use off-road – for the rest.

I don't believe riding a bike needs to involve any suffering. To me, it's there as a tool for exploration and adventure. As with most of my other trips, if I got tired or wanted to change course, I would. I would go where the NCN took me and sometimes where it didn't, and I'd explore as much of it as I could, to understand what makes it what it is and what could make it better. The goal was not to break any records. I'd do the trips around my other work schedules and around train stations.

When the idea of cycling around the country on the NCN occurred to me in late 2021, I instigated a recce along a hitherto undiscovered segment of the network near me, south towards the Thames. It was a mild Sunday in December and my boyfriend, a recent convert to cycling, was tempted outside by the prospect of a mini-adventure on his brand-new bike. I packed a thermos of coffee and two mince pies in a rucksack and off we went. We'd cycle as far as we fancied and then head back, hopefully in time to see the last few laps of a Grand Prix race on TV.

NCN1 runs the length of the UK's east coast all the way from Inverness to Dover. It passes within a couple of miles of my home in east London and I've cycled the 13 miles north along the Lea River to Waltham Abbey scores of times. It's one of my favourite mini-adventures, taking in a nature reserve, dipping under echoey bridges and past morsels of the river's hundreds of years of industrial heritage. However, on weekends when walkers and cyclists are confined to a narrow gravel path with an open body of water inches away, it's less attractive.

Keen to avoid any hint of a towpath, I pick a point on the Ordnance Survey map's NCN layer close to home, after NCN1 leaves the River Lea. We ride my local cycle superhighway, a protected main road bike lane that starts just over a mile from my house, and runs past Mile End Park and all the way into the city. Our first indication we are on NCN1 comes just as we leave the park, at an unassuming pedestrian crossing; the kind bordered by narrow, fenced-in pavements, where you have to waddle astride the bike to press the button and then wait for the green man.

The NCN is often invisible to the casual observer for two reasons, the first being its signage. When I pull my phone out to take a photo of what feels like a symbolic first sighting, I'm asked what I'm doing. I point out a blue sticker on the far traffic-light post, with a red square containing a number '1'. My boyfriend seems astonished by this discovery. I realise at this moment how weird it is that while drivers get large, dedicated road signs for every occurrence (ducks crossing, anyone?), a fairly significant route traversing almost 700 miles along the spine of the country gets a large print-run involving a lot of sticky-backed plastic.

Undeterred for now, we cross and make our slow way down a thankfully brief section of towpath, stopping to pull into the foliage each time we meet someone coming the other way, because my other half, an uncertain cyclist, is understandably afraid of falling in the water. The second reason people often don't notice the NCN is because it mostly doesn't involve any dedicated cycling infrastructure – it is parasitic – hence the shared pavements, the pedestrian crossings, the narrow towpaths. We meet 'Cyclists dismount' signs at busy road crossings. We budge out of the way of runners and by now my other half is enthusiastically photographing cycling signs, too, half in fascination, half dismay.

After this we are in business, though, finding the NCN at its best: a beautiful segment of cobbled street with the pale magnificence of St Anne's Church in Limehouse and its crown-like tower to one side, and Georgian terraces overlooked by the overground railway. 'Let's live here,' I hear – one of his favourite refrains, whether we can afford it or not. Old warehouses, still painted with names of their owners of a century ago, and gantries with pulley wheels overhead flank a quiet neighbourhood square with a café and corner shop. These give way to newer gated apartments, built during the 1980s redevelopment of Canary Wharf. 'I want to live here,' he calls out again, demanding we stop to look in an estate agent's window.

We finally reach the Thames. I always love the moment of meeting the river, the sudden broad views across the sparkling water, in this case towards Canary Wharf's towers and more former warehouse buildings. We stop for another photo and weave gently among the many people out taking a Sunday stroll. The Thames Path is gorgeous, following the north side of the river before crossing via the Greenwich foot tunnel and continuing towards Erith on the Thames Estuary. On the way it passes old London pubs, expensive apartment blocks and crumbling wooden piers topped with cormorants, which eventually give way to post-industrial dereliction.

We're not going that far today, though; we'll stay on the north side of the river before returning home. A couple of times we miss our tiny blue signs and have to backtrack or check the OS map, but it's shown us bits of London we wouldn't otherwise have seen. We discover a delightful little wharf surrounded on three sides by brick-built warehouses overlooking a tranquil square of water. We pass beautiful houseboats, the homely, adventuring kind that look like they may have even been to sea and made friends with the odd whale.

We stop at a second wharf where a group of windsurfers are practising and I put on all the extra layers in my rucksack. We sit on a wall and gaze across the water, passing the tiny thermos cup between us and trying to stop the mince pie cases blowing away. My other half is delighted with our ride, as am I. It will be a good 20km there and back, which is a lot for him. I ask him what he thinks of the NCN. His answer: 'It's good but it's not a network.'

That festive bike ride was both the beginning and the end of a journey. In early February our relationship exploded in a huge and largely unexpected argument, after which I returned home and realised he had taken everything he valued and moved out. We tried to patch it up over the coming days and weeks, but had to admit our relationship, which had spanned two and a half years and a pandemic, had ended.

The roof emergency had left my bank account at the edge of its overdraft, so I said yes to every bit of work I could. The deadlines kept rolling in and I kept meeting them, if not quite on time, then forgivably close. In the evenings I'd paint the attic walls and put up wallpaper, listening to podcasts about self-care and compassion. From the start of the year onward, my heart thumped in my chest, accompanied by a constant sense of rising dread, and things stayed that way for months. I'd wake up at 3 or 4 am, not knowing where I was, my heart racing, and lay there for hours unable to sleep. Occasionally, in a daze, I'd catch sight of myself in a mirror looking, as PG Wodehouse would have described it, like an owl with a secret sorrow. I'd pick up objects, turn them over and put them down again, as if unable to solve a puzzle. Outwardly everything seemed normal, and friends remarked on how well I was coping. In truth I hadn't had time to process what had happened, I was just surviving.

Even in the worst moments a bike ride, or indeed any time outdoors, has a supernatural ability for healing, and thankfully I had a lot of time ahead of me outdoors if I was going to explore the NCN for this book.

It was a dry, warm spring, so I began my first forays in March and carried on riding through the summer and into the following spring, catching trains and cycling for anywhere between a day and a couple of weeks. I would end up criss-crossing the country, meeting all sorts of people along the way. I'd meet those I knew and those I didn't. I wanted to talk to people who worked at all levels on the front line of improving the lot not just of people who call themselves cyclists, but of those who don't yet cycle. As well as being a personal process of healing and renewal, the purpose of the trip would be to take the pulse of the NCN; to understand how sick the patient is and, ultimately, how we can put cycling at the heart of how we get around.

2

FOUNDING A NETWORK

Living without a car in the UK can be a challenge, because while roads take us everywhere we need to go by car, the same cannot be said for public transport, walking and cycling. Right now, even using those alternative methods in combination requires a level of determination and a gung-ho spirit that understandably puts most people off.

In spring 2022 I set off for the weekend to visit some much-loved friends near Hay-on-Wye and, because I don't own a car, I had just such a challenge on my hands. It's 20-ish miles between Hay and Hereford Station as the crow flies and 21 miles by the most direct road route, but I'm fascinated to learn, studying the map, that it is a full 49.5 miles via the NCN, detouring along the undeniably beautiful edge of the Brecon Beacons, with three times as much climbing (3625 feet) as the main roads.

I'm a little less fit than usual after winter, so I decide to bring along Lily, my pink electric bike. A former hire bike and pre-named, she changed my life. Even as a regular cyclist, clocking up thousands of miles a year, she makes far more trips possible by bike, including if I need to get somewhere and not be sweaty. However, even with Lily's 50-mile range, such a long and hilly a detour doesn't make sense, so it's a case of studying maps to avoid the worst main roads and hoping for the best. Because we don't have a network of cycle routes, this means making up my own way, using the roads and any likely look-ing off-road paths.

My cycle navigation app routes me along a hodge-podge of pave-ment cycle paths outside Hereford Station. A half-decent cycle lane saves me from the main road traffic out of town and then I'm led along a dirt path on a former railway line. It's boggy from the winter's rain. Birds sing loudly as the bike fishtails through the mud, rolling fields give way to the deep blue of distant hills and I take a deep, grateful breath. I have that feeling I often do when cycling of just being glad to be alive and out on the road.

Trying to avoid the direct but terrifying A-road, I have the choice of trespassing through a field or taking a farm track. I opt for the latter and end up knee-high in a puddle that looked innocent enough on approach. The ebike motor in the rear wheel is entirely submerged, but somehow keeps on working. I miss the country lane I've been aiming for and woman-handle the bike for a further two miles through waterlogged orchards and field margins. I occasionally pause and consider the beauty of the rolling countryside and fields, and I marvel with some passers-by as a military plane flies so low overhead I can practically count the rivets. I'm pelted with hail so emphatic it rings my bicycle bell and stings my eyelids, and by the time I arrive at my friends' house, a good three hours after disem-barking in Hereford, my lips are blue and me and the pink bike are thoroughly caked in mud, although thankfully everything inside my trusty panniers is dry.

———

In 1977 a group of Bristolian renegades were similarly frustrated at a lack of decent cycle routes in their area. At that time there was almost nothing by way of cycling infrastructure in the UK. The country was entering a decade of rapid growth in car ownership, while cycling rates had plummeted.

In the 1950s, cycling was a very normal means of transport in the UK: around a third of distance travelled was by bike, which was more than in the Netherlands at the time. However, within two decades cycling had become an outlier in Britain, as with much of Europe. By then, UK roadbuilding programmes and growing relative prosperity had accelerated car ownership, and the roads became deadlier places. Many UK bike builders went out of business as everyday cycling declined and leisure models dominated the remaining bicycle shops – as cycling historian David Hembrow puts it, heavy mountain bikes with knobbly tyres, and not a practical mudguard or pannier rack in sight.

Similarly, rail travel was being sidelined. In 1961, partially cannibalised by the growth in motor transport and air travel, the railways were running at an operating loss of £86.9 million. While vehicle taxes funded roads, the Treasury was subsidising train travel and the UK government believed that transport, unlike healthcare or education, should fund itself.

The Beeching Report, named after its author Dr Richard Beeching and published in 1963, recommended maintaining the profitable intercity services and high-speed lines, and cutting many of the stopping services on single track branch lines. Around half of all stations and a third of all route miles should be closed, it said – and, a few exceptions aside, saved by local campaigns, they were. At a time when less than 12% of the population owned cars, it left communities on the scrapped lines the choice of taking the bus if there was one, buying a car or cycling.

Cycling wasn't particularly tempting. In 1966, as traffic volumes had grown, so had road casualties. That year 7895 people were killed on Britain's roads, the highest peacetime traffic fatality rate. By the late 1970s and early 1980s the situation had improved slightly (even as the population increased by two million in two decades and vehicle miles tripled), thanks to drink driving legislation, vehicle and road improvements, and road safety campaigns, but the roads still claimed almost 6000 lives annually: per mile travelled, road users back then were between two and six times more likely to be killed than today.

Towns, cities and the countryside were being reshaped and bulldozed to facilitate a rise in motor traffic, while new motorways, at the time tourist attractions in their own right, were rolled out at pace. Pedestrians and cyclists were sidelined and, as motor vehicles were increasingly prioritised, traffic volumes grew, and walking and cycling felt less and less safe or appealing. Public transport was on the decline, too, and access to the streets – a public space – increasingly required access to a car.

Although the cause of death and destruction was clear, public safety announcements turned to the most vulnerable to protect themselves from this onslaught. The Green Cross Code was relaunched in 1978 with David Prowse, the actor who played Darth Vader in the original *Star Wars* films, instructing pedestrians on how not to get run down in the street. This is a trend that continues today in road safety campaigns that hand hi-vis jackets to children walking to school, but fail to tackle the driver behaviour that puts them at risk.

Cyclists weren't always on board with cycling improvements, where they did happen – and some opposed separate cycle routes, fearing it would erode cyclists' right to use the roads. This went as far back as the 1930s, when experimental, physically separated cycle routes were being built in Britain, albeit not always very good ones. As cycling historian Carlton Reid put it, though, 'there was little appetite to provide anything at all for them, despite the fact that they far outnumbered motorists'. This debate, whether cyclists should simply be brave and ride in the road with traffic, has rumbled on ever since. I will say, if that were an acceptable solution, everyone would surely be doing it. The fact is, in a nation with few decent cycle routes, only the fit and the brave are cycling.

In 1977 the Bristol branch of the environmental campaign group Friends of the Earth held a rally calling for cycling provision in the city. At the time the A4, the main road from London to Fishguard, ran right through its heart, past the cathedral where the protesters gathered. It was busy, dangerous and noisy, and made for a presumably fairly hairy cycling experience for the few still attempting it.

One Bristol resident, a tall civil engineer named John Grimshaw, was asked to address the crowd. John, then in his early 30s, was an imposing, well-spoken man with curly hair and a deep voice. He was tired by the lack of progress from campaigning alone and part of a growing movement within Friends of the Earth, and beyond, concerned about the future of the planet and our impact on the environment. Not entirely sure what to say, he launched a campaign group with a fellow resident, George Platts, to try and force change.

In 1974 John had written a 22-page report making the case for the bicycle as everyday transport in the city. Titled *Cycling in Bristol*, in almost every way it could have been written today. In it, John questioned the focus on motor car provision to the exclusion of cycling, walking and bus travel at a time of soaring energy costs, and when most commutes were less than three miles long – hardly efficient use of a private car.

By the autumn, protesters organised themselves under the new campaign group, Cyclebag, which stood for Channel Your Calf and Leg Energy into Bristol Action Group. Around 75 men and women lay down in Bristol's Castle Park, forming the spokes of an enormous wheel, with bicycles on kickstands sporting colourful balloons as its rim. Grimshaw later claimed this act was deemed so offensive to a nearby hotel that the council was persuaded to landscape the park to prevent it happening again. The council was less keen on landscaping the city for cycle routes, however, and the group quickly realised their protest tactics weren't working.

When my forays into the NCN began, I knew I needed to talk to John Grimshaw, its founding father. Early emails and phone calls led to later meetings in person and over the coming year or more we were periodically in contact. John explains circumstances 'just came together' by chance for what came next. 'Basically, in Bristol in 1974 you knew the name of every cyclist you met, there were that few,' he says. 'And there wasn't a millimetre of cycling infrastructure.' Naturally, those few cyclists started to get together to push for change.

He recalls, 'After about 18 months of hopeless campaigning, because the politicians weren't interested, Cyclebag turned its attention to the resources that we did have.' As an engineer one resource he identified was the land for potential cycle routes – and while such land generally belonged to Avon County Council and British

Waterways, it was a resource they could lobby to use. The obvious options for cycling in a very hilly city like Bristol were its relatively flat disused railways and river valleys.

In 1978 Grimshaw and his colleagues were confident young men from upper middle-class backgrounds with the belief they could shape the world around them – and they believed they had right on their side. They mounted their bicycles and began exploring those potential routes, drawing up designs for new cycling and walking paths as they went. At the time, Grimshaw says, they didn't think they had the muscle to obtain use of one of the now disused railways and settled on a riverside path between Bristol and Bath. At the time, anyone wanting to cycle the 13-odd miles between the two cities would face not only the growing volumes of motor traffic, but some stiff climbs along the way.

Things moved quickly. Defying expectations, in 1979 Avon County Council leased the group a stretch of disused railway near Bath for £1 a year and Cyclebag, under its new construction company, Sustainable Transport Ltd, began work. While Avon County Council had granted planning permission for the work, there was no funding, so John persuaded a charitable trust of the Clarks family shoe empire to give them £10,000 for materials on the half-joking promise he would build them a rough path that would wear out plenty of shoes.

In just three months, in the summer of 1979 a 'small army of committed volunteers' constructed what would become the first five miles of the NCN, by hand, on the former railway line from Bitton Station to Bath. Fulfilling John's promise to Clarks, on top of the flat ballast they poured around 1600 tonnes of limestone dust.

It's hard to overstate what an achievement this was, against a prevailing wind of automotive growth, no municipal support and laughably small sums of money. With this significant success under their belts, they ramped up their efforts.

John and the group's knack for networking and PR began to shine, attracting an official visit from the Secretary of State for Transport, Norman Fowler, to view the new path. The day Fowler and his wife arrived, Grimshaw 'made sure everyone in Bristol was on it' to prove its popularity – which worked until everyone broke the fourth wall and stopped to introduce themselves to the minister.

In 1981 the UK government, seeing the potential for other traffic-free paths, commissioned John Grimshaw and Associates to produce a report on the rest of England and Wales' disused railways. Bill Clarke, then Cyclebag's secretary, co-ordinated the survey and in 1985 a Scottish equivalent followed. Of the 10,000 miles of lines decommissioned by Beeching, Grimshaw and Clarke estimated 8000 were 'impossible to recover', having fallen into fragmented private ownership. The remaining 2000 miles became the starting point for further cycle routes. 'Now of course, no-one took any action on it because, like every other government report, every time nothing ever happened,' John tells me wryly, after four decades' first-hand experience.

Meanwhile, Cyclebag kept digging, taking on some fairly ambitious projects. They built a path on an inaccessible part of the River Avon between Bristol and Pill by hacking at a rock face and constructing a new causeway above the high tide mark (although it would later periodically flood). On the job 'conditions were fairly rudimentary,' a report from the time reads, 'with the main site base . . . nothing more than a nearby railway arch, and the tool store a cache hidden under a bush.' Even in the early days, recognising the potential of the path for the whole community, they stipulated shallow gradients for wheelchair users. They then turned their attention to the Kennet and Avon Canal from Bath to Bradford-on-Avon. Construction was a community affair with a celebratory element: families with young children would come along and someone had often cooked something for everyone to eat at trestle tables on site.

Officials would arrive to view progress, and grant permissions and funding, often apparently in bad weather, with sometimes slapstick consequences. One horrible day in 1982 a man from the Countryside Commission, on a grant-funding inspection, slipped off the Kennet and Avon Canal towpath, piled high with years of dredging silt, into the water. On a visit to the waterlogged Staplehill Tunnel, which was filled with fog during a temperature inversion, a planning committee chair fell over 'something soft and soggy', an unidentified horror lying in the flooded tunnel.

These mishaps didn't harm the cause: the Countryside Commission official granted the funding, while the planning chair gave the necessary permission to use the Staplehill Tunnel, bringing them closer to realising the full 13-mile Bristol to Bath route.

Trying to break the council's ongoing apathy, Cyclebag repeatedly turned up outside Avon County Council's offices with slogans daubed on rolls of polypropylene fabric used as path underlay. In huge lettering they called for funding and support for the completion of the Bristol and Bath Railway Path. The team continued work on the former railway line that cut between Bristolians' homes and schools in the north-east of the city, softening the featureless path with trees and landscaping. Around 500 volunteers finished the final quarter of a mile of the route in four days over the spring bank holiday of 1985. Within six years, 13 miles of route were built – with little funding from the council. For the path's grand opening, a band turned up to play under a bridge, double bass, clarinets, violins and all. By 1992, the charity claimed, using manual counts, the Bristol and Bath path carried a million cycling and walking journeys per year.

Meanwhile John was working full time as a consultant, 'building reservoirs and multi-storey car parks and all that sort of stuff.' He was also one of the engineers who built the Ffestiniog Railway in North Wales in the late 1960s and knew what could be done with volunteers. 'It's easy to motivate people, really. You have to give them a challenge, don't you?'

In 1978, the then Labour government launched a youth training scheme, which expanded under Margaret Thatcher's Conservative government. The Youth Opportunities Programme's purpose was to help 16- to 18-year-olds into employment, providing employers with free labour, and informal on-the-job training for participants. John saw an opportunity and grabbed it.

Using hundreds of these workers, construction ramped up on salvageable disused railways, with up to nine routes being built in parallel at one time. 'We just jumped in,' he said, adding, 'At the peak we had about 900 people working for us, all paid for by the government. At that stage we were still a tiny organisation – I was the only engineer, plus those 900 people, plus a few office support people. Crucially, the scheme provided supervisors on site, some of whom became core professionals at the heart of [what later became] Sustrans.'

They were hard times for the scheme's young participants, John recalls. Some were in fairly desperate situations, the extent of which became evident when they turned up to work. 'They would come without food because they were impoverished,' he says, matter-of-factly. As with other challenges that came their way, the group found a solution. 'We would buy a sack of potatoes, cook them over a fire under a bridge and feed them before we started work.'

YOP, and similar employment schemes that followed it, weren't uncontroversial either as some questioned how useful this informal work was for the participants themselves and the supposed goal of getting them into work. For right or wrong, though, these people, who had nothing, played a crucial role in the early construction of the NCN.

After building a handful of routes across the country, in 1984 John and his colleagues set up the charity Sustrans, a shortening of the earlier construction company name, Sustainable Transport, to buy and sell the land necessary to build and finance these routes. Their first commission outside the Bristol area involved converting an eight-mile stretch of disused railway between York and Selby. Local cycle campaigners had raised a petition with 1000 signatures, and wrote to the Prime Minister and the National Coal Board, who owned the tracks, urging for the cycle route to be built.

Permission was granted, the Countryside Commission would fund it and John agreed to do the work, 'because you always say yes to everything,' so Sustrans agreed to buy the land for £1. This nominal sum resulted from a piece of theatre allowing one body to dispose of a liability and another to gain an asset. The two worked out the value of the structure or piece of land on one hand, and the cost of its upkeep on the other, and the difference would always conveniently come to £1. Then, selling the crushed stone ballast from the former railway line to the York ring road project helped fund construction of the path.

Sustrans worked in areas of the country with strong cycle campaign groups, places they knew there was a groundswell for safe routes. John says, 'We relied entirely on local groups and then key players from those local groups came across to join our staff when we had money to pay people.' New paths also had to be accessible by train and bike from Bristol. By the mid-1980s they had constructed links between York and Selby, and Derby and Melbourne, along with the Liverpool Loop, and Consett and Sunderland paths.

Over time, John's network of campaigners and local officials grew. However, he recalls that not everyone was on board: 'There were campaigners who were very much against what we were doing, because they said it was a local authority's job and, if we did it, the local authorities wouldn't. But I took the view that if the local authorities weren't doing it, nothing would happen.' This debate rumbles on today.

The matter of funding was a tangled maze that Sustrans became adept at navigating and, as work ramped up, so did their considerable fundraising efforts. Central government didn't fund cycle routes in the 1980s, so the list of sources reads like the periodic table song – a bewildering array of names.

While the Countryside Commission was a major funder, along with British Waterways, John explains each project came with its own local entanglement of contributors. 'Typically, you had money from the county [council], money from the district, money from a parish, money from the Countryside Commission, money from the job creation scheme.'

This confusion didn't always play well, however. John says, 'I remember an auditor coming in from the government and he said, "How many sources of funds do you have?" And I said, "Well, we've got five projects on the go at the moment and each has on average five funding bodies. Therefore, I'd say we've got 25 sources of funds." And he looked at me and said, "If you've got 25 sources of funds, you must be corrupt. We only fund organisations that have one source." Would you believe the Department of Transport then decided to remove the small grant they had given us? They felt we couldn't possibly be managing things properly.' John dismisses my suggestion it was an administrative nightmare; it was just how things were done back then or 'the background drudgery' as he describes it.

Construction of the paths themselves was fairly straightforward, John says, not least for a civil engineer. 'It's not like building a motorway. It's just a question of doing a few sketches and assembling contractors.' It was then up to a growing team of workers to translate those sketches into paths. In the early days those contractors were the youth workers and volunteers, and once those individuals had done it once or twice, they knew what they were doing and could replicate the work. Some of the old railways' drainage systems, often a combination of humps and ditches, had failed over time and needed rebuilding, but in essence you'd clear some trees, flatten the ground, and lay a surface with the limestone dust or, with sufficient funding, tarmac on top.

The big challenge was connecting the railway paths to the road network, neighbourhoods and town centres. Ideally people could easily reach these traffic-free paths from homes, workplaces, shops and schools along the way. Work teams constructed as many access points to the new paths as they could, but the time it took to make the necessary agreements with local authorities and a lack of funding for urban routes meant there were often fewer than John would have liked. Some of those routes still conceal the famous slogan-daubed polypropylene used as protest banners.

Then the wind changed. Free labour and the funding that came with it threatened to dry up as YOP and its successors ended in 1989. Anticipating the end, Sustrans' staff were put on a month's notice, though many clung on until the end in the hope the money would appear. The loss of funding came as a recession hit and local councils reorganised. Meanwhile, motor travellers were receiving ever more largesse. That year Margaret Thatcher launched 'roads for prosperity', dubbed 'the biggest roadbuilding programme since the Romans'. Back then cars, not bicycles, meant aspiration and in many places they still do.

In the nick of time, a funding-savvy powerhouse appeared. Then development director of Friends of the Earth, Carol Freeman had heard about this charity turning disused railways into cycle routes and, enthused about its work, moved over to Sustrans. Carol says, 'I just walked in. I said I could raise money for them, including raising my own salary (they were broke as usual!). John gave me a budget of £1000 and said get on with it.

'When I started it was less than 20 people spread across the country. Sustrans was in debt. It kept getting grants for construction work which were not big enough to do the job and then doing the job anyway. It had no core funds, no supporters.' Carol set about turning Sustrans into a membership organisation, helping grow the charity's supporters from 178 friends of Sustrans to 9000 by 1995. Supporters believed in the cause and as well as fundraising, offered a prospective pool of volunteer labour and credibility to potential funders. With Carol's help, which included 'piecemeal funding from a potpourri of sources,' Sustrans managed to cobble together enough funds to maintain their staff and keep building.

They also started thinking about knitting the until then disparate routes together. In 1991 the charity proposed a 1000-mile route running the length of the country, from Inverness to Dover, linking some scraps of existing path. The cost of the entire project, they estimated pointedly, would be equivalent to that of widening just two miles of the M25.

Sustrans also produced a map comparing the Dutch and UK national cycle networks at the time. While by the early 1990s the Netherlands boasted thousands of miles of routes, broadly crisscrossing the country, over here it looked like a disoriented moth holding a pen had landed on the map a few times on its meandering journey elsewhere. Still, by 1993 Sustrans had built over 300 miles of traffic-free paths and designated many hundreds of miles more across Britain. There were segments in Glasgow, Edinburgh, County

Durham, Cumbria, York, Liverpool, Derby, Bristol, Sussex and many other places, but, as John Grimshaw acknowledged at the time, it was far from being a network. The idea of how much they could or should achieve began to grow.

The first long-distance NCN route was the Sea to Sea, or C2C, which opened in 1994. Stretching almost 140 miles from two westerly points, at Whitehaven and Workington, converging near Bassenthwaite, and running to Newcastle or Sunderland, it was pieced together by David Gray. Gray built the Consett to Sunderland portion, working with John Naylor of Groundwork, who delivered the network of railway paths in West Cumbria. Within its first year Sustrans claims 10,000 people had cycled its length, including a police drugs squad and a pair of 69-year-old women keen to do something meaningful before they turned seventy.

Sustrans wasn't alone in this work. In 1993, the Danish national cycle route network opened and the following year the idea of a European-wide network was born. What would become the Eurovelo routes were funded by the European Commission in 1998 to harness the economic power of international cycle tourism and would go on to span the continent, to varying degrees of quality. Campaign groups across Europe were beginning to form, pushing for construction of off-road 'greenways', traffic-free walking and cycling paths. These were later taken up by governments, and national networks began to expand and link into the Eurovelo routes.

With the turn of the century looming, the National Lottery launched the Millennium Commission, offering grants of up to £50 million for ideas that would help define an era. John, Carol and the team decided to put in a bid for a national cycle network. By this point Caroline Levett, a similarly energetic civil servant, had become integral to Sustrans' operations and brought a level-headed presence to the organisation.

Unlike the Millennium Dome, Sustrans' bid wasn't for one big project, but for a series of small ones, as the charity later described in its book, *Millennium Miles*, 'in places no more than a thin line on the ground', but nonetheless they hoped it would touch millions of lives up and down the country. In fact, Caroline believes a national cycle network was the only bid to meet all five grant criteria: it was genuinely national, socially inclusive, would improve health, was good for the environment, and included an artistic or historical element in artwork proposed for along the routes.

To expand the network nationally, they would continue in a similar vein, 're-us[ing] redundant railway lines, neglected tow-paths and derelict land, transforming urban and rural wasteland into popular and attractive public space.' For an organisation used to doing things on a shoestring, it was a case of plucking a figure out of thin air and applying, but keen to avoid bidding for the full £50 million on the assumption that lofty figure was reserved for more iconic structures, the final bid came to £42.5 million, which, coincidentally, was close to the answer to 'life, the universe and everything' in Douglas Adams' book, *The Hitchhiker's Guide to the Galaxy*. Although pure coincidence, this became a fun PR lever for the NCN bid and part of the NCN's mythology.

From a handful of routes, the plan was to build 2500 miles of network by the year 2000 – in just five years – and 6500 miles by 2005, with a tiny team, beefing up the existing network – travelling the country and drawing lines on maps. The appendix to the bid, listing the routes that would make up those miles, is like a motorway-scale plan for cycle routes spanning the whole country. Indeed, Sustrans' account of the plans, in *Millennium Miles*, claimed it was 'the most extensive transport construction since the motorways'.

They included a 155-mile route between Bristol and Reading, using 67 miles of minor roads, 60 of towpath and 20 of derelict railway. Another 158 miles spanned the entire north coast of Wales, from the Menai Strait to Liverpool, an astonishing 86 miles of which would run along seafront promenades. The beginnings of Lon Las Cymru, the epic route spanning Wales, from Cardiff to Menai, are written out as two heroic stretches totalling almost 300 miles, across maps numbered 804 and 805. Another 151 miles, from Pitlochry to Inverness across the Cairngorms, followed 97 miles of minor roads, some forest track and required almost 37 miles of new route.

If the millennium routes looked like a motorway network, the later phase of routes, to be delivered by 2005, were a finer-grained mesh of A- and B-roads linking them together. The Lottery would provide less than a quarter of the funding for the first phase and councils, the government, public bodies, private trusts and donations, and general fundraising would need to find the rest.

The vision was bold – it was to be the makings of a transport and leisure network. John says, 'We were going to go from city centre to city centre, because we'd already made the decision that really, if you wanted to encourage people to start cycling, every city needed a Bristol and Bath [railway path]. It needed somewhere where you could regain confidence, so the idea was to have a traffic-free route in or near every city in the country.'

These would differ from motorways in very obvious ways, one being that the cycle routes would allow cyclists to travel to high streets and railway stations, the other being the inclusion of sculptures. John says he was 'very anxious about the travelling landscape'; the idea that the journey mattered, not just the destination. In his mind these routes would be linear parks, not simply thoroughfares. They were also part of their local communities, speaking to each area's history and culture, and its people.

The charity's PR campaign included a reception event at St James's Palace in London, hosted by the then Prince Charles, in which John cornered the new chief executive of the Millennium Commission, Jennifer Page, to encourage her to back Sustrans' bid. Caroline recalls, wryly, 'Jennifer Page turned on me and said, "I have never been pinned up against the brocade so hard in my life. We have got the message. Alright!"'

Over that summer Sustrans organised a mass ride, a promotional exercise with 200 people cycling from Inverness to Dover, to drum up support from local and national politicians, meeting more than 50 local authorities along the way.

On 11 September 1995 their efforts paid off. The NCN won the bid and the singer Meat Loaf handed John Grimshaw the £42,500,000 cheque on *The National Lottery Live* TV programme. The Millennium

Commission was taking a gamble, giving such a gargantuan task to a largely unproven organisation, but they knew if they succeeded the results could be genuinely transformative for the UK.

Sustrans also knew there was a substantial risk of failure. The then finance director, Malcolm Shepherd, says, 'It was risky; we all knew that. Which of course motivated us all to get the hell on and do it.' They wanted to prove themselves worthy of the trust placed in them, so Sustrans staff up and down the country, who numbered about 25 at the time, got to work. On top of the Lottery cash, they had to set about finding the remaining 77% of the funding the network needed from local authorities, other charities, landowners and supporters.

They went to councils, flashed the cash they hoped to invest in the local area and asked for contributions. While the idea of a national network helped focus councils' minds, the willingness for material change varied.

'Cycling was so different,' says Isobel Stoddart, who organised the Inverness to Dover mass ride, a promotional exercise to drum up support from local and national politicians. She adds: 'You had to fight your corner. Now it's commonplace, it's policy, but in those days we were really having to do a lot of diplomacy and persuading. Local councillors needed convincing and there were negotiations with farmers and landowners, and communities.

'I distinctly remember John saying to us, "Don't look like cyclists when you go to these meetings,"' she recalls. It was so people would take them seriously. Cyclists were outliers back then, far more so than today, and were quite often seen as eccentrics, going against social norms. What's more, highways authorities – the councils in charge of roads – didn't have staff tasked with cycling; they had staff who designed roads for motor traffic. 'We were having to deal with highways people. The whole concept of thinking about cycling in the highway design . . . well, it wasn't thought about. We would fight and fight to get it considered,' says Isobel.

'There is a slide show John used to give; really the basic stuff about cycling, what it could do and its contribution and the arguments [for it]. For a lot of people listening, I think it was quite a revelation. It was positioning the bike in a totally different way.'

The idea of leisure routes in rural areas often appealed to local authorities; they didn't require reallocating space from drivers. It was when the routes reached the city and town centres that negotiations became fraught, because land was more contested and few councils were willing to tackle the growing supremacy of the motor vehicle. Shared paths were developed in pedestrian areas through Birmingham and other cities. Narrow cycle lanes were painted, intermittently, on roads and, although it was considered ground-breaking at the time, the paint invited people to ride in close proximity to moving traffic, without any protection. Needless to say, few were tempted. Truly transformative were the traffic-free routes and the new bridges hoisted into place to carry cyclists and pedestrians across rivers, railways and main roads as the network gradually took shape.

Mark Strong was there at the start. Mark is energetic and passionate about cycling, with a singular focus on his narrative, and a startling knowledge of cycling routes and their history. Once he starts talking, he'll keep going until someone stops him. Now a transport consultant with his own firm, in 1991 Mark joined Sustrans from the London Cycling Campaign, becoming regional manager for the south east. He was one of the team drawing lines on maps to create the national network.

When I meet him in a café on a rainy morning in Brighton, he recalls the scrappy early days at Sustrans. 'They started off with this 1000-mile network and then they suddenly realised that 1000 miles isn't very much when you add up all the bits, and then it morphed. Somebody in marketing said "Let's call it the National Cycle Network." Slightly over-inflated, but let's call it that.'

Of course, making it happen was another thing.

Mark remembers John and his team 'went round buying bits of unused railway lines', picking up land and structures no-one else would touch – they were seen as liabilities to most people. John has a way of making things happen, through determination, his formidable book of contacts, an incredible memory and, sometimes, sheer force of will.

Mark laughs, recalling those times. 'Everyone else was saying "I'm not buying that . . . it's got five bridges with roads on it . . . they're gonna fall down" and John was saying, "Just buy the thing. We'll sort the bridges out. They haven't fallen down since the Victorians built them . . . They're not gonna fall down."'

John would go with a British Rail Board regional director to their archive in York and wade through stacks of documents for each area, title deeds for stretches of disused railways, scooping up what he thought was useful. He was, as a colleague described it, 'like a kid in a sweet shop'. Sometimes the maps were so poor it was hard to tell what they were taking on, but if they looked interesting, John grabbed them. I imagine these visits like the 1990s *Crystal Maze* finales, where contestants were put into the crystal dome with frantically whirling bits of gold paper they had to grab before the clock ran down – except with John in a stuffy archive in York shovelling maps into his panniers.

In the 1990s, Mark says, 'What Sustrans had was this map, lots of little tadpoles of A to B, either actual routes or potential routes. They're all completely unconnected. They're just little short sections of routes, some of which are really useful, some of which are in the middle of Loch Earn, up on the A9 near Aviemore. Some of them are great and some of them are in the middle of nowhere.'

In the town centres, where the railway land was sold off for housing, sometimes you could forge an alternative urban route and sometimes you couldn't. In the mid-90s Mark and his counterparts around the country were asked to link these bits, quickly, to form something worthy of the NCN moniker, 10,000 miles of it.

At the time of the Lottery bid in 1994, the plan was that by 2005, 6500 miles of network would span Britain, reaching within two miles of 30 million people. Thanks in part to 'very enthusiastic local authorities', as John recalls in *Millennium Miles*, by midsummer's day of the millennium year, almost 5000 miles were already on their way to completion across 2000 separate construction projects.

This included 219 miles of new railway path – derelict railway tracks repurposed and renovated for walking and cycling – and 107 miles of new canal and riverside path. There were 272 miles of new route – one heck of an achievement for a small charity. Each yard would have involved at times long-winded one-to-one negotiations and considerable persuasion skills on the part of Sustrans.

Off-road miles paled in comparison to on-road miles. The vast majority, 3000 of those 5500 miles, were on 'minor roads' and another 464 miles on 'town roads' or their pavements. In total, around 150 miles of network were on footpaths or 'converted footways' – things like widened pavements with a painted line separating walkers and cyclists. Sometimes it was a strip of narrow pavement next to a main road. While it wasn't ideal, it did a job of linking up sections of network; the idea was that later someone would come along and finish the job.

Local authorities had chipped in another £69.4 million from their own funds, the more enthusiastic even extending planned routes. These councils were and still are the key players in the network, owning the roads that make up most of the routes, along with the footpaths, painted cycle lanes and promenades. Sustrans, meanwhile, owned less than 5% of the network.

By 2000 the NCN founders had been working for two decades and, while scores of routes remained unopened at that point pending land negotiations or waiting for other construction projects to finish, much was completed. By the 2005 deadline there were a whopping 10,000 miles of designated routes.

If their early work juggling funding, multiple construction projects and a far-flung workforce on a shoestring was impressive, this achievement was truly monumental. When the dust settled, they had raised £200 million for the work, more than quadrupling the original Lottery fund. John Grimshaw says this epic achievement was the work of 'thousands of people' working 'with over 400 local authorities, government departments and other bodies' to form 'a coherent network of use to local people'. He adds, 'The actual number of players is far too numerous to list, but their input and efforts do need to be recognised in the effort to make a real change in Britain's transport realities.'

The NCN's purpose, John says, was 'simply to popularise cycling', to provide 'safe and attractive' places people could ride a bike, walk and use wheelchairs, 'making possible all sorts of everyday trips to school, work, friends, for recreation, leisure and tourism – by cycle.'

In *Millennium Miles*, the NCN is described as follows: 'From Land's End to the Shetland Isles, the west coast of Ulster to the belly of East Anglia, it links together ancient travelways, including Roman roads, canal towpaths, disused railway lines (including viaducts and tunnels) and drovers' roads,' with a handful of brand-new bridges now connecting them. Revived, once again these ancient travelways linked places and landscapes. They connected city, town and village dwellers with green space, artwork, history – and one another.

'Whilst it has created wonderfully scenic swathes of track for all to enjoy, it is the daily journeys, to school, to work, that are the key to its future success. Sustrans is not about putting your bike on the back of the car, driving to a cycle path, going for a spin then driving home again.'

Many of the urban sections that were needed to get people from their homes to the scenic routes used a patchwork of residential streets, pavements and country roads, and some weren't the original alignment or quality Sustrans had hoped for. Many routes were frankly circuitous, unimproved but for new signage. However, for a charity in Sustrans' position to achieve all this with diplomacy, a little cash and a lot of goodwill, it was a people-powered miracle.

3

FRIENDSHIP AND WAYFINDING ON THE THAMES PATH

In spring, I begin my clockwise exploration of the NCN, following NCN1 from London to Dover, via the Thames Path. Ducking under the river through the Greenwich foot tunnel, where cyclists must dismount, the NCN weaves together London's architectural treasures and history. It passes the grand Royal Naval College, narrow streets of ye olde maritime terraces and delightful pubs, heading towards modern flats offering acres of glazing to the waterfront.

Broad riverside cycle lanes slowly become more cracked and crazed, turning to gravel amid the gritty decay of London's riverine industrial heritage. Behind the regional distribution centres of supermarket giants at Erith, jutting out into the Thames, are rusting and grey concrete structures that loom over the concrete path. After that the NCN meanders between the waterfront and the glass- and pothole-strewn roads and pavements of industrial estates, main roads and, briefly, alongside a slip road of the thunderous A2, a motorway in all but name.

On the last weekend in March, I head east along the Thames to meet an old friend for a bike ride. Beccy, juggling parenthood and a freelance photography career, and long out of the saddle, suggested weeks ahead we cycle somewhere together. I hunt around online for a short-ish ride which starts and ends near Gravesend. I scour Komoot, a cycle navigation app, for recommended rides around the Isle of Grain, where a new section of the England Coast Path has recently been opened, but it's too far from any train station. Eventually I discover a route following a canal towpath east from Gravesend to an RSPB wetlands reserve, if we make it that far.

Among the route highlights flagged on the app by other users is one feature that gives me pause. Dubbed 'atmospheric alley' it looks for all the world like somewhere you'd go to get mugged: a narrow graffiti-covered snicket between an industrial building and a heavy-duty metal fence with spikes on top. I have to believe that if the people of the internet think it positively worthy of note, it can't be all bad. Besides, after at least an hour staring at the map for something suitable this is the only route that ticks the boxes for being traffic-free, not too long and with some decent scenery (atmospheric alley aside).

After two days of high air pollution, it's a relief to leave London. I'm not sleeping well and regularly wake up at 4 a.m., but this means I can leave home early. To sidestep engineering works I catch the high-speed Javelin train at my nearest mainline station and disembark at Ebbsfleet, where trains are terminating, to cycle to Gravesend. I soon realise I'm following NCN1; it's like the network is sucking me in. Either way, it's doing its job and connecting two places I need to cycle between. I find a pavement cycle path which, despite switching inconveniently from one side of the main road to the other, is largely newly surfaced and well signposted. I slow down and ding my bell politely for people walking, including one woman with a pushchair who, to my embarrassment and horror, immediately grabs a young child by the coat collar to yank him out of the way. We are in a deep gully seemingly carved out of the rock, where a vast amount of road space is given over to motor traffic and everyone else is shoved on to a pavement at the edges.

As tradition dictates when visiting Gravesend, I become lost in the town's fast-moving one-way system and pedestrianised shopping areas, each hostile to cyclists in their own quirky ways (the latter prohibits cycling altogether). Eventually, after an NCN sign treasure hunt around the town, some dodgy road crossings and a three-sides-of-a-square tour of some choice pavements, I locate Beccy in the station car park.

While we take turns to use the station loo, I notice Beccy's brakes seem to be rubbing. She hasn't used the bike for a while. I fish out my multitool from a pannier, first making things much, much worse by screwing something the wrong way until the wheels barely turn and then, by the time she reappears, I've got the brakes in roughly better shape. I've brought my cheap, heavy hybrid bike with supposedly shock-absorbing front forks, so I can match Beccy's likely sedate pace, and it turns out to be a good choice, if not for her pace, then at least for the terrain.

We couldn't have chosen a better day: the sun is shining, and it is surprisingly warm for the end of March. It is a tonic to see a dear friend and we cycle in T-shirts, chatting happily. I worry excessively about other people's safety and, once in traffic, I nervously lead Beccy out of Gravesend's busy roads, between multiple lanes of queuing traffic with drivers on all sides, forgetting she'd happily cycled in London for years.

The GPS route I've downloaded leads us through a park and into an industrial estate. It looks far from promising: the road is rough and rutted, with alarmingly deep gullies down the middle for presumably industrial levels of rainwater, but to my relief Beccy views it as an adventure and chuckles happily. The road skirts a huge factory building and seems to reach a dead end. We are almost next to the blue and red NCN sign before we notice it. It apparently leads riders on NCN1 east from the Thames Path; we've just approached it from the wrong side. What looks like a solid metal fence conceals a narrow gap. If someone intended to create a cycle route reminiscent of a bookcase that was really a door to a secret passage in a mouldy old castle, I don't think they could have done a better job.

Not only is this part of a national cycle route, it's also part of the England Coast Path and the Thames Path, and we stop to take ironic photos before proceeding. After a couple of metres, we follow a 90-degree turn and I instantly recognise the internet's 'atmospheric alley'. If anything, it is worse than its pictures: narrow, long and claustrophobic. As we ride in single file, I point out patches of broken glass to Beccy behind me. She is a characteristically good sport about this inauspicious start to our adventure. As the end grows closer, though, it appears to be barred by a fence. We know from recent experience to persevere and ride to the very end, expecting a gap to suddenly appear. However, not only is this fence for real, it has, in fact, been welded shut on both sides. We are trapped.

I reach my fingers through the narrow gaps between the bars, like a prisoner in a medieval jail grasping for a scrap of bread just out of reach, and manage to turn around a laminated sheet of paper attached to a lamp-post. It tells us, slightly alarmingly, that the route is closed – for safety reasons! – and there is a diversion in place. The alley is so narrow that, to turn our bikes around, we have to stand them on their back wheels. I worry what specific hazards caused someone to weld the entrance to this alleyway shut. Is the wall on one side about to fall down? Are bandits known to hang above it, dropping down on wires, and trapping unsuspecting walkers and cyclists like animals in a cage? Is there a really angry badger that patrols it at sundown, charging at cyclists with bloodied teeth? I shudder at the thought of finding myself alone in such a place at night. Even during the day I am supremely glad to have Beccy with me.

Once freed from the atmospheric alley, I notice on the NCN sign-post evidence of another laminated sheet, presumably warning the way is closed. Someone has apparently torn it off or perhaps it blew off in a violent gust of wind. Glad to breathe the free air again, we make our way around the diversion, along a wide road with vans parked on the only pavement and a few drivers overtaking slightly too fast. This is clearly not a place many people walk or cycle.

I always want to like Gravesend. Beccy moved there for a spell and I loved strolling the ancient pedestrianised streets near the river. There's a lovely restaurant in a modern waterfront building and we once visited a ship anchored in the harbour that featured art and music events. Pocahontas died here and there is a statue denoting the end of her journey, far from home in a land of strange diseases and horrible weather. There are the usual decaying shop fronts and chain

38

stores, day drinkers and various characters that make up British towns, but it always seems full of promise.

I was excited, therefore, to learn that Gravesend has its own canal, but I wasn't sure what to expect. I hoped, not least because I'd chosen it for today's ride, that it wasn't simply a dry bed of stinking mud and empty Coke bottles. We find the canal. It literally stops with a blunt end, as if someone drew it in marker pen and thought 'that's far enough', but it turns out to be rather lovely: the water sparkles between aquatic plants and a line of trees.

To reach the traffic-free path at the end of a narrow concrete road, there is a barrier and a sign politely telling us this is private land, on which the NCN and its users are kindly permitted, with the subtext we'd better behave ourselves while we are at it. The barrier tapers from a wide base to become quite narrow at the top, and I have to rotate my handlebars to get through it.

These barriers are mostly installed with the understandable purpose of keeping motorbikes off foot and cycle paths, but in doing so they keep anyone with a non-standard cycle out, including tricycles and cargo cycles that carry children or luggage, and some even require panniers or even less conveniently, a child seat to be removed. Sustrans' barrier removal is a slow process and often landowners permit cycling and walking on the condition that anti-motorcycle barriers are installed, even though they may not comply with disability legislation.

It's an almost supernaturally perfect day's cycling. The path is rough, a chalky colour, peppered with chunky, angular stones and steep-sided craters large enough for a badger to bathe in (hopefully not the same angry alleyway badger), but it is car-wide, so we ride side by side, avoiding the worst potholes and catching up on life, love and work news. During the pandemic Beccy took up environmental campaigning, sensibly calling for homes to be built on brownfield rather than greenfield sites, with decent transport links, including cycling and walking, not just provision for cars.

Exhausted from her efforts and parenting her two young children, she is delighted to have the day to simply ride her bike. From the towpath we glimpse marshlands to our left, at the verges of the Thames Estuary, and the canal on the right. We can't believe our luck. We both brought picnic food and come midday we set up on a grassy bank in a field beyond the track. Several people pass on foot and by bike, and we give a cheery hello. Mid-picnic there is a buzzing sound and two youngsters on a motorbike whoosh past at speed, headed toward the riverbank, before returning 20 minutes later. So much for those anti-motorcycle barriers.

After lunch we continue along the canal, and then follow generally quiet country roads with NCN179 signs. The countryside here is gorgeous – cottages and fields of horses nestled in a rolling landscape. We could be in Italy or France. 'I feel like I'm in an Enid Blyton book,' Beccy shouts out as we fly down one hill. We agree the only thing missing from the day is tea and cake, but we can't have it all.

At around the point we need to turn back for Gravesend, we spot a sign for the RSPB reserve, which boasts a complex of wooden buildings, including a café. We head in, stunned by our good fortune, order rocky road slices and pots of tea, and plonk ourselves down on picnic tables overlooking the water. Across the wetlands rows of trees and hedges are smudged in a gentle golden mist that renders the scene almost preternaturally beautiful in the afternoon sun. It is a view I'd happily frame on a wall. Part-way through our second helping of cake, the woman serving discovers she's overcharged us (neither of us have noticed) and emerges with our change.

Later, realising NCN1 continues to Higham, Strood and Rochester stations, Beccy decides she'll bring her daughters and partner back one day soon. With the sun getting low, we rejoin the road, dodging clouds of midges and bumping back along the gravel path to Gravesend. Beccy mulls over getting a mountain bike too, given the jolts her arms have received. I can't help but think that if my entire NCN adventure is this good I'm in for a treat.

4

BACK TO THE BEGINNING ON THE BRISTOL AND BATH RAILWAY PATH

At Bath station, early one Thursday morning in June, there are two people with bikes waiting in the pedestrianised plaza to meet me. The man, in his late 70s, a good 6'4" tall with grey curly hair, has a large black electric bike propped up beside him. His slender companion is in her late 60s. She has a grey bob, a smart, multi-coloured skirt suit and a vintage racing bike. This is John Grimshaw and his right-hand woman, colleague of 30-plus years and constant voice of reason, Caroline Levett.

The years haven't slowed either of them down. Despite having left Sustrans 14 years ago, John and Caroline are still designing and building cycling and walking paths, with Caroline as company secretary and John as route designer – and sometimes human bulldozer – at their current organisation, Greenways and Cycleroutes Ltd. We sit down in a café opposite the station for a briefing on the early days, locking our bikes together outside. Armed with a cycle pannier full of documents, John leafs through his archive and spreads a series of maps, books and reports out on a coffee table. Handing me a few copies to borrow, he takes me back to those first days.

He recalls his early adventures in 1982 with Cyclebag's then secretary, Bill Clarke, trying to map out England's disused railways for use as potential cycle paths. Back then, and through the years of construction, John spent much of his time on the road. He lived with his young family in a kind of commune in a big Georgian house in Bristol. At one point there were two other families – 15 people – living in the one building, with the future mayor of Bristol and fellow Sustrans founder, George Ferguson, living next door. He says he doesn't know how he did it all, but then, he adds, 'We had different energies back then.'

John would go off on week-long trips by train. 'If a project wasn't on the mainline railway, we didn't do it,' he says. Travelling between Bristol and some of the early routes in Birmingham, Derby, Consett, York and Edinburgh, he'd spend two or three hours on a project and then get back on a train to the next one. 'It was incessant travelling,' he says, 'but in those days we were fortunate: we had a sleeper train from Bristol to Scotland, which made life a bit easier.'

John admits he probably travelled too much in the early years, but in civil engineering, travel was the norm. Eventually his employer let him go; the NCN was taking too much time and interfering with his work. He acknowledges it was an obsession, but one he doesn't regret. He was motivated and nothing was going to stop him. At some point he was paid by Sustrans, but for many years he says he doesn't know what he lived on. Caroline took a decade of unpaid leave and lived on her husband's income – back then, that was possible. Today John and Caroline are hardly well paid, but they say at this stage in life, their needs are few.

I ask what kept him going back then, traipsing up and down the country and leaving his family for substantial periods of time. Then we get to the heart of the issue and he replies, 'I felt that, with a family particularly, the fact that they couldn't cycle anywhere really upset me. When they were old enough to cycle, I wanted them to have routes that they could cycle on. There are photographs of my children when they were very young, coming on to building sites and things, supervising the work, which was going to become a route that they could use. That was quite a powerful motivation: to create a better world for one's children.'

John starts to explain how he got things done on the ground – apparently through sheer force of will, a total refusal to take no for an answer and in the face of some quite substantial hazards.

'You can't ask permission to do this work,' he says, bluntly. 'That's why we had to survey one line at night, because we knew we'd be shot if we went through in the daytime.'

'By who?' I ask, not sure if I've heard him right.

'By the landowner.'

John claims this particular landowner had broken planning regulations by removing part of a railway embankment, which was key to a route they wanted to build. John and his colleagues 'got the planners to force him to rebuild this embankment,' adding, perhaps unnecessarily, 'so he was a very unhappy man.' You can't help but admire his determination, although I wonder what would have put a halt to his efforts if an angry man with a shotgun didn't do the job.

Caroline mentions that Bennerley Viaduct, on one of the lines they surveyed all those years ago, on the border of Derbyshire and Nottinghamshire, has just opened for walking and cycling. Owned by Railway Paths Limited (RPL)* and funded by National Highways, the final reopening of what's known as the Iron Giant, near Ilkeston, was decades in the making, but it was work that started with them.

John hints at other routes they are developing, including one near Tintern Abbey and Shepton Mallet, which apparently creates constant work. It seems to be a full-time job, requiring meetings, his drawings, and her negotiation and diplomatic skills. Caroline says while she and John are equally driven – mad, she calls it – they couldn't be more different.

It's easy to complain about a lack of safe routes, and I know I'm guilty of doing this, but these two have made a genuine, positive difference in the real world. It's humbling to spend time with two

---

*Railway Paths was originally Sustrans' arm's length land management body, but is now a separate charity. Established when British Rail was being reorganised for privatisation, its purpose was to hold assets, like bridges, that might be of future use for routes. It still exists and still owns some of those structures today.

such driven and positive people, who have so fundamentally shaped the landscape for cycling in the UK and continue to do so.

Our briefing complete, we head out on our bikes. John sails across the busy road outside the station on his ebike in the same way he probably has for the past four decades – seemingly regardless of traffic. Caroline and I, on regular bikes, give chase. It's a warm summer's morning and we turn off a busy road to the river path where it all began more than 40 years ago. I notice John's shorts have a rip on the back of one leg – like him, all his clothes look as if they've seen some adventures.

The narrow riverside path is busy today and we ride single file to allow riders in the opposite direction to pass. I ask what keeps him doing this, after all these years? 'Lack of imagination to do anything else,' he answers, deadpan. When I ask him to be serious, he adds, 'No, if you look at all these people coming towards us, who wouldn't have been here otherwise, it's worth it.' Of course, no-one else knows this is one of the people who started it all.

The Bristol and Bath route follows a short stretch of road before reaching the former railway line. At the entrance are some chunky metal pipes, bent into shapes to prevent motorbike access. Caroline says these were heating pipes discarded during the bulldozing of a local hospital and commandeered in typical John fashion. They went on to form a standard, albeit non-wheelchair-friendly, design across the network.

We're on a long section of former railway embankment somewhere outside Bath, with established trees and views out across fields. 'I like to build a meander in,' says John, 'so walkers don't get intimidated by a long, straight path.' It's something I wouldn't have noticed, but sure enough, there it is – it's lovely.

John planted many of these trees, now established specimens, but gaps were deliberately cleared over the years so users can see through to the countryside beyond – part of John's 'travelling landscape'. We spot a train in the distance, and John recalls, 'When we were building here, we would hear a train on the nearby line, just over there, and we'd think they were coming on our line – it was really weird.'

It's sometimes hard to separate myth from fact, as John has a dry, mischievous sense of humour and the ability to spin a good yarn. 'We had our most successful fundraising event ever here,' he says, further on. 'We were a bunch of thugs with sharp tools, planting trees' – I wonder where this is going – 'and we decided to stop everyone and ask them for money. We raised £400 that day in £10 voluntary donations – the only time we ever made a profit.' You may have seen Sustrans staff today stopping users and asking them for money in a similar fundraising vein, but without the sharp tools.

John still has a proprietorial attitude to the path. At one point he declares, 'I think a tree has fallen on the fountain.' He dismounts, leans his bike on its kickstand and descends a grassy bank to where a fallen tree conceals a large granite block. Beneath an enormous trunk you can just see a tap with a button on the side, for drinking water. It's too big to move and John says he regrets siting the fountain here. At the time, before the route was complete, the path temporarily went down this bank.

We carry on and I duck for a low-hanging tree that's sticking out just at eye height. John calls out and we stop again. 'Do you have your saw, Caroline?' he asks, adding 'I didn't bring mine.' Caroline delves into a pannier and, sure enough, produces a small pruning saw, which John employs on the half-fallen tree. 'Dutch Elm disease,' Caroline says sadly. After a few moments of sawing there is a crack and the eye-stabbing tree is felled and pushed to the side of the path.

As we remount and carry on, I admit, 'I often see things like that on paths, fallen trees and branches, and want to do something about it, but I don't feel like I've got permission.'

'Well, I give you permission on all the bits I built,' says John, which feels like I've had some kind of formal honour bestowed on me.

He says that, over the years, part of what kept him from getting fed up with building paths was the construction of fountains, sculptures and seating along the way, which Caroline translates as 'coming across delight.' John's philosophy, one that Sustrans certainly embodies today, is that cycle routes shouldn't simply be like roads, but should bring together landscape, sculptures, seating, water fountains and a sense of the history of the area you're riding through.

It also makes people want to look after them, which is handy because most cycle paths, unlike roads, don't have maintenance budgets. They rely on a lot of goodwill. John notes that they recently had a hundred volunteers planting trees by a new route in Aylesbury. 'People get excited if they can make a contribution to building their own paths,' he says.

We pass massive semi-circular benches made from railway sleepers, their seats low to the ground, with towering backs. Some of these, built in the early 1980s, are decaying now and some are concealed by foliage. On the Bristol-Bath route there's also the head of a huge stone man drinking, which is an enormous water fountain.

Today we are headed to Bitton, and then Caroline has a lunch meeting and John is off somewhere or other, but we stop at a section of path with a fingerpost pointing in three directions and a spur leading away from the main route. 'We started here because when you're building, access is one of the most important things,' says John. 'The lorry would back in here with the limestone dust,' he says, pointing off the path. John is very matter of fact and unsentimental, but this feels like a momentous place to me – the start of the NCN.

Nothing about the location would tell you this, though. The fingerposts, metal signs fashioned like flags kinked in a light breeze, pointing users away from this spot, are the same kind you see all over the network – the Millennium Mileposts – but this is mile one, where it all started. Where all those people dug and raked, sweated and occasionally lifted their heads at the sound of a ghost train. Where potatoes were cooked on fires under bridges to sustain workers who couldn't afford their own food. Where, day after day, equipment was dragged along half-made paths on Heath Robinson-style trailers by men and women with tanned limbs on racing bikes and at times reluctant children. While I'm pondering this, John recalls in his usual factual way the mechanics of the construction process.

Suddenly, though, it's time for us to part and in a slight daze I ride off, back in the direction I've come. I stop a few hundred metres down the path at an information board. I expect to see the story mirrored here, but it's mainly about the former railway line and other details of the current route. I look up and realise John has returned.

'I wanted to take you to see some geology,' he says, by way of explanation. We go back up the path, past the Bitton sign, and stop beside a rock-face cutting. 'You see those bumps,' he says. 'They're sea turtles, fossilised.' We walk over to the wall, where turtleback-sized lumps are embedded into the rock. I lean the bike and kneel down to touch them. 'No way,' I breathe, as John explains that 200 million years ago these creatures were swimming in what was a great shallow sea. There are about 15 of them, clustered together, perhaps engulfed in mud while swimming one day and now frozen forever in that moment. One of them has a visible flipper or head and there's an ammonite among the pack.

I look up. All around us is green pasture land and only a small information board under a nearby bridge tells the broad story of this area, a vast shallow sea that stretched as far as Newton Abbott, in which prehistoric sea creatures swam together. At the time of the cycle route's construction, Sustrans' geologist revealed their identity, but you could pass this every day for a decade and never know what you were looking at.

Finally, John leads me on to where they built the path alongside a working stretch of railway. A leisure train line still operates on one track and the other track is given over to cyclists and walkers, with a fence dividing the two. He wants to show me what's possible. 'Now you really must go,' he says, conscious I'm cutting it fine to ride the 20-odd miles to my next meeting, back in Frome.

5

MAPS, A MURDERER AND MUD ON THE KENT AND SUSSEX COASTS

A cycle network is, essentially, a simple thing: it's hundreds of thousands of connections between homes and schools, shops and hospitals, and green space further afield. If you want to be able to cycle from your front door to any of these places, near or far, you need routes joining your neighbourhood, to every part of the place you live in – the town centre, local shops, school, the place you work.

These routes could be on protected main road cycle routes, direct, low-traffic routes through back-streets or green spaces away from cars. In most places the principal network looks like a spider web for every town and village; in coastal areas it's more like a ladder, with one main waterfront route, an inland route or two and rungs linking them together. You need bridges or tunnels across things like rivers, big roads and railways, and decent junctions so people cycling don't need to stop and slow down all the time, or make daring dashes between fast-moving vehicles.

Then we join the towns, connecting them to the village three miles out, then the next one, working our way out to gradually build a network. Hundreds of these inter-urban routes exist already in the UK, in Sustrans and others' old rail trails, towpaths, greenways and quiet country roads. We just need to connect them up, make the standard high and consistent, and make them a little less wiggly on the map, so a three-mile distance doesn't involve seven miles of hilly cycling.

Not every road needs a bike lane, or could fit one, so to make people feel safe cycling you might also have low-traffic routes: shopping streets, residential roads, well-surfaced bridleways and even quiet rural lanes, where people can drive in and out, but not through, as part of that network.

Although commuting trips are prioritised in transport planning, we do twice as many leisure trips as work trips. This goes for both driving, where just 15% of journeys are commutes, and cycling, where 27% of trips are commutes. In fact, just under a quarter of our trips (23%) are for leisure. I'd argue these journeys are just as important as any other. According to Sustrans, the NCN is used for both: 56% of journeys on the network are for 'functional reasons, such as travelling to work, taking the children to school, visiting the shops or visiting friends.' The remaining 44% are for leisure. The pandemic transformed the working week, bringing with it more home working and more time spent in the places we live. Given this, a focus on commuting makes even less sense, and access to green space and movement outside our homes becomes even more important.

With 26% of people inactive between 2021 and 2022, and walking and cycling the most substantial contributor to physical activity, growing the network is a public health intervention as well as a transport one. One thing I learned when I studied for a year to be a dietitian, before changing careers, was the easiest way to get regular exercise is to incorporate it into our everyday lives. Just like roads, the local cycle routes that take us out of town, city or village, give us respite, a place to exercise and fortify our mental and physical health, be together with family and friends, be alone or be a tourist – as well as acting as crucial commuter infrastructure. Of course, delivering these networks is easier said than done. The hard bit is getting together the money and the political support to build them.

From mid-April I take day trips between high-speed rail stations around the coast from Whitstable to Brighton, picking up each leg where I left off. This is an area that could benefit substantially from a connected cycle network. Thanks to its dense population, research has found that on the busy Kent coast anywhere between 15% to above 30% of commutes are short enough to be cycled or e-cycled, while up to half of school commutes are cyclable. Expecting some off-road paths and with no need to carry luggage, I deploy the gravel bike – drop handlebars, steel frame and wide tyres – which feels like it needs some accompanying heroic music. You can attach panniers to it or tiny bikepacking bags. It also goes fast, when provoked, so I call it the Adventure Rocket.

A favourite route of mine is the Crab and Winkle Way, a popular 7.6-mile, mostly off-road route between Whitstable and Canterbury. From there you can cycle to Dover, NCN1's start or end point. Traversing delightful rolling countryside on gravel paths and country roads, it follows in part an old salt trading route where men in ancient times travelled with donkeys from Seasalter to Canterbury – and a sign midway tells visitors all about it.

It's an image I love to conjure. Those were tougher times when people probably smelled pretty bad and it certainly makes me glad to be alive in the 21st century with modern medicine and running water – though you can't argue those men and their donkeys didn't have great views along the way. Today, you follow the little blue NCN signs, first along the coastal path at Whitstable, then inland, through forest and field, on dusty dirt and gravel tracks, across the undulating landscape to Canterbury.

I'm trying to enjoy the ride, but I keep getting distracted by the details – the frustrations, the time spent getting lost, the inconvenience and discomfort of sharing roads with drivers who don't seem aware of how scary it is being overtaken too close – close passing as it's known – at speed. The NCN, I realise, follows a pattern: glorious stretches of rural road and former railway paths that are a puzzle to find from their nearest train stations. If the signage isn't throwing you for a loop, in built-up areas there's a fierce dance of pavements, roads, odd-shaped anti-motorcycle barriers and a maze of backstreets, requiring constant vigilance to avoid missing one of the tiny blue direction signs. With 43% of all urban and town journeys in England shorter than two miles, the in-town sections of routes are really the bits we should be getting right.

At Canterbury I traverse a mud path through woodland that was clearly a bog all winter and the signs are hard to follow, pointing me here, there and everywhere. At the Whitstable end, on a newly surfaced, wheelchair-accessible, zig-zag section of tarmac, leading users gently up on to an off-road path through woodland, some perverse soul has installed a dastardly tight wooden chicane fence. Presumably meant to deter motorbikes, in one fell swoop this fence renders these wheelchair-friendly improvements inaccessible in an actual wheelchair, or any other non-standard cycle without some serious manhandling and the risk of falling in a ditch.

On my second visit of the year, during a press trip, after the rain has washed away the various obligatory scrawled phalluses from the brand-new tarmac, a child has added their own artwork. Beneath a picture of a rainbow emerging from clouds, in chalk, is written, 'Welcome to Paridise'. It seems the perfect testament to our love for these quiet, traffic-free places, surrounded by wood and birdsong just on the outskirts of town.

I meet some interesting people on trains. There's a woman in a mobility scooter who travels at the weekend to the coast with her small dog. She wears a tiny bicycle brooch and, as I'm keen on talking to strangers, I ask her if she likes cycling. She used to, she says, but she had a stroke at 40 – my age – and can no longer ride a bike. She looks at mine and says, 'I envy you. Make the most of it.' It feels like an invocation.

I'm also getting used to navigating the NCN digitally, via a layer on the OS map. From the early days of the NCN, Sustrans was all too aware that cyclists need to be able to find out about the network, and then successfully follow routes. While PR, formal and informal, performed the first role, maps and signs had to perform the second. These, Sustrans wrote in *Millennium Miles*, would denote 'not only the route but also difficult road crossings; sections which are not yet of an acceptable standard; the line of proposed improvements; distances along the route'. The philosophy was that the network would be navigable without a map. In 1997, formalising the Network, Sustrans persuaded Ordnance Survey to include the NCN on its Landranger maps, both traffic-free (an orange-yellow line) and on-road (blue).

The OS map web page on my phone offers 'low accuracy', for some reason, putting about a mile between where it thinks I am and where I actually am. The combination of that and a multitude of missing, obscured or oddly placed NCN signs and stickers leads me perilously towards massive roundabouts in towns, on to frightening main roads and on a couple of lengthy detours. I ask a man for directions. He claims he knows where the NCN goes, even though he doesn't, sending me on a long and hilly loop. While UK government policy now says cycle routes should be navigable without technology or maps, in reality few of them are. Eventually I realise the OS map has an app – I'm a slow adopter of technology – which solves the accuracy problem.

Despite the frustrations, once I've settled on the best tools – the combination of OS map app and on-road signage – the NCN is navigable, albeit with a few wrong turns. Across a succession of day trips I reach the end of NCN1 at Dover and the start of NCN2, which heads west all the way to Land's End. The Adventure Rocket and I discover the many seaside towns and villages along the south coast. We traverse country lanes through farmland and nature reserve. We cycle close by the creepy old power station of Dungeness, nestled in a seascape of shingle and wind-blown wooden houses and shacks. We ride right along the seashore and down the white cliffs of Dover under the blue skies of a gloriously sunny spring.

John Grimshaw and his team borrowed the NCN signs' design from Denmark's burgeoning cycle route marking system: a red square with white characters on a blue background. The early Sustrans routes were numbered 1 to 8, 1 being Dover to Inverness and John O'Groats, 2 Dover to Bodmin, 3 Bristol to Land's End, 4 London to Fishguard, 5 Reading to Holyhead and 6 London to Keswick. Scotland was given number 7 – Sunderland to Carlisle, Glasgow and Inverness – and

8 spanned Wales from Cardiff to Holyhead. Additional routes have two-digit numbers running clockwise from the original route, so 21 is Eastbourne to London, 23 is Southampton to Reading and 27 is Plymouth to Okehampton.

Sustrans also produced simple adhesive signs for use by route rangers on a temporary basis to cover for any missing or damaged signs. These route rangers are the network's volunteer maintenance crew, each tasked with caring for a patch of the NCN. While initially intended as temporary, like the bad bits of the NCN, these stickers have now become part of the street furniture. Ahead of each summer, when volunteering work ramps up, Sustrans can send out 2000 new stickers per month to its rangers. I'm already becoming well acquainted with these little stickers, when I can find them.

After I've been riding around in circles for some time in Dover, directed by confusing NCN stickers and a metal sign pointing the wrong way, a local cyclist, Steve, takes pity on me and guides me out of town. We cross between various bits of pavement, up 'Death Valley', his name for the debris-strewn pavement cycle path beside the dual carriageway that leads steeply out of town.

On some residential streets away from the roar of traffic, where we can hear each other a bit better, Steve tells me he's lived in Dover his whole life, was born there and has always worked there. 'It's gone downhill a bit,' he says, 'but then a lot of places have.' Steve tries to cycle all year round, but tends to put on weight in winter, being tempted after each ride to indulge in biscuits and pies. 'There's something wrong with my masterplan,' he admits, puffing up the hill. We cross the massive main road out of town on a neat little cycling and walking bridge. As we're about to part, another cyclist stops to chat. This is Lewis, a young man with curly golden hair on a touring bike. He's cycling home from Hastings to Broadstairs, having ridden all the way there yesterday to camp overnight. He says the next section is lovely and I'm in for a treat.

Bidding Steve and Lewis goodbye, I climb up a headland nature reserve, on a new, wide, smooth tarmac path. The morning is overcast, there are ponies in an adjacent field and a morning haze smudges

53

the sea and white cliffs. On clear days I imagine the view would be outstanding, but even slightly out of focus it's enchanting. I'd say it's the kind of morning that makes you glad to be alive, but every morning on the bike does that for me.

This path, which runs two and a half miles, in parallel with but separate from the dual carriageway, was recently resurfaced by Sustrans, funded with more than half a million pounds from the trunk roads body, National Highways. The charity hopes the route will help local people cycle for everyday journeys as well as improving access for visitors on foot and bike. Formerly it was a potholed dirt path. Now it's easy riding over lovely rolling grassland, with beautiful views towards the Battle of Britain memorial at Capel-le-Ferne.

It feels like a small win for cycling. It's less than 10 miles between Dover and Folkestone, albeit with some hills – less than an hour's ride, and eminently cyclable, particularly with an ebike. Though you won't tempt everyone to cycle for every journey in and between town centres, along the way are homes, businesses, sightseeing spots and places of historical importance – the kinds of short daily trips where it's useful to have other options than driving. Plus there are people like Steve who come out for exercise and peace and quiet, when not interrupted by lost journalists. I notice there's still some work to do to connect the remaining seven and a half miles, aside from the disappearing pavement path leaving Dover.

As a kid, growing up on a steep little hillside smallholding in rural west Somerset, one of my favourite outdoor games was to invent escape routes from imagined pursuers via an elaborate series of holes in fences, alleyways and steps. I would run, duck, scramble and dodge, always making it to safety and slipping away from my pursuers undetected. In places the NCN takes me right back there, the route down into Folkestone being a classic of the genre. In the spirit of things just imagine, if you will, James Bond-like leaps and general feats of daring.

Off the Old Dover Road, a quiet street lined on one side with quirky clifftop houses, is a narrow, potholed little path heading downhill into Folkestone. It's crowded by undergrowth and when I ride through that April it contains a couple in Lycra struggling single file uphill. I wait for them and we exchange good mornings in that absent-minded way, though it's past midday. I hear French accents and wonder briefly what they make of our NCN.

From there, the chase is on: at the bottom it's out into a main road you have to ford, using your wits alone, to a narrow traffic island. Safely across, there's a zig-zag of arrows leading down a steep pavement path matted with dead plant matter and scattered with loose stones, before you plunge left down an even steeper side road into a housing estate. Someone has painted a cycle lane in a comedy U-shape at the end of a cul-de-sac, as if its author had heard of bike lanes but wasn't really sure what their purpose was. 'As long as the lane follows the pavement,' I can imagine them being told, 'you can't go wrong . . .'

Then an arrow shoves you unceremoniously on to a potholed pavement that probably saw better days a decade ago and then, at another right angle, into a narrow, fenced path between two gardens and back on to another residential road. From there the NCN drops through Folkestone via a long, straight descent on the road (painted cycle lane only, I'm afraid) and out the other side of town, surprisingly, right through the middle of an adventure play park. Cycling at more than walking pace is unwise, I decide, if I hope not to bump into any children.

The rest of the day runs the gamut of NCN experience: gravel on the Royal Military Canal towpath, a zig-zag of quiet country lanes, a mostly potholed path through a sheep field, some gates, pavements and even some ancient stairs requiring riders to dismount, leading up into Rye. Sustrans is resurfacing a path away from a bad main road, with views of lakes and wetland, and isolated little houses. While the tarmacking isn't finished, it's a bank holiday and no-one is about, so I sneak round the 'Cycle route closed' signs. This is more like it.

A couple of weeks later I return on a press trip, retracing much of the route from Folkestone to Rye, and one of the more hardened adventure cyclists complains he preferred the gravel. If you're designing for fit young men, fine, but if you want people with disabilities, those with heavier or non-standard machines, or even those without a special gravel bike to use the path, it needs to be well surfaced. One friend, spooked after a fall, cycles at walking pace or dismounts whenever faced with a gravel path. Cycling should be as much of an adventure as you want it to be, in my opinion – with the option you can just get there as smoothly and easily as possible. The tarmac feels like a victory for inclusivity to me – and it makes for much easier riding.

One Sunday at the end of April my friend Claire joins me to ride from Hastings to Brighton along the coast. This is Claire's first daytrip without her infant son and she's delighted to be by the sea, which glitters in a bright haze of morning sun. At the seafront in Hastings we stop briefly to talk to some Rotary club volunteers staffing a charity ride and are given the rundown by one chatty man in his late 60s about what makes Hastings so great.

Part of me is considering leaving London, so I'm making mental notes and have to admit Hastings does seem fun. For him, it is the quirky residents that do it. 'Where else do people paint themselves green and dance around the streets for May Day?' he asks proudly – adding the slower trains from London stop it from getting too busy. It reminds me of what Prince said of Minneapolis – that the cold weather keeps the bad people out. Here it's the bad train connections. When the man starts running through Hastings' many other festivities, I realise we aren't going to get away without interrupting him.

As if to underline the point, around a corner we almost bump into a man coming the other way on a penny farthing. Neither of us can believe he just navigated the pebble-littered beachfront path from up there, unscathed. We dodge the pebbles ourselves, singing, 'Oh I do like to be beside the seaside', and stop to eat our packed lunches on the shingle. The ocean shines silver like a mackerel's back, dazzling us as we shovel away our salads and sandwiches.

The coastal promenades give way to narrow roads littered with potholes and treacherous crumbling edges, spiced up by some dangerous overtaking. Spring has sprung and there are bluebells, and the new leaves on the trees are acid green in the bright sunshine. NCN2 merges very briefly with the start of the Cuckoo Trail, billed as one of the most popular family cycle routes in the south east. Running 10, 12 or 14 miles, depending who you ask, between Heathfield and Polegate, it's another former rail trail, opened by Sustrans in 1995 and, curiously, by the then TV gladiator, Jet.

Perhaps more curious is who built it. Former Sustrans regional manager Mark Strong recalls driving some ex-offenders to the trail for a day's work. 'I got in the minivan and there was a bit of shouting, so I asked what was going on and someone said, "I'm not sitting next to him, he's the murderer – I was only inside for fraud!"' When the men enquired what their task was, Mark explained they were going out to do some tree clearance with axes and chainsaws. He remembers this made him feel a little uncomfortable, but the man in question tried to reassure him, saying, 'It was only the once and I was angry. I'm not angry now. Don't worry, I'm not gonna kill anyone again!'

On a narrow, wood-shaded path, the trees draw shadow veins on the dry mud below; the sky is an improbably bright, clear blue, and the leaves luminous. Some dog walkers are out, enjoying the day. 'Apparently this is a cycle route,' a woman dog walker says, apropos of nothing, and mildly incredulous.

'I know, it's a bit narrow,' I respond.

'We tried cycling on it once and gave up and went somewhere else,' the man says as I wait for Claire to photograph some bluebells.

Claire, an adventurous spirit and a strong cyclist on a fairly rugged road bike, is enjoying her discovery of the NCN, saying, 'It's like an adventure, because you never know what you're going to find next!' We are both delighted by our surroundings, the wind turbines peeking out from behind hedges, amid the roadside buttercups. We ride through quiet country lanes and try to duck past some 'Road closed' signs – you can usually sneak through on a bike – but our way is eventually blocked by fences and we have to haul the bikes over a field gate. This is the third NCN blockage I've encountered in just a few weeks. I'm keeping count. They're building a new roadside cycle path, it turns out, connecting to one of England's best new cycle routes, but I won't discover that for some months yet.

On a scary main road, I put feet to pedals to get through as fast as possible. Claire, unusually, lags behind. I wait for her at the next turning, with a van driver tailgating me, in case she misses the NCN sign.

'Are you OK?' I ask.

'I got lost in thought,' she says cheerily, 'and when I do that, I stop pedalling.' It seems incredible, and perhaps indicative of our different characters, that I was pedalling for my life on that main road, while she was happily daydreaming.

I was already aware, from coworking with Claire, that she disappears into her own thoughts to a remarkable degree. It gives her a formidable focus at work, but it can sometimes take a while for the external world to filter in. While cycling, I notice she has an unnerving habit of swinging suddenly towards oncoming pedestrians or traffic and I'm never sure if she's seen what's up ahead until, after a couple of panicked warnings, she calmly pulls in. As an excessive worrier about the safety of others it concerns me. A southpaw, she naturally dismounts on the right, on the traffic side. A couple of times on today's ride she simply dismounts and steps backwards into the road without looking. The thought occurs to me that cycle routes don't need to just be safe for a 'sensible 12-year-old', the aspirational standard for the NCN, coined by John, they need to be suitable for life's daydreamers. After all, why should we need constant vigilance on a nice day out?

We stop for tea at one of a series of cycle-friendly cafés in the area, this one in a brewery complex, complete with themed sandwiches (the 'Chris Hoy' involves thick cut ham and vintage cheddar), cake and excellent coffee. The area is a hotspot for leisure cycling, close to the off-road mountain bike route, the South Downs Way (NCN21), so on a sunny weekend the café is busy. We park up at the bike racks and sit outdoors with road cyclists and e-mountain bikers in the sun trap of the brewery yard, enjoying lovely views across the green fields of the verdant Cuckmere Valley.

The countryside around the chocolate-box pretty village of Litlington, with its flint and sandstone houses, is eye-poppingly beautiful. As the quiet country road sweeps Claire and me around the river valley floor, a herd of dark brown cattle grazes the foreground, on the floodplain beside the Cuckmere River. Behind this, tinged blue in the afternoon light, a lump of hillside displays a great white horse, etched at its top in the chalk earth. Generations of people have likely looked at this unchanged view. There's a roadside warning of toads for the next half a mile, but sadly we don't spot any.

We ride through an NCN-marked field – it's that or the main road – and greet the local sheep. Between Seaford and Newhaven someone has considerably built a smooth, wide path set back from the main road and shaded it with now established trees. This is the kind of route we need around the country. There are even rabbits hopping along in the grass verges. Newhaven's harbour holds a fleet of little white yachts, lined up in the turquoise water. It's cycling heaven. Then we climb up to clifftop dirt roads, before greeting the ocean once more, on a flying pavement path into Brighton.

As if to remind us of what's possible, in Brighton the seafront road, Madeira Drive, has been upgraded during Covid to a wide, two-way cycle lane, removing one lane of traffic and making it one-way for vehicles. It continues on to the border of Hove, a tantalising glimpse at a future route.

It feels like I'm embarking on a big adventure around the country, but by the time we reach Brighton it's the end of April and I'm conscious that if I'm to complete my journey before the autumn I'll need to get moving on my patchy circumnavigation of Britain. With the NCN west of Brighton intermittent to Chichester, now seems a good time to leave the south coast behind. That means the day trips are done and I'll need panniers where I'm going next. The subsequent trip is to the Isle of Wight to meet someone working hard to make the roads safer. But first we need to understand how we got to where we are today.

6

MILLENNIUM MILES, MOSS AND AN OMERTA

At its launch, Sustrans believed the NCN had three purposes: to be attractive for novices, memorable for visitors and useful for local cyclists. It needed to be traffic free or low traffic and link with local networks, so you didn't have to drive to reach it. The NCN was always intended as a core network to which councils would add their own routes on the roads they controlled – the fine-grained networks that would make everyday journeys cyclable. Although Sustrans works with local councils on developing these networks, they have no powers to ensure their delivery.

Over the years, some local authorities held up their side of the bargain, if you could call it that, on roads and through parks, and some didn't. Routes generally became part of the NCN where they aligned with the core network, but in built-up areas they were often of mixed quality, requiring some skill and confidence to navigate, and hardly attractive to a novice. The rest were on roads, which gradually became busier.

Many cycle paths crumbled and faded under a lack of maintenance. The UK's cities and countryside are littered with these cycle lanes that time forgot, bike routes of Avalon: traffic-free paths tucked behind industrial estates, mossed over and collapsing; laughably short, unusable pavement bike lanes that appear beside rural roundabouts, now carpeted in brambles. I often wonder, when I encounter them, were they intended to link into future routes that never happened? Were they the efforts of a well-intentioned council officer who moved on or retired before their dream was realised? Or were they contributions by a developer who hoped someone else would pick up the baton?

It's hardly surprising in this context that some NCN routes – the well-maintained ones away from traffic on peaceful, flat paths surrounded by trees – became victims of their own success, where at peak times high-speed cycle commuters mixed in with dog walkers and school children on a three-metre-wide strip of tarmac.

Once the Millennium lottery funding that founded the network was spent, with no more millenniums on the horizon, Sustrans found ways to keep going. The charity won another £50 million from the National Lottery in 2007, for more than a hundred crossings and bridges, linking communities across railway tracks, rivers and main roads. Sustrans estimated the 30-year return on these bridges to be up to £8 for every £1 invested – much of this in health benefits. By comparison, road investment tends to return just £1 to £1.50 (if we're lucky), so we don't lose money on them, but we don't gain much. The closer these safe cycling and walking connections are to people's homes, the easier they obviously are to get to and the bigger the benefits.

In 10 years, Sustrans had transformed from a group of radicals with elbow grease and persuasive skills to an organisation responsible for a national piece of infrastructure. The charity kept refocusing its efforts to attract grants, depending on current policy trends, from building safe routes to schools, to connecting cycle routes with railway stations and behaviour change programmes helping support people to get cycling. Bits and bobs of funding came from government bodies, local councils, Heritage Lottery funds for the old rail bridges and EU grants, as well as private trusts.

Despite their success, getting anything built was a slow process. For each metre of route, Sustrans had to line up planning permissions and support from local councils and communities – often without the funding yet in place to deliver – and the degree of feast and famine was remarkable. It wasn't, and still isn't, uncommon for tens of millions of pounds of taxpayers' money to suddenly become available in winter due to departmental underspend. The charity became adept at lining up designs and agreements for potential projects ahead of time, so that if and when money appeared they could rapidly spend it by the end of the financial year.

By now, many NCN routes had become world famous – from the family-friendly, traffic-free Camel and Tarka Trails in Cornwall and Devon, to the epic C2C (Sea to Sea) route from Cumbria to Tyneside. Others, like the Bristol and Bath path, were crucial commuter infrastructure, too.

While outwardly Sustrans was busy and thriving, by 2007, within the charity itself, a power struggle was coming to a head. A kind of omerta hangs over what exactly happened, with different views on who was involved. Even the incoming CEO, the charity's long-standing finance director Malcolm Shepherd, says he wasn't aware of events at the time, which he says emanated from the board. However it happened, though, in 2008 John Grimshaw, who some people felt was possibly the only person with the drive, engineering knowhow and charisma to have delivered such a mammoth achievement on a shoestring budget, was summarily ejected from Sustrans.

Simon Talbot-Ponsonby was the project director responsible for delivering the many paths that made up the new network – with just two engineers. He says regional staff would phone him up needing counselling 'because the whirlwind had just been in.' He continues, 'John had a vision and when he told somebody to do something, he was generally broadly right... My job was to translate what John wanted [in]to something that was practically achievable. John's very practical, but not necessarily when it comes to dealing with other people.'

Some local authorities 'loved to work with John because he was charismatic and others couldn't cope with him,' he says. 'I dealt with all the ones that didn't like him.' It was the same with staff: because there was no money for hotels, staff would host each other at their homes and John's appearances for inspections were treated like royal visits. One local member would even give up his bed for John.

Office staff would jokingly pin a *Bike Mag* article on the noticeboard describing John as a military leader who 'never looks round to check whether [his troops] are still with him or are lying bloodied by the wayside' and 'a thorny bastard and arrogant with it, who has no time for terrestrial concerns like being nice to people, or even polite'. 'God in the office' was how one 'underling' described him to the article's author. This characterisation, John says, is 'unfair'.

In a similar vein, Caroline says that for around a decade someone kept removing John's name from Sustrans' Wikipedia page. She would write him back into the charity's history, only to see him removed again later.

John, tellingly, describes his removal as a 'palace coup'. He acknowledges he was growing very frustrated – 'I couldn't stand various procedural meetings and stuff on diagrams . . . it wasn't my scene at all' – and while he feels bitter about what happened, he admits building paths is where he excels. He accepts his methods could be abrasive but, to him, delivery of the network within a tight timeline and with limited funds meant pushing people. 'My style of management was constantly touring the country looking at the work that was on the ground,' he says, 'praising things which were done well – and a lot was done well – but of course on a complex project such as we were doing there were always things which were falling behind.'

More broadly, staff from the early years, John and Simon included, were increasingly torn on the charity's direction of travel. Although Sustrans was founded by environmental campaigners, Simon Talbot-Ponsonby felt the focus on the NCN had been lost in 'trying to solve the problems of the world,' including climate change and health. Meanwhile, the new miles that were introduced weren't always quality miles – they were, perhaps more accurately, holding miles. Sometimes, faced with a mile gap between two good bits of NCN staff would do their best to link them up, however inadequate that link might be. It could be as little as a 50cm path on the verge of a dual carriageway if it meant joining up two lovely sections of route.

Malcolm Shepherd acknowledges some of this took place under his watch. 'At one stage we were getting a bit carried away about distance of the NCN,' he says, adding staff wanted to prove the trust and investment given them by delivering more than they promised.

They wanted to demonstrate its positive impact. He added that if they'd had more money, they would have focused more on quality, and not just quantity.

There wasn't a huge amount of quantity, though, either. If before 2010 the NCN's growth looked a 45-degree slope, after 2010 it resembled a flat line. Between 1999 and 2005 the total mileage had rocketed, at a rate of roughly 2000 miles per year, to 12,000 miles, followed by another five-year spurt to 15,000 miles by 2010. Progress under Shepherd slowed to around 250 new miles per year, eventually reaching its peak of 16,500-odd miles by 2016.

Nonetheless, by 2014 Sustrans had gained a place on the UK's top 100 charities list, spending £70 million a year on anything from path upgrades to behaviour change programmes. In some ways, though, they were thinking on the scale of a charity, rather than a body delivering a piece of national infrastructure. Shepherd recalls a conversation with a minister. 'I said, "Look, why is it we're not able to get through to Government as we should by now?" And he said, "To be absolutely honest, you don't ask for enough money."'

The money Westminster did spend on cycling had an impact: between 2013 and 2018, eight English cities were allocated funds for 14 projects, including in Bristol, Cambridge, Manchester and Newcastle. In five years cycling in those cities grew, for the most part, by 25% to 50% by the end of construction, and kept on growing. The biggest cycling increases happened on high-quality, on-road routes that replaced car parking spaces or traffic lanes, giving people cycling the priority they need on the road, just as we do for people driving. More women and people from ethnic minorities cycled thanks to these routes, and at least a million car trips per year were switched to cycling – health, equality and decongestion benefits, all for just £191 million, which is small beer in transport terms.

This was yet another in a long line of stop-start funding initiatives, however – trials that were never scaled up, despite their clear benefits – and the money inevitably ran out. As roads became busier, and funding and support to improve the NCN's signage, surfacing and accessibility failed to materialise, Shepherd and his team started a conversation about the NCN's declining quality. While they wanted a 12-year-old to be able to navigate the NCN unaccompanied there was a lot of it, Shepherd admits, 'where you wouldn't dream of doing that, so it had to change. Either that or we had to accept something quite different and I don't think we would ever want to do that. Use of pavements was never a good idea, but there was a lot of it that was being done.'

In places, councils didn't seem to know the NCN existed, and unless there happened to be a local champion and some funding, paths built by the people were overtaken by other forces. Routes turned to mud in winter, tarmac broke up and potholes formed, and many roads, by then 67% of the network, became so overrun with motor traffic that cycling on them was inconceivable for all but the hardiest of cyclist. Ownership of the remaining third of the network was split between bodies like the Canal & River Trust, the Forestry Commission, Network Rail, the National Trust and private landowners, and only around 2% was owned by Sustrans, further complicating matters.

As a minority landowner and 'custodian' of the network, rather than a national body with the necessary money and power, Sustrans couldn't make councils build, maintain or improve routes, and while compulsory purchase powers are almost ubiquitously used by government bodies in roadbuilding projects, for cycle routes it doesn't happen. While some NCN routes thrived and became ever more popular with tourists and commuters, others languished.

As a result, the NCN's reputation, and with it people's opinions of Sustrans, was mixed. Along with the beloved iconic sections of traffic-free route through some of Britain's most beautiful landscapes were the sketchy, potholed roads shared with heavy industrial traffic and the endless obstructive barriers cyclists struggled to negotiate on rocky paths. For some cyclists and campaigners, the NCN had become a byword for the shoddiness of British cycle routes. While the Dutch, having largely nailed the urban cycling environment, were developing intercity high-speed cycle routes on which users barely needed to slow down, let alone stop, UK cyclists still had to negotiate space with pedestrians on pavements or with speeding motor traffic on A-roads.

Some of the criticisms levelled were that quality standards were being 'lost in Sus-translation' and some of the NCN represented little more than a 'notional cycle network'. While some of the criticism was fair, the charity had become a lightning rod for people's frustrations about a lack of decent, safe cycle routes in the UK and the increasingly hostile traffic conditions that were driving cyclists away from ever-busier public roads. Many of the decisions resulting in NCN routes, from path alignment and quality to traffic speeds and volumes, were beyond the charity's control, but it did have one card up its sleeve.

In 2015 and 2016, as Malcolm Shepherd was leaving and a new CEO, Xavier Brice, taking the helm, a team of freelance surveyors set about examining the network through a magnifying glass. They categorised things like surface type, width, lighting, barriers and signage, as well as road classification for on-road sections. They also asked users, supporters, volunteers and stakeholders what they thought of the network. The vision behind the 'For Everyone' approach Sustrans' new CEO was leading was for 'a UK-wide network of traffic-free paths for everyone, connecting cities, towns and countryside, loved by the communities they serve'. The surveys revealed just how far away that vision was.

While the review characterised more than half of the network (53%) as 'good', just 1% was very good and almost half was below par, 42% of it involving things like busy roads with fast traffic, poor signage, inadequate surfaces and barriers, and even the odd ford or beach crossing. There were a staggering 16,435 barriers on the network, including steps and steep ramps unusable in a wheelchair, roughly at a rate of three per mile on off-road sections. There were also 473 crossings and junctions that needed attention, mostly where traffic-free sections crossed a road, and '15,680 incorrect, missing, obstructed, confusing and damaged signs' hampering user navigation. In total, 7596 miles of route were below standard and Sustrans calculated it would take £2.8 billion – and 22 years – to make them good.

Intuitively, its users knew much of this already. When asked what one change they would like to see on the network, 6000 NCN users, surveyed online as part of this reckoning, unleashed a litany of requests. Surging into the online form from computers, phones and tablets up and down the country was a river of strong feeling, fed by thousands of tributaries. While some users voiced enthusiasm for beloved routes, far more expressed anger and frustration at their absence or insufficiency. This cascade of remarks was delivered in comment-box staccato, 10 words of bewilderment and a deep desire to be able to cycle, walk and wheel safely, year round. In many places it is like reading one-star Google reviews.

One soul, bereft of local cycle routes, simply pleaded for anything but the existing 'big black hole' on the map where they live. Another, angrier, demanded: 'Make your network useful and people will use it.' Another said: 'Build decent quality infrastructure and maintain it,' with examples of its failings including 'badly surfaced mud tracks' 'full of obstacles: cobble strips, gates, barriers,' 'impassable even on a mountain bike' and 'too many busy roads'. One listed an alarming gamut of possible hazards on their local routes, including 'being thrown the wrong way into bus stops on 60mph roads, overrun with trees, constant blind turnings and poor surfaces'. 'The "network,"' they added in sarcastic quotation marks, 'is a disgrace.' 'Stretches of brilliant path fizzle out when they get into towns, or send you on ridiculous convoluted routes around back streets,' another observed.

Signage, accessibility and surface quality were a big issue. 'No signs telling me to get off and walk, no speed bumps, no chicanes. Tarmac,' was one person's battle cry. Respondents blamed Sustrans and some felt they should no longer manage the NCN or put their signs, seen as a seal of approval, on routes that were clearly not up to scratch.

Sustrans' new CEO, Xavier Brice, and his team accepted that if they wanted a network people could rely on, some of it was going to have to go. As I mentioned in the introduction, in 2018 he admitted to me, for a piece I wrote in the *Times*, that people had had enough of the crap bits of the NCN, and they needed fixing. It was the start of a new cathartic era of honesty. In 2020 the charity removed its branding from the worst quarter of the network, reducing it from 16,575 miles to less than 13,000. This was more like the standard that was safe enough for that 'sensible 12-year-old' to use unaccompanied, but it was also a sad admission of the various limitations holding back progress. It wasn't a story entirely about decline, however: as part of the new era, in 2018 Sustrans proposed 55 'activation projects', a pledge to fill key missing links on the network, where local authorities and landowners were on side. In time-honoured tradition, within six months, thanks to this vision of improvement and again to departmental underspend, the project was fully funded and by 2023 297 network improvements were completed.

While the review didn't change the power dynamics surrounding route delivery – councils still controlled the roads, and private landowners many of the off-road sections – it began a much-needed improvement process. That included that loch-side path near Oban, whose launch I went to in 2019. The ribbon-cutting event that April was attended by children who were suddenly able to cycle to school year-round and, as if to underscore the 'for everyone' title, while riding the new tarmac we passed a large group of seniors out for a sunny morning hike. In partnership with local authorities and landowners, the charity also wanted to improve the network and its signage – the network lives or dies by decent signage – so users didn't need to use a map or smartphone. It also pledged to deliver 5000 more traffic-free miles within the next 22 years.

Sustrans had purged most of the crap from its network, but with many miles still 'very poor', 19% of the network was designated for experienced cyclists only – represented by dotted lines on the OS map. If nothing else it perhaps served to embarrass some councils into action and since the loss of some routes at least one council, Norfolk, which lost some of its tourist attraction routes in the process, began improvements to bring the NCN branding back.

The charity's ambitions ramped up again. In February 2022, writing for the *Guardian*, I broke the news of Sustrans' new target to link every settlement of 10,000 people or more with a traffic-free, barrier-free network 'suitable for a sensible 12-year-old travelling alone'. This was a massive statement of intent, reiterating its founding purpose as a national network and extending its 12,786 miles to reach all corners of the UK with decent routes, but delivery remained an issue.

It is now unusual for a charity to run a national piece of infrastructure, but it isn't uncommon for civil society to be the driver for cycle routes. Decades of marketing and lobbying by the motor industry kept cars high on the agenda, sidelining the humble bicycle around the world, but in the 1990s cycle clubs, campaigners and citizens in the Netherlands, France, Germany, Denmark and other European countries kickstarted early cycle routes, too. The difference is, in those countries the local and national governments soon stepped in to fund, expand and improve those networks.

The UK may have been the first nation to conceive of a national cycle network, but it's no coincidence other countries have rapidly overtaken us. The Dutch national cycle network started in the 1920s and 1930s as a campaign for rural and suburban cycle paths, led by cyclists pressing for investment in leisure routes. Those rural routes kept Dutch cycling levels relatively high, even as cars dominated across Europe. Recognising an opportunity for wider support, campaigners began to position routes as rural transport networks, providing cheap and accessible mobility. It took another 50 years for urban cycle campaigns and the Stop de Kindermoord (Stop the Child Murder) movement, which came from a growing horror of children increasingly being injured and killed in traffic collisions, to get going. Now, regional governments develop, maintain and expand cycle routes in cities and towns and, also crucially, beyond and between them.

In 2015 I spent a month in the Netherlands, part of which was spent cycling around the country, almost entirely on a network of dedicated bicycle roads. I even rode a surreal 32-mile-long cycle path alongside a motorway crossing the Afsluitdijk, the dam protecting the land from the North Sea. After decades of planning for cycling, there wasn't a place you couldn't go by bike, just as for cars. I was undoubtedly a tourist, with my panniers full of camping gear, tepid cheese slices, bread and apples, but on my way I saw the sheer variety of users, from elderly couples riding side by side on electric bikes, heading from the villages into town, to kids cycling from school through windswept field cycle paths. I witnessed Amsterdam's epic bicycle rush hours. At the weekends, fit folks in Lycra use the bicycle roads for fast training rides.

In 1997, just as the UK's NCN was taking shape, a group of French activists began lobbying for construction of a network of long-distance tourist routes across France to connect with local cycling infrastructure and greenways. The following year the relevant government department took the ball and ran with it. By 1999 a new body of regional governments and national establishments, Vélo et Territoires, had a plan to deliver a 9000km national network of cycle routes and greenways, to new design standards. They would connect the main towns and French regions with Europe-wide cycle routes on the Eurovelo network. The routes were initially understood as tourist attractions, but later local authorities realised cycling was becoming a commuting option, even in France's large rural areas, linking to train stations that connected onward to towns and cities.

In 2010 and 2019 the plan, and the standards, were revised upwards again to improve social inclusion and in 2011 the cycle routes became part of the national plan for transport infrastructure. By 2020 the 193-member-strong body of regions, départements, towns and cities involved had delivered a 25,000km network of cycle routes, 46% traffic free, and the remainder on roads shared with traffic.

Following a growth in new cycle routes during the pandemic, the French government claimed there were now 50,000km of cycle routes – more than 18,000 miles more than Britain's, albeit in a much larger geographical area. In early 2023 France pledged to spend €2 billion on cycle infrastructure and supporting measures over the following four years, with €250 million a year for bike routes alone, to double the cycle network by 2030 to 100,000km. Meanwhile, in Britain, cycling was still fighting for scraps.

In the UK, by December 2023, Sustrans had completed just 233 miles of improvements and removed or redesigned 1414 (9%) of more than 16,000 barriers in three years, while new barriers were still being introduced elsewhere. While still an undoubtedly impressive achievement for a charity with no legal powers to deliver and reliant on patchy funding, at that rate it will take 235 years to match the cycle route mileage French government regions, départements, towns and cities had achieved in just 31. Meanwhile, if local authorities and landowners don't add new ones, the network will finally be barrier-free, or close to it, in 34 years. Each one of those removed barriers, Sustrans points out, has made a big difference in its local community, each one potentially enabling education, work and social opportunities. The realisation of Sustrans' masterplan, meanwhile, would see the NCN increased to approximately 17,000 miles. The rest of the network would have to be delivered by highways authorities, regional transport bodies and volunteers, working in isolation with little to no co-ordination or a national plan to link them together.

7

CRIME AND ACCIDENTAL PUNISHMENT
ON THE ISLE OF WIGHT

The main reason most people don't cycle is fear of traffic, yet movement on this issue has been painfully slow. In the decade since 2011 fatalities on Britain's roads, per billion miles, have barely budged. Cuts to roads policing have left forces across the UK starved of resources to temper the worst impulses of the worst drivers, arguably dragging the general driving standard down with them, while tensions between cyclists and drivers forced to share the same crowded roads – fuelled by parts of the media – are left unchecked.

Attempts to keep those on foot and cycles safe have, perversely, tended to focus on those least able to prevent the carnage: cyclists and pedestrians themselves. Perhaps unsurprisingly, these patchy initiatives encouraging the use of hi-vis, helmets and constant vigilance from anyone on foot or bike from childhood onward have not yielded the hoped-for improvements in road safety.

In this surreal landscape, Detective Chief Superintendent Andy Cox, National Police Chiefs' Council lead for fatal collisions, appears, mirage-like, as a rare voice of reason. Through an apparently relentless one-man campaign, he's trying to shake us out of the apathy that lets us accept, almost unquestioned, five people dying each day on Britain's roads.

I'm crouched at the side of a gravel path on the Isle of Wight with my back wheel in my hands, while Andy and his brother Dave stand by, waiting for me to fix a puncture. It could have been embarrassing, but Andy and Dave are taking it all in their stride – while trying not to laugh. There is no getting away from it: I drove the bike over some dog poo just before my back wheel punctured and now the poo is on my finger.

No-one has any hand sanitiser with them, only some tissues and some fruit-flavoured water. We watch a Labrador and its owner walk past, and wonder collectively if this dog is the culprit (it isn't; we see the man responsibly use a bag). Regardless, I spend the next few miles, middle left finger raised off my handlebars in a rude act of quarantine, lest it contaminate all it touches.

Slapstick aside, we're here for a serious purpose. Andy is embarking on day one of his second annual countrywide challenge to shift the dial on road danger. His plan is to ride and run in different locations with various police forces across England, meeting bereaved families and hapless journalists. He is also raising money for RoadPeace, the small charity that helps loved ones and victims of traffic danger pick up the pieces after a collision. The first day of his challenge starts here, on the Isle of Wight, with 30 miles of cycling.

Cycle network or not, if you ride a bike, you're going to encounter drivers at some point: at road crossings, on country lanes, in neighbourhood streets. Cycling isn't fundamentally a dangerous activity; it's actually more dangerous not getting regular exercise, in terms of our health – but while most people are careful and considerate behind the wheel, things can and do go wrong. That's why people like Andy are so important, not only in enforcing the law but by raising awareness of where the danger is coming from and what we can do about it.

I crossed the Solent the night before under a dreamy pink sky, before a night of epic thunder, flashes of lightning and heavy rain. The storm was so loud it woke me in my haunted-looking room above a pub, convinced for a moment someone was wheeling a large cart along a cobbled street beneath the window. In my mind it was big and plastic and yellow, and possibly filled with fish.

In the morning I take the 'floating bridge' – a very slow chain link ferry that apparently keeps breaking down – like a cycling salmon against a tide of children catching the ferry to school on foot. Riding towards West Cowes seafront, I think I see Andy and give him a wave as I approach, but it's not him, it's Andy's brother Dave, with their dad, Douglas. It turns out Andy's family is from the Isle of Wight and they still live here. Andy chose the island to start partly because of his connection to the place.

Detective Chief Superintendent Andy Cox arrives moments later, a tall, athletic, broad-shouldered man in his early 40s. He's wearing a purple Andy Cox Challenge T-shirt under a softshell jacket. His girlfriend, Ciara, and her son are also here, in the bright yellow electric car loaned to them by the AA for the challenge, complete with L-plates and, apparently, a second set of pedals. Ciara's car is being repaired and the yellow car adds a perhaps unwanted comedy note to proceedings, which Andy seems mildly embarrassed by. He may be a senior police officer and a public figure of some standing, but he still removes his helmet for photos, so Chris Boardman doesn't see him on the internet wearing a lid. While wearing one is a personal choice, the general feeling is it makes cycling look more dangerous than it is. You're in fact more likely to contract a head injury in your own bathroom. It's not that there's anything wrong with helmets, rather that they can end up becoming a distraction.

The first time we met, in December 2019, Andy was head of Vision Zero in the Metropolitan Police, with the objective of eliminating road deaths and serious injuries in the capital by 2041. I'd suggested a morning meeting in Victoria to talk generally about his work for a potential article, not realising this would mean a 5 a.m. start for him, travelling from Northamptonshire. He talked through his strategy to target lawbreaking drivers as a way of not only making the roads safer, but catching criminals who, he says, stand out because they are likely to break other laws, like driving without a seatbelt and speeding. It was the first time I'd heard a police officer talk in this way and it felt revolutionary.

Andy keeps reiterating the fact that four to five people are killed every day in the UK because of road collisions and 24,000 people a year are permanently disabled – and yet it's something we've come to accept. In 2022, 85 people were killed cycling in Great Britain and 376 people were killed while walking. Each of these deaths devastates both the victim's family and often the person behind the wheel.

He uses social media, interviews and, each year, the Andy Cox Challenge to highlight this problem that's often hiding in plain sight. It takes a lot to create a societal shift in how we perceive and tackle road crime, as Andy terms it, but that's what he's trying to do. He jokes about how mouthy he is on social media and he can sometimes be seen wading into Twitter debates to correct misinformation or outdated assumptions. He even quietly has words with other police forces who fall foul of prejudices that focus on the victims of road danger, rather than the culprits – the outdated helmets, hi-vis and 'share the road' initiatives.

Before moving to roads policing, Andy had exactly the kind of attitude he's now trying to change: that crashes are just one of those things, an inevitability. Another common misconception is that cyclists are to blame for causing danger and, while people cycling through red lights and on the pavements is unacceptable, there's a much bigger problem, as Andy knows from the crash data.

He says, 'The stats would be that 99.7% of fatalities are linked to a driver rather than a cyclist.' He points out there's a road danger reduction and congestion benefit to targeting offending drivers, and banning the worst of them from driving again. At the moment, thousands of people are out there, behind the wheel, with more than 12 points on their licences, claiming 'exceptional hardship', because, after their fourth offence, they claim they need their driving licence. However, as Andy puts it, it's those who are killed, injured and bereaved by dangerous driving who experience the hardship.

Andy wants to change what's considered acceptable on the roads and for crashes to be treated not as inevitabilities, but as the product of poor decision making. He calls speeding and mobile phone use 'road crime' to reflect their lethal potential. It may be socially acceptable, but even driving while using your phone hands-free is so distracting that research shows it's similar to being drunk at the wheel.

Part of Andy's mission is media coverage, and he's expecting local journalists to come and cover the start of his week-long challenge, a slot on James O'Brien's LBC show at lunch time, and me. When the local media don't turn up and a slot on another major radio show is cancelled, Andy is undeterred.

I've been warned about how hilly the Isle of Wight is and I brought the Adventure Rocket with me, but Andy's brother, Dave, who still lives and works on the island, has found us a relatively flat 30-mile route following quiet roads, NCN routes and dirt paths. Their dad, Douglas, joins us for the first leg of the ride, but before we've left Cowes, at the first incline, he peels off without a word. Andy says, enigmatically, that he'll probably turn up again later. We pass a church that looks like a castle, where Andy's parents were married and where Queen Victoria attended church services when she visited the island.

As we leave town for some leafy country lanes the gradient changes, and I hear some clicking and sounds of consternation coming from Andy's bike. It turns out he's learning to use the gears on the rather fancy road bike he's been loaned for the challenge. I'm astounded when one of the key figures working to improve road safety, not least for cyclists, admits he hasn't touched a bicycle in 20 years. Thinking back, last year the challenge involved 30 miles of running per day and no cycling. I soon learn Andy is ambitious and competitive, from a sporty, cricket-loving family, and doesn't like to do things by halves – so mastering this machine is a small matter.

Leaving university to join the police in 1999, by 2012 Andy had been promoted in record time to superintendent. Then a detective working on violent crime, his chief constable moved him to the role of 'specialist operations' in Northamptonshire police. This involved road policing and guns. Andy recalls saying, 'I've never issued a traffic ticket, and I've never held a gun, so why on earth would I want to work there?'

In the hierarchical world of policing the move was non-negotiable, but Andy says it was the best thing that ever happened to him, pointing out that 'More lives are lost because of a speeding driver than murder and terrorism combined every year.' In fact, it's double. This was an area in which he could have a real impact.

Joining roads policing, Andy was instantly struck by how few resources were allocated to such a substantial cause of harm. On a murder investigation, he says, they'd have 50 or 60 staff. For road collisions, it's a fraction of that. 'They were all working in a totally disorganised way,' he says, 'and no-one was talking to each other.' Immediately apparent were the huge volumes of data police had access to, including automatic number plate recognition (ANPR), which can detect lawbreaking behaviour such as disqualified drivers, but which was barely being used.

'Every second, drivers are triggering ANPR across the country, so we're being absolutely overwhelmed by it,' he says. Andy asked officers working with ANPR what they were doing with those drivers they saw breaking the law and the answer was 'Nothing'. In London, as head of Vision Zero, he identified and targeted the most dangerous roads and the 250 most dangerous known drivers. 'Essentially, day and night we targeted those drivers and blasted them relentlessly with ANPR.'

It was a fruitful initiative. 'Surprise, surprise, we found weapons, guns, drugs, counterfeit currency, stolen vehicles, disqualified drivers, wanted people – and they didn't drive for very long, because we really targeted them.' They even caught a wanted murderer. This is all replicable on a national scale and using the same tools he believes we could easily target the most dangerous 5000 drivers.

Andy also fought to change how contributory factors are recorded in collision reports. Previously, attending officers' initial assessments, made at the side of the road, about what has happened and why, weren't being updated following a thorough collision investigation. Without accurate information about why crashes are happening, it's hard to detect trends and effectively target resources at preventing them – it's just guesswork.

In trials in Manchester and London, proving Andy's point, updated collision reports increased the proportion of crashes in which speeding was a factor by three to four times. What was assumed to be the cause of around 250 deaths a year nationwide is now understood to kill somewhere between 750 and 1000 people each year. That's the equivalent of my entire secondary school dying each year because of people breaking the speed limit. Speeding is, in fact, a factor in around half of all road deaths. There are now plans to roll this change out nationwide.

We're riding through some stunning countryside, partly following NCN routes and partly quiet roads, thanks to Dave's route-planning skills. I worry about Andy from time to time – because that's what I do – though he does admit to poor road awareness and has a tendency to veer towards the middle of the road. 'If I get killed on this ride,' he jokes, 'RoadPeace will be set for life!'

There are picturesque houses on country lanes wherever we look and Andy talks about moving back, if and when work permits – once an islander, always one. It's sunny, but last night's rain sprays us all with dirt and we're relieved to stop for a coffee on the shore, with waves crashing gently on a beach beside us. It is idyllic. I scrub my finger for a long time in the washroom basin before touching anything.

Each day of Andy's countrywide challenge has a theme and today's is about trying to change the language around road collisions, so it's apt that I'm here. In 2021, with the University of Westminster's Active Travel Academy, I researched, consulted on and published the UK's first and only road collision reporting guidelines, to try and improve the language media and professional bodies use when talking about road danger. Words shape how we view the world around us and the degree to which we see a need to act on problems. Using the word 'accident' for road crashes before the facts are known perpetuates the view that there's nothing we can do about them – because accidents just happen.

Cox sees the impact of this language in the real world. 'Number one, it's offensive to bereaved families who see the word "accident" and see the way that it's just assumed to be one of those things when it really isn't. But number two, really the reason this is important is to change the narrative, to make society think differently, so that we don't accept five people dying every day – and that we recognise that's a choice. It's driver choice.'

It's a long road though. Roughly 1600 people are killed on our roads each year; violent deaths that are for the most part preventable. Among the 10 guideline clauses was one that encouraged media and professions to mention a driver, rather than just saying things like 'the car mounted the pavement.' Semantically removing the driver from the scene, evidence indicates, obscures their presence and potential role in the crash. It's not about blame, but recognising there's a person behind the wheel in crashes and that collisions aren't inevitable. I also recommended collision reporting shouldn't focus on the less serious outcomes – like traffic delays – or claim speed detection that catches lawbreakers is somehow victimising drivers.

As Andy puts it: 'Once we change the narrative, we change our behaviours.' Fatal road collisions, horrific as they are, are still way down the priority list in the media and across the various agencies tasked with tackling it. Andy, like me, wants to change that.

Roads that feel dangerous are a huge barrier to more people cycling and walking, wherever you live, but research shows roads are dispro-portionately dangerous in rural areas, and in poorer communities and neighbourhoods where more people of colour live. Women, older people and people with disabilities are less willing to walk and cycle on streets that feel dangerous, so it's an equality issue too.

Cox wants vehicles fitted with automatic speed limiting technol-ogy, because with a national 70mph limit it makes no sense that cars are rolling off production lines capable of achieving speeds more than double that. As well as an end to 'exceptional hardship' clauses, he wants graduated driving licences for new drivers, as under-25s are more likely to be involved in fatal collisions.

We drink our coffee and get back on the road. Andy's work life sounds more intense the more we talk. All the national leads in England's police force also have a day job and, when we meet, Andy is both the national lead for fatal collision investigations and head of crime and intelligence for Lincolnshire Police. He tells me he can receive a phone call in the middle of the night, after an 18-hour day, from a firearms officer on the ground asking him for permission to take a potentially lethal shot. Between dodging puddles on a muddy path, I can't help but look at this mild-mannered man with his easy smile in a different light.

You get the feeling Andy's ambition is a little wasted in policing, though. At one point I ask him what's wrong with roads policing, and he stifles a laugh, as if it's too long a list. He obviously loves the impact of his work, the ability to save lives and prevent crime, but there are entrenched views to deal with and change is slow. One way he has a big impact is with his awareness-raising work, like this week, but as with everything, there's always a next step.

'I don't know how I'd make it work, but I'd like to do a year-long challenge around the world,' he tells me. 'I remember my eldest going on a cricket tour to India and me running round a circuit by the pitch, which was part indoors, part outdoors, while he played.' His son, Andy's spitting image, spotted him. 'He said the first-time round there was just me; the second time there were a handful of people running with me, kids and adults.' The third time sounds like a scene from *Forrest Gump*, a mass of people running along with him. 'People saw me as a curiosity,' he says.

Andy also talks about America, where he's had interest from road safety groups about his previous challenge and where he has given a talk. 'Their road deaths are four or five times higher than ours, per capita,' he says. 'It didn't go anywhere, and I thought, well I still have a lot to do here.'

We join the Squirrel Trail, the Isle of Wight's famous family-friendly cycle route, NCN23. Following an old railway trail and mostly off-road, it leads, via the gentlest incline, 32 miles from East Cowes, across the floating bridge, to Newport. As predicted, partway along Andy's dad reappears from the opposite direction, as if from nowhere, and follows us slowly to a pub where Andy does his James O'Brien interview while we grab tea and soft drinks.

There's a final traffic-free trail back into Cowes, with glimpses of the shore through trees. Douglas tells me this traffic-free path is well used by workers at some of the local industrial units and low-level lighting was installed after a couple of people strayed off the path into the trees after late shifts. Once we're in Cowes a driver impatiently undertakes Dave as he moves to turn right – the only one to have annoyed Andy on our ride so far. Due credit to Isle of Wight drivers, everyone else has been very considerate and careful. In fact, by London standards they've been an absolute delight.

As we ride Douglas keeps inviting me for lunch. I don't want to impose, but Andy insists I'd be welcome, so I follow everyone back to Andy's childhood home for a delicious cottage pie and vegetables cooked by Rosemary, Andy's mum. Ciara has bought snacks for us, finger food, which I'm still reluctant to touch, because no amount of washing will make my hand feel hygienic. We listen back to Andy's James O'Brien interview, Andy analysing how he might do better next time and then, over lunch, talk turns to the grandkids and Andy's challenge.

I think I sense Andy's posture stiffening slightly when Douglas makes a comment about badly behaved cyclists. It's not that they're not a problem, it's just that there are so many other, empirically worse problems on the roads. Even at home, we need to be able to have these conversations. Realising a ferry is leaving soon, I head back to the terminal at top speed, catching the floating bridge just in time and passing the children again, on their return journey from school.

Policing attitudes have gradually changed during my 10 years or so covering cycling and road safety, and helmet camera and dashcam submissions have made a huge impact in educating drivers and reducing the worst behaviour, but there's still a long way to go. People like Andy get it, but roads policing is still drastically underfunded: during austerity road police numbers were disproportionately cut, newly recruited officers are less experienced than those lost in the cuts, and it will take time to regain the same level of expertise, let alone change the culture. It's hard to think of any other area of life where so many people die and face life-changing injury and so little action is taken to change it. People like Andy remind us road deaths are not inevitable, but until we tackle them properly, the streets will still feel – and will be – unsafe for vulnerable walkers and cyclists.

8

CYCLING ACROSS CORNWALL
WITH A SHRUB

Cornwall is one of England's most rural counties. At the south-west end of the country, with substantial volumes of coastline, it also boasts some uniquely brutal hills. If there's anywhere that will offer up a challenge to the creation of a cycle network, it's here – and yet, even in perhaps the most unlikely of places, the bicycle's potential is substantial.

Anyone who's cycled from Land's End to John O'Groats (LEJOG) will tell you it's this end, with its beautiful but horrific little hills, they dread the most. They're steep enough to really hurt, long enough to really, really hurt, and regular enough that any brief descent is of little comfort, because you know another climb will be along directly. When I cycled LEJOG on (a rather fancier) borrowed electric road bike in 2019, I was most glad of the electric assist in Cornwall, so bringing my pink ebike with me on the Cornish leg of my NCN trip not only made sense, I considered it essential.

Even in the hardest cycling territory in the UK, 10% of people could commute by bike. In 2017, using census data and cycle journey planning tools, researchers from the universities of Leeds and Westminster developed the Propensity to Cycle Tool. They calculated a Dutch-style network of genuinely quiet roads and traffic-free paths could raise current cycling levels by five times their current 2%. With widespread e-cycle availability, it's 17% – more than one in six. Across England, with both a network of safe cycle routes and widespread ebike availability, one in four commutes could be done by cycling. This data showed cycling is not a niche pursuit – it's a genuine mass transport option.

Commuting is only part of the story, though. Among the attractions of rural cycle routes in places like Cornwall are their leisure and tourism benefits. Tourist spend in Cornwall was £970 million in the three years 2016 to 2018, which was more than the next top three English holiday destinations combined, including Cumbria's South Lakeland. Since it was completed, the famous Camel Trail, one of the jewels in the NCN's crown, quickly became Cornwall's second most popular attraction, with an estimated 300,000 users a year, rising to 400,000 by 2004. It is trumped only by the Eden Project.

Each year visitors swell motor traffic by 12%, clogging up even quiet roads and causing substantial challenges for local residents and businesses. While I'm not hoping to find a solution to those problems, a ramble across Cornwall is a crucial stage in my journey, representing the start, or end, of the network and presenting me with the kinds of challenges typical of much of the UK, 90% of which is rural.

It's mid-May and I leave home in a rush. In the 18 hours since I got back from the Isle of Wight I have shoved my camping gear and some dresses into my panniers, slept and stuffed the ebike's basket with food. I haven't really thought the dresses through, but I'm trying not to wear out the seat of the two hole-free pairs of trousers I own. I'm not keen on shopping for clothes, and besides, the idea of cycling across Cornwall in a dress seems delightfully whimsical. Part of me hopes I can cycle the entire trip in normal clothes, in the longstanding spirit of making cycling normal, but we'll see.

I'm also bringing a shrub with me, wedged into the bike basket in a cardboard box. During the pandemic I grew it from a cutting, from the overgrown garden next door, a pink flowering weigela. It's a gift for my sister Ele. I don't own a car and know to make the most of extra carrying capacity when I can. As I'm planning on cycling to Ele's house in Somerset from Land's End, this represents an ideal delivery opportunity. It, like the dresses, adds an element of fun. Plus

I relish the challenge of delivering a plant unharmed across potentially hundreds of miles of country road and cycle path.

It's 9.40 p.m. when the train pulls in to the station and dusk has fallen. I turn my synthetic down jacket inside out, figuring the orange liner will make me more visible to drivers in the gathering gloom. I reattach my panniers and the basket, and bump the hefty bike down the considerable step to the platform. Penzance: this is where the adventure begins. On catching my reflection in the train windows, I am quite obviously wearing my jacket inside out and my reflective sash makes me look like Miss World of the Apocalypse. Pushing a massive pink bike with a shrub in the front basket I am very much on the wrong side of eccentric, but probably no-one notices and I'm looking forward to being on the road, where everything will make more sense.

Once a-sail it feels like I'm piloting the bicycle equivalent of an articulated lorry, the substantial metal frame flexing gently under the combined weight of me and the luggage. It requires some concentration to keep upright: we're probably 100kg between us. Along the coast road out of town the evening air is mild and it's pelting me with something. I look suspiciously at the seabirds overhead, then at the road, before realising I'm being hit by some kind of large fly. It doesn't matter much, as long as none of them go for my eyes: there's a bit of light left in the sky and I'm on the road.

Climbing a hill, a stone memorial in the shape of a Celtic cross stands sentinel over a pretty harbour. Below, little boats bob beneath the royal blue evening sky, framed with strings of white lights. I could stay there, watching the scene, until the last of the light disappears, but I need to get camped and am immediately delighted with the ebike as my navigation app directs me away from the NCN and up an impossibly steep road. At first I can't believe it leads anywhere. Up and up me, the ebike and the shrub go, between cottages, stopping mid-way to look back down at the harbour. At the top we pass a woman and her dog. 'Steep around here, isn't it,' I call out and she says something like, 'You're brave,' perhaps failing to hear the ebike motor mooing like a perturbed cow.

Leaving the houses and street lights behind, on the narrow country lanes I realise the extremely bright front light I've attached to the handlebars only really illuminates the cardboard box with the plant in it. The effect is like the floodlights in a shrubbery of a stately home and it dazzles me into the bargain. I shade my eyes with one hand and try to aim the light at the road. For now, though, the sky is still pale with light and a couple of the shrub's leaves waft pleasingly from the top of the cardboard box, like tiny hands waving.

It's a magical if slightly tense ride. Through evening air spiced with wild garlic I follow narrow lanes with high hedges, peppered with the tall ghostly flower heads of cow parsley, before joining a couple of wider roads I'd rather not be on at night. There are some extremely cautious drivers, clearly unaccustomed to overtaking cyclists. At one point I think, 'It would be easy to get complacent about the quiet roads,' seconds before a driver appears around a sharp, narrow corner. We both slam on our brakes, and as we pass one another the driver looks as glad as me of her good brakes and fortunate timing.

At a crossroads in a faintly lit village, I stop to check I'm still going the right way and reposition the light again. I'm pleased to see a man on a mountain bike, apparently on his way back from his own evening adventure. We say hello before resubmerging into the night. As the sky fades, the bright front light illuminates parts of the passing hedge and the basket casts an ever-darker shadow just where I need to see.

Towards 10 p.m. the road becomes a phantom, the faded tarmac only slightly lighter than the hedges, and my eyes strain to see. My depth perception is going, too, in a kind of strange reverse version of snow blindness, and I can't tell if the road ahead goes uphill or down. A couple of times I almost slam on the brakes, certain I'm about to plunge off the road into darkness. From nowhere a bat whistles, inches away, past my left ear, and I whisper, 'Wow' into the night.

It's 10.07 p.m. when I arrive at Tower Park Camping, seven minutes too late for check-in. The map of the campsite, posted on the door, goes in one eye and out the other, so to speak, so I ask a passing camper for directions to the tent area. She laughs at how floodlit I look and points me towards some trees. The wind has picked up and I spend an implausible 45 minutes wrestling with my usually familiar tent as the branches above me blow alarmingly in the wind. I fight and force, and let out various straps as the whole thing flaps around like a flag. Every few minutes the front light of the ebike turns itself off, leaving me alone in the eerie wind, before I rush over to turn it back on.

I'm relieved to eventually climb into my sleeping bag and fall asleep, after releasing a gigantic moth that flies into my face. The shrub looks as happy as a shrub can look, tucked away in the tent's tiny porch and unscathed so far. I quietly bid it goodnight.

The next morning, with rain threatening, I wonder what kind of person would cycle across Cornwall carrying mainly dresses. Everything is badly crumpled and I thank heaven for the ugly baggy shorts I packed at the last minute.

It turns out I've bent my tent pole out of shape, which explains last night's struggle, and the slapstick continues. By the end of the morning I've fallen waist-deep into some rocks and stinging nettles with a half-eaten cheese sandwich mid-picnic, and snapped the kickstand off the bike trying to move it out of the way of a passing tractor.

I've also managed to get toothpaste in my eyes. Long story short, the only contact lens case I've brought was the one I keep toothpaste and Sudocrem in, when bike packing (cycle camping). I'd washed the separate lens compartments out in the train toilet, but evidently not that well and apparently only after mixing the lids up. Still, I'm in a beautiful part of the country at the start of a big adventure.

Little country lanes eventually lead to a view that stops me in my tracks. The broad expanse of Sennen Cove stretches out under a clear sky with rocky cliffs bookmarking it, as gentle little waves wash towards the shore. I follow NCN signs along a narrow road running parallel with the bay, almost colliding with a van driver talking on his phone. I stop several more times to view the bay from different angles before the van driver returns, smiling obliviously.

While LEJOG riders may head for the famous white fingerpost denoting the start and end of the land, I'm after a different sign – the one that marks the start and end of the NCN. My plan is to cycle there before doubling back to meet Simon Murray, Sustrans' network development manager for Cornwall, at St Erth. The NCN joins a narrow gravel path along the cliff top for its final metres, sharing with the epic South West Coast Path. I take a photo of the bike with the big blue sign – a milestone – and begin my journey east.

I've planned my route, 225 miles from Land's End to my hometown of Wiveliscombe, in Somerset, as best I can. I estimate it will take about six days. At the time of writing there is no way to plot a route digitally using the NCN, so I make my best guess by adding in towns I know the NCN traverses as waypoints and loading it on to a GPS device attached to my handlebars. The Ordnance Survey map app with the NCN layer is there as a backup.

Just south of Penzance there is a pub called the Lamorna Wink, a 400-year-old establishment atop a stunning bay favoured by early 20th-century Post-Impressionist painters. The pub's own painting, hanging on a pole outside, of a pirate giving a hammy wink, makes me giggle out loud. I imagine generations of residents telling visitors, 'Oh you can get contraband rum from Pirate Pete, just use the Lamorna wink.' Shortly afterwards the road turns steeply down towards the ocean and I stop to check my map, narrowly avoiding being mown down by an angry man in a Land Rover. I've gone the wrong way and retrace my steps over some violent speed bumps that threaten to catapult the shrub out of the basket.

In another incredibly picturesque little dell with pretty stone cottages I notice my GPS device is telling me something. Instead of the usual map with a line depicting my route, there is a wedge across the screen with yellow, red and green sections on it. 'Climb 2 of 56,' it says in text underneath, rather ominously. I realise the coloured stripes denote gradients. This hill apparently has a couple of yellow and red sections, which I guess probably isn't good news. Part-way up I stop to let a driver pass and am forced to push the rest of the way. I start to see a major problem with the 'quiet roads' routes – in Cornwall they are the ones no-one really wants to use on foot, bike or, I'd hazard, by car. I've owned vehicles that would have struggled up this incline.

Past Penzance, a brand-new seafront path on the beach has been laid in shining white concrete. It isn't as wide as it is popular, sadly, and quite a few people are out walking in the beautiful, blustery morning. They are fully relaxed and unheeding of anything but the wind in their ears, St Michael's Mount off to one side, and the general majesty of the scene, as befits such a place.

I ring my bell 30m out, giving strollers plenty of time to look back, move in opposite directions and finally settle on a configuration through which I can pass. If there is no response to the first ring, I ring again at 20m, then at 10m, then at about 5m. By this point travelling at walking pace, I call out, 'Excuse me, could I squeeze past?' Approaching one family from behind, the male of the pack remains wilfully oblivious of me until a woman flatly says 'Dave!' and practically drags him out the way. I can't help thinking why go to all the trouble and expense of building a brand-new path, force cyclists and walkers to share the space, and make it so narrow it's bloody inconvenient for everyone using it?

It is near lunchtime when I meet Simon at St Erth station. He is instantly recognisable by his hi-vis tabard and I bet he wouldn't cycle across Cornwall in inappropriate clothing, carrying a shrub in a basket. He leads us away from the NCN via some horrendous painted main road cycle lanes, barely wider than our handlebars. There is a safe route, he explains, but it's 'circuitous,' so we take a risk – but not as big a risk as the refuse truck driver takes with Simon, squeezing past him at a traffic island, leaving centimetres to spare. The bike lane vaporises at a colossal roundabout, as high-speed traffic bears down on us. We sit on an outdoor terrace at Birdies Bistro café overlooking the Hayle Estuary, with little egrets, ducks and geese wandering about. I eat some delicious bubble and squeak, and the removable ebike battery has its lunch at a wall socket.

In his soft-spoken voice Simon explains how he helps develop Cornwall's NCN for Sustrans, using a combination of funds from the Department for Transport (DfT) and local authorities. Simon is a lifer at Sustrans – 15 years and counting. He's a man on a mission with a fear of seals – they bite, apparently, and can get underneath you when you're swimming. He gets a kick out of helping more people cycle, even if the pay is a fraction of what he could earn in a private consultancy.

Simon is in the process of drawing up two Local Cycling and Walking Infrastructure Plans, also known as LCWIPs (pronounced 'Elsie Whips'). The theory is councils work out where cycle routes are most needed and prioritise delivering those routes. Many local authorities have found the Propensity to Cycle Tool useful for deciding where new or improved cycle routes could go, but drawing up these plans is a slow process, partly because cash-strapped councils have to fund the process themselves and there's no money to build the routes. Simon is working on LCWIPs for Cornwall's 10 major urban areas, where most cycling trips will take place. He explains a key part of the process is community engagement, understanding local needs and trying to avoid 'concerns' developing into a 'backlash' as ideas develop into plans.

They also need to help people safely across things like roads, rivers and railways. The A30 is one of Cornwall's arteries, running from London to Sennen. While I'm in the area, National Highways (NH), the body tasked with managing and developing England's trunk road network, has begun widening the A30 from one to two lanes north of Truro. This will cost £330 million, part of England's five-year, £27 billion roadbuilding scheme. Despite being dubbed a 'congestion-busting, economy-boosting route in Cornwall' that will improve safety, it's unlikely it will achieve any of that.

The sums involved in roadbuilding are almost insultingly large, given how little active travel (another term for walking and cycling) receives and how problematic road schemes are. In an NH review of evaluations of 80 of its own road projects, along with long-term evidence from four road schemes completed in the last 20 years, the Campaign to Protect Rural England (CPRE) found that roads schemes of this type rarely delivered on their main promises. Across 13 schemes, on average, traffic increased 7% after three years and a staggering 47% after eight years. Bigger roads encourage further car-centric developments (like new housing estates on major road junctions far from shops, schools and services), driving up traffic. This is not a new problem: it's one we've known about for decades. The trouble with having a well-funded body whose sole purpose is roadbuilding is that they will find ways to keep building bigger and faster roads.

Of the 25 reviewed road schemes justified on economic bases, CPRE found only five had evidence of economic effects and those 'may have arisen from changes incidental to the scheme.' The report noted, 'Any respite from congestion provided by a new or widened road is temporary,' and the case for roadbuilding is based on a flawed understanding of what happens when you widen roads. Increasing road capacity, it turns out, generates more car trips, first by making it easier to drive and secondly by squeezing out other options – surrounding roads get busier as more people drive, and cycling and walking feel increasingly dangerous. Add that to declining investment in public transport and you are left with few other options. This long-understood phenomenon is known as induced demand. It's the same with new cycle routes: more and better increase cycle journeys. Ultimately, you get the users you build routes for.

Let's compare the roadbuilding process and the resources behind it with that of cycling. Compulsory purchase orders (CPOs) are invariably used to buy land for road schemes on the basis roads are strategically important pieces of infrastructure. Government or local council compensates landowners and consults them on the details, without offering them veto powers over the plans. For cycling this almost never happens. Instead, if we need a cycle route a charity or volunteers end up engaged in endless negotiations spanning decades.

With roadbuilding, multi-year funding settlements also allow for strategic long-term planning. For cycle routes, it's common for the financial year to be well underway before that year's funding is announced, including for the NCN, when the money needs to be substantially spent within that financial year. Every year Sustrans rides this rollercoaster: the zero-gravity moment, suspended over a precipice, before the track ahead comes back into view and the height of the drop is revealed. What follows is a high-speed scramble to spend whatever sum is granted in whatever time is left – usually less than 11 months – and deliver most of the project before the deadline.

While Sustrans has become adept at delivering under these conditions, and there is some flexibility on deadlines, it puts them at a clear disadvantage. Cycle routes generally take three years from conception to construction to complete: a year to think and talk about it, a year to get the permissions and funding, and a year to build it. That's when things go well. Living hand to mouth year-on-year makes forward-planning difficult and favours smaller projects that can be delivered quickly. This short-termism and the frantic scrabble it creates is enraging: while dedicated individuals fight to deliver something so unquestionably beneficial as cycle routes, we clear the way for roads with their frankly questionable outcomes. The difference seems to be simply that the body in charge of delivering the road network, unlike the one for cycling, is powerful and well-funded, and has the status quo on its side.

Perhaps surprisingly, National Highways is one of the NCN's biggest funders, after Government – and boasts it's the biggest builder of cycle routes in Britain. It may seem counterintuitive that trunk roads would need cycle routes. However, anyone who has tried to cross a dual carriageway on a supposed cycle route, with no crossing, or who has driven around a bend at 60mph only to see a pedestrian or horse rider making a dash for it across their path, will know just how dangerous it is when we fail to think about the two networks at the same time.

The purpose of the NH cycling and walking fund is to attempt to mitigate the negative impacts of their roads. Bridges, tunnels and safe, protected routes, ideally away from main roads, are essential if you hope for people to cycle locally, but they aren't always built where cyclists need them or to the standard that makes cycling around trunk roads feel safe.

NH is, quirkily, no longer part of the Civil Service. It's a company with a single shareholder – the Secretary of State for Transport. It has 6000 staff to the 98 delivering cycling and walking under the government's relatively new cycling and walking delivery body, Active Travel England. Its money and clout means it can push boundaries. In 2016 NH set new, high design standards for its cycle routes, the likes of which England hadn't seen before. These were better than the national standards at the time. Excitement soon faded, though, when it became apparent regional departments were using a loophole to avoid using them. It turned out the new standards didn't apply when building pavements and on-the-ground observations suggested that's what NH was delivering, not cycle paths. While shared-use paths are fine when it's a rural area with low usership, shared pavements next to trunk roads that force users to give way at each side road are less good. NH denies it's a loophole, but it is hard to see it another way.

By 2023 NH had spent £84 million of its five-year £106 million active travel pot. While relatively modest in transport terms, it's more than the DfT awarded the NCN in the five years to 2023. Incredibly, NH can't seem to say exactly where the money went, what exactly they've built, if any of it is any good or if anyone is using it.

Several FOIs by me inspired west London MP Ruth Cadbury to forward some written questions to the transport minister, the answers to which confirmed NH not only hadn't assessed its own existing cycling provision, it didn't know if what it had recently built for cycling with public funds met its own design standards. It couldn't even say whether the investment offered any sort of benefit, because it doesn't count cycling and walking users on its network. Without knowing user numbers, its targets to reduce cycling and walking casualties create a perverse incentive to simply reduce cycling and walking. By the end of our round of questions, under increasing pressure from ministerial questions and public scrutiny, NH submitted a proposal to start assessing its cycling and walking provision

On 11 March 2020, Westminster announced a £27.4 billion settlement for NH to spend on England's trunk roads over five years. That same year the NCN got *nothing* from the DfT, nor did it receive anything from NH the next year and it hadn't received anything in the previous two years. I put the two five-year sums on a bar chart for a talk I gave, using the previous five years' NCN funding for comparison. Between 2018 and 2023 the NCN received a total of £77 million from the DfT. You could barely see it on the graph.

The cause of the gap in NCN funding was, in part, an administrative one: while National Highways' five-year funding pot was allocated in 2020, negotiations on its cycling spend took so long Sustrans didn't receive its £3.6 million until October 2022 – halfway through the funding cycle. The money still had to be spent within the five-year term, only by then just two and a half years remained.

These delays obviously have real-world impacts. Cornwall Council had big plans for their cycle network. They wanted to deliver almost 20 miles of multi-use routes for pedestrians, cyclists and horse riders. It would cost £19 million, £17 million of which would come from NH. The money arrived, but the funding agreement with NH was delayed and by the time the council had approved the Saints Trail, that left just 15 months to acquire the land and complete the work.

More than halfway into the funding cycle, it emerged less than half of the routes would be delivered. Despite, as reported at the time, the 'overwhelmingly positive response from public consultation' and the best efforts of council officers, the routes were undeliverable within the timescale.

An independent review identified that landowners along the way were reluctant to sell land and that costs would be higher than initially thought. Separately, I was told the initial designs didn't meet current standards (one apparently scaled a hill only an elite athlete could cycle up), so the council was encouraged to deliver better but fewer routes, that would cost the same as the full complement and take an equal amount of time. Originally, routes would connect Perranporth with Newquay, Truro and St Agnes, St Newlyn East and Carland Cross, Trispen with Idless – substantial constituents of a network. In the end a little over eight miles would be delivered, linking Perranporth with Goonhavern and Truro to St Agnes.

After the pandemic there was a three-year government funding settlement for England's NCN for the first time – Scotland had long benefited from multi-year funding. This was transformative, Simon says, allowing longer-term planning for a pipeline of bigger and more ambitious routes. 'We can begin to have those sustained conversations with not just local authorities but major landowners, like the National Trust, the Canal & River Trust, and others that we work with to deliver improvements or new routes.' With routes already in the discussion and planning phases, it becomes quicker and easier to deliver the third phase, construction, at short notice, if additional funds become available.

Sadly, the good times didn't last: in early 2023 the second two years of the NCN's funding settlement were cut, in a footnote to a money-saving announcement about HS2, and by December Sustrans was still waiting for that financial year's funding settlement. In April, the home page of Sustrans' website featured an 'urgent repairs appeal' for public donations to deal with the effects of extreme weather on the network over the previous 12 months.

Around the same time campaigners revealed England's ongoing roadbuilding spree would blow our chances of meeting net-zero goals. Decision-makers were being required 'to ignore the negative climate impact of roadbuilding and traffic but to give weight to tree planting around schemes as a nature-based solution to climate change,' ignoring any increase in emissions. NH doesn't have a great track record on trees, though: in March 2023 it was revealed half a million trees, planted by NH on 21 miles of upgraded A-road, had died because of a lack of aftercare, costing the taxpayer £2.9 million – just less than its annual NCN settlement.

I can't help but wonder what we are doing subsidising a body whose efforts, whose very existence, is in direct conflict with our ability to maintain a liveable planet, while defunding things like walking and cycling with real, demonstrable benefits. That's not to say they don't make environmental efforts. According to NH the A30 dualling would include 'new badger setts and tunnels and animal crossing points, including 11 underbridges, two overbridges, five drainage culverts and two dry tunnels – for otters and other species – as well as a 'green bridge' at Marazanvose.' Some newts were re-homed and even their rare insect food source was moved with them in swathes of turf.

If the great crested newt rears its head during a project survey for a cycle route, it can halt construction for a full year. Things like ecology surveys, though important, can be onerous and if you miss a window to survey the behaviour of species at a key point in the year, you can wait 12 months for the next opportunity. All that aside, there are plans slowly forming. Cycling and walking links need to avoid the worst hills – which isn't easy in Cornwall. After our peaceful estuary lunch, Simon and I collect the charged ebike battery and set out to explore some of his domain.

'The railway engineers took the best bits of land,' says Simon – and often the road engineers got the next best bits – 'but in Cornwall . . . riding to the station, travelling up the line then cycling at the other end is very much an option for people.'

A route between Falmouth and Truro, about seven miles apart, would be an obvious one to deliver. 'Cornwall [Council] have an aspiration to link those two towns together,' says Simon. 'There's some particular challenges because there's a very busy A-road; there's a branch line railway [to cross].' And while people might not want to cycle alongside a main road, 'There are options but they're probably not as direct as the commuting cyclists would like.'

Simon and I head off to explore some of the new and to-be-improved sections of NCN on his patch. Beside the café a road was made one way to make space for a new safe cycle path. There was significant local backlash from drivers against a short detour, but it was a needed link. We ride an off-road path rippled by tree roots that's due to be resurfaced and its users given priority over motor traffic where it meets the road. This is a small detail that feels a little bit radical – it's not often you see cycling and walking given precedence over driving.

We follow the NCN signs through the heart of Hayle and Cambourne. 'John Grimshaw was way ahead of his time when he said the NCN should link train stations and town centres,' says Simon, adding John 'did the hard bit of identifying the network and linking between towns.' He saw the NCN, after all, as a transport network as well as nice leisure routes.

'You do get criticism about the NCN in Cornwall; that it's not the route that cyclists want to take,' says Simon. It's often circuitous and hilly, but those are the quieter, safer roads. Without dedicated infrastructure those are your options: flat but busy main roads, the chosen path of generations of travellers, with all the dangers that accompany them, or quiet routes that go around the houses and the hills. I try and modulate the ebike to Simon's speed. He's a good sport, but it's not an equal match; my 250w ebike motor against his leg power.

On one dirt path alongside a school Simon astonishes me slightly. 'A lot of councils don't know the NCN is here – I had to point out to them this route existed,' he says. I find this mindboggling. I know a lot of the public haven't heard of the NCN, but you'd expect officials in the boroughs it travels through to know. Whether councils know about it or not, as there's no maintenance budget, unpaved routes like this, of which there are many, become a bog in winter and unusable by all but mountain bikers, who enjoy mud and don't mind getting changed after a ride. For local kids, commuting by bike to school is only possible in the dry. After heavy rain they presumably have to be driven by parents instead.

On cue it starts to rain, which the shrub enjoys. Simon and I pull our hoods up. We notice some NCN signs are missing and Simon explains he doesn't have the budget to put up dedicated signposts either, so if a new housing estate is built and there's no street furniture, like a lamp-post, near the junction that a sticker can go on, turnings can easily go unsigned. I'm once again astonished the network isn't allocated enough money for its own signs and I wonder about Sustrans' target to improve signage across the network with no money. With insufficient funding, which tends to come from individual councils, and limited staff, however, it isn't a priority, and it will be a long time before all the network is properly signed.

A big part of Simon's job is winning hearts and minds over plans for cycling routes. It's a crucial, but often underfunded, part of the process. Word reached a landowner about a potential route Simon was looking into before Sustrans got a chance to talk to them. 'Suddenly, they wanted more and more information about the project, and we weren't in a position to share it,' he says – because there were no designs at this early stage, it was still just an idea. This can be disastrous, turning people against a scheme based on fears or rumours and ending any chance of a safe cycle route. Unlike NH, Sustrans doesn't have the power to compulsory-purchase land and so the conversation ends there.

The drizzle intensifies as we part ways near Redruth. Simon is off to make dinner for his kids, but asks that I text him I've arrived in the dry OK. I head for my B&B, the battery emptying at the top of the final hill. The flustered young woman who runs the place lets me and the bike inside. She looks at me. 'Travelling around on the bike with no kids, sounds like freedom,' she says wistfully.

The following morning I realise not only have I left my glasses in the campsite bathroom, but one contact lens has torn to the shape of a gibbous moon. Without spares of either I put the broken contact lens in and set out to find replacements as quickly as I can from one of Cornwall's branches of Specsavers.

On the way I head to Bike Shop Bissoe on the outskirts of Redruth to get a new kickstand fitted. The shop, it turns out, sponsors an elite-level competitive cycling team, Saint Piran. Although I have my route plotted out, I idly ask Steve, the manager, the best way to St Austell. He makes me a complementary espresso, while he explains, 'I'd go on the main road. It's about a third faster,' adding, 'but I'm happy to ride on the main road.'

'And it's less hilly, I presume,' I say.

'Not particularly.'

I'd experienced my first dangerous overtakes on the road to the bike shop, on the outskirts of Redruth. Steve says it's a local custom to blame dodgy driving on 'Emmets', the regional name for tourists, but he believes it's actually local drivers disowning their own bad behaviour.

Out of Redruth NCN3 follows a dirt path through a former copper mine, Wheal Maid, that is very picturesque, but very much resembles Mordor. The route runs between huge industrial tailing ponds and rocky hillocks that crowd in on the path. It is awe-inspiring in its bleakness. I dodge granite blocks half sunk into the ground, jutting out just enough to threaten a broken wheel and a possible crash. This is puzzling and inconvenient given I am very much trying to get somewhere. There is a nice little bridge over a main road, built just for cyclists and pedestrians, so I forgive the route a little eccentricity, for now.

Back on the road two signs point to Truro in two different directions – one says five miles, one six. Without any further information about either route, I pick what seems like the most likely option and head merrily along little roads like a pirate aboard a two-wheeled frigate, with the shrub and one scratchy eye.

My fairly jolly mood is soon punctured by various pavement cycle paths that meanly send me the long way around the exit roads of high-speed roundabouts, forcing me to give way every few metres while drivers enjoy unhindered progress. Pavements become narrow, foliage scratches my arms from overgrown hedges and the signage deteriorates. At one roundabout a van driver accelerates towards me as I cross, actually leaning his upper body into the turn as if he's riding a bobsled on a deserted ice chute.

By this point I'm in low spirits at the generally depressing state of English cycling infrastructure and growing increasingly angry, when things get markedly worse. I spend the next several hours missing signs and going the wrong way down hills so steep the ebike can't pull me and the luggage back up them. I make short, maximal efforts on roads and a horrific wall of a dirt path that's actually part of the NCN, shoving the bike on foot, clinging on to the brakes to catch my breath, to return to the last sign I missed. My GPS, losing signal, keeps switching itself off.

I finally locate King Harry Ferry, which offers a gorgeous crossing over clear blue water in another deep, wooded valley. As the chain ferry rattles along, a small brown and white sailboat glides past in our wake. It is idyllic. The shrub wafts happily in the breeze and it is frankly a blessed relief to have a breather. Cyclists embark and disembark last, after all the car traffic, but at least I'm on the road.

I'm on an urgent deadline. I need to get to Specsavers at St Austell before it closes at 5.30 p.m., hoping to get hold of some new contact lenses, but the NCN is being wilfully obstructive. Time is ticking down and St Austell is barely crawling closer.

I cycle down a road overlooking yet another stunning, cliff-encapsulated bay: the sea is a startling blue and little houses cling gamely to vertiginous slopes. A sign says the way is closed to vehicles, but it's next to one proclaiming the plucky NCN still open for business. I am rightly sceptical. I forego lunch at a pretty little hut with outdoor seating overlooking a delightful cove, even though it is past 3 p.m. I'm almost in tears, exhausted and worried about my eye, on the phone to Specsavers again, trying to work out which of their stores carries the right kind of lenses. Fearing for my schedule and my eyesight, I push on miserably to St Austell.

Here the NCN descends, via a narrow path made of broken pipes and rocks, on to a beach where I shove the bike through soft golden sand dunes, trying to guess which sandy trail might lead out. I use a handy public loo for a wee, but it practically explodes after I flush it, sending water pouring suddenly out over the bowl and across the floor. It feels as if the whole bay is about to explode. Another impossibly steep hill means my escape happens in extreme slow-motion.

At the top I opt for a road marked perversely with a dotted line on the Ordnance Survey map as 'for experienced cyclists only'. It doesn't make sense: this is one of the best roads I've ridden all day, mostly because it's flat and there's barely a car in sight. I pass a gorgeous hamlet with white cylindrical houses, small, squat towers guarding the roads in and out.

After hours of torture, the worst is over. I turn off the road to a wonderful, wide, smooth, brand-new tarmac path, freshly resurfaced from a dirt path by Simon's team. It runs through the Lost Gardens of Heligan – one of Cornwall's most popular tourist attractions. There are junctions on the bicycle roads with little fingerposts. This is a proper cycle route, I think. One of the hills is still too steep for my waning battery, though, so I am off and pushing again in the hot afternoon sun.

I reach the outskirts of St Austell with just 10 minutes until Specsavers closes, when the battery dies on a double roundabout. It's rush hour and gung-ho desperation sends me sailing across, miraculously unscathed, between vehicles. The fully laden bike is too heavy to pedal uphill unaided, yet the pavement is barely wide enough for me and the bike. I eventually pant through the shop door with less than five minutes to spare.

While my big pink bike draws some admiring comments, the shop staff apologises they don't have my contact lenses in stock. My best bet, they say, is to head to Truro in the morning. I sit outside the shop on a bench, dirty, tired and deflated, and look on my phone for a hotel that's located downhill. The St Austell Travelodge staff are kind and let me bring the bike into my room to recharge. I shower and lie on the bed in the foetal position, googling whether my eye warrants an A&E visit, while all the boy racers of Cornwall gather at a drive-thru outside, competing over who has the loudest exhaust.

There is more kindness to come: thankfully a driver lets me across the dangerous roundabout on foot, blurry-eyed, on my way to dinner. Somehow, the next morning Truro Specsavers has a cancellation and I get the only appointment in the county for two weeks, a pair of contact lenses, and a mild but fair telling off by the optician. The kind proprietor at Tower Park Camping and Caravan, St Buryan, posts my glasses to my sister's house in Somerset. The stinging in my hands is finally subsiding, but the nettle rash from my fall into the rocks at breakfast has left about 20 red welts across my fingers.

9

CAMEL WALK

Deciding I've seen enough of Cornish hills, and frankly feeling a little traumatised, the pink ebike and I catch a train to Bodmin Parkway to ride one of the UK's most popular stretches of NCN. A route built on a former railway line, it's flat and, I've heard, incredibly picturesque. But first I have to find it.

There's a solo jazz dance step called the camel walk, which you start by tilting one shoulder downward and sliding the same foot forward simultaneously, before lifting each heel consecutively in a little switch-switch rhythm. Then the first foot slides behind the second foot, which slides forward and you perform the sequence on the other side. It's tricky to learn, but very satisfying once you get it. The camel walk and the Camel Trail have much in common.

To perform the route as intended, without driving there, visitors can take a train to the nearest station, Bodmin Parkway, and cycle – or take a taxi. I am too cheap to take taxis unless in tears and I have already got those out of the way, so I choose pedal power. Arriving at Bodmin from St Austell visitors first need to carry their bikes, panniers, baskets and shrubs over the tiny footbridge, because there's no lift. St Austell, I learn, is the only station in the whole of Cornwall with a lift.

In fact, anyone in a wheelchair travelling to and from Bodmin Parkway in the direction of London Paddington will need to first get on a train in the opposite direction to St Austell, use the county's only station lift and board another train back via Bodmin. Two decades of disability legislation requiring services to be accessible seem to have escaped this part of the country: of 36 Cornish train stations, just 12 offer step-free access, a problem the rail operator, GWR, puts down to the constraints of Victorian infrastructure. If you're a wheelchair user in Cornwall you apparently either have to rely on expensive taxis or a private vehicle, or face endless frustration and delay. In at least one case there's a shuttle bus between platforms of the same station, and in others the option to cross the railway tracks between trains, supervised by staff, but only when there's someone on duty. All of this is also inconvenient for anyone trying to get about with a heavy bike.

Bodmin Parkway is, for some reason, set in a secluded valley five miles outside the town of Bodmin. The cycle route signage between the two is very bad. In those five miles, I perform 19 wrong turns, U-turns or pauses to read the map. By the time I've found the famous Camel Trail almost an hour has elapsed. I could almost have walked it quicker.

All frustrations are soon forgotten, though. The Camel Trail is glorious: two long, flat, traffic-free stretches of former railway line split in the middle by the small town of Wadebridge. The Bodmin end skirts a pretty woodland vale and the Padstow end, the stunning Camel Estuary. Running for 12 miles, it is flat, straight and about as relaxing a bike ride as you could imagine.

I'm glad to be here on a weekday, as the trail is jam-packed on weekends, particularly during holidays and in good weather. I have whole stretches all to myself, and I'm like a kid in a toy shop after closing time. The plan is to cycle to Padstow and back. The shrub in the basket wafts happily in the breeze and I stop at regular intervals to take photos and gaze into the distance. I also have to stop once to grumpily open and waddle through a gate, where cyclists on one of Britain's most popular family cycle routes are forced to dismount and give way at the driveway of a private house, and once for a cycle chicane at a quiet country lane.

A couple of miles in, I stop for lunch at a delightful café, right beside the Camel Trail, leaning the bike on a grassy bank with 12 other bikes. There are benches across a slope of lawn under a small orchard where, when I visit, the world's prettiest kitten, an athletic creature with spotted markings like a leopard, is climbing the trees and generally charming all the customers. Returning to get a jacket from my bike, I invite a couple in their 70s, who have just arrived, to join me at my table.

Once dismounted the man moves with some difficulty and has to be helped up the steps to the seating area by his wife. Though they are incredibly reserved and don't tell me their names when I introduce myself, talking partly among themselves in low voices, they do tell me they cycle a lot. They have driven to the start of the Camel Trail today and are cycling halfway, where they say most people stop and turn around. He converted his cycle into an ebike, because of a condition that reduces his mobility and strength. However, his wife points out, once on the bike, you can't tell he is disabled. She still rides a regular pedal cycle and intends to for some time. They are very relaxed together and lick each other's ice creams unselfconsciously.

We bid each other goodbye, remount and head off in opposite directions. The tarmac gives way to a fine gravel surface leading through a tunnel of spring-bright green foliage, with red campion and valerian growing at the verges. Railway cuttings come and go, and sunlit fields appear behind the trees shading the path. I take a very deep breath and feel myself relax, happy to be on the bike somewhere actively designed for cycling.

At Wadebridge users are led through the town via residential roads, on painted lanes that bus drivers seem to consider fair game and via a wacky crossing to a pedestrian island at a roundabout. At least it's fairly well signed and it's worth the bother. The stretch from Wadebridge to Padstow is one of the most stunning rides I've ever taken, with almost uninterrupted views of the Camel Estuary, its acres of sand at low tide and presumably acres of water at high tide, all framed by verdant hillside.

The tarmac path alongside the estuary is comfortably wide, like a road, meaning I can enjoy the view without worrying about drifting into a hedge. A strip of water, a broad river in itself, cuts through the middle of the estuary's vast golden sands, which are rippled by water and stippled with white gulls. I pass a rail carriage turned into a café, with large picnic benches – closed today. I stop every few metres just to stare at the view and take photos, which means I have to weave slowly past the same couple walking a pack of small dogs more than once. It rains and then the sun comes out, and the shrub and I cross the former rail bridge, now a trail bridge, buffeted by astonishingly strong winds being funnelled down the estuary floor. My baseball cap threatens to take off.

The Little Petherick Creek Bridge is a marvel in itself: three great trapezoid wedges of steel girders, each 133m in length, span a junction in the estuary just outside Padstow. It not only affords you access to a highly effective blow dryer, but to vast views across the Camel and Little Petherick Creek. It seems delightfully extravagant for a cycling and walking route. It literally takes your breath away. It is truly magical, very bracing, and quite the antidote to my ordeal further west. I can understand why so many visit this route each year, though I'm totally poleaxed by how difficult it was to find.

The route ends, rather unceremoniously, in the car park of a large fish restaurant, where users of one of Britain's most popular cycle routes are commanded to dismount. Parking before biking! I cycle aimlessly into town, dodge SUVs on narrow roads, gaze at the pretty harbour and, because there's no train station, I turn back for a second blast of wonder.

I cycle back to Bodmin, trying out an off-road route through Lanhydrock, which rattles me and the bike so severely the battery gets jammed into its casing and won't come out. I'll have to drag the whole bike to a plug socket the next time I need to charge it.

I leave Cornwall with mixed feelings: relief the hills are behind me and sadness at the patchy state of our much-loved NCN. The Camel Trail was as wonderful as I'd hoped, but I'm genuinely shocked by how hard it is to reach without a car and that, despite its clear worth as a tourist attraction and leisure route, whenever it reaches a road, even a cycle route of its stature comes second. If we can't ask drivers to give way so people using the Camel Trail can do so with safety and ease, where can we?

10

LAKER CLOSE, AND A REUNION OF SORTS, IN SOMERSET

One of my earliest memories is of the moment I first rode a bicycle. On a sloping expanse of grass beside a local reservoir, my dad held on to the back of my pale blue folding Peugeot bike, with its white basket and white tyres, and ran with me. We rumbled along, across the grass, until suddenly I looked back and he wasn't holding on: I was riding, thrilled, panicked, alone down the hill.

We lived in an old stone cottage near the foot of a steep, north-facing, pine-covered hill, surrounded by forest. It was a 400-year-old woodsman's house with ceilings so low anyone taller than 5' 9" would brush their heads on the doorframes and ceilings. My dad, my sister Ele and I would cycle from the house, down a short stretch of country road overhung with trees, to a little stone humpbacked bridge, where a dirt track runs away from the road. It follows the river Tone along the floor of the steep, wooded valley – the only level surface going – and we would ride for what felt like miles beneath a canopy of beech and oak and acres of pine, with bracken smells, forest smells and the sound of running water.

Each winter there were pheasant shoots and the hapless birds dotted the woods for what felt like much of the year; some of them were so tame they would eat cat biscuits from our hands. There were deer bridges across the river, four planks of wood covered with chicken wire, but we almost never crossed the boggy grass around the river to reach them; for us, the woods were for cycling. We would pretend we were driving cars on the dirt path; one patch of decaying tarmac underneath an enormous oak by the stream served as our petrol station. Dad's bike was a bright pink mountain bike, which seemed radical for a man back then – and part of his charm. I think he figured no-one would want to steal it.

For my dad, cycling changed his life when, aged 16, he was hit by a driver, somewhere in the Kent countryside, and almost lost his right leg. He recalled lying on the road beside his bike and looking down to see bone poking out of his knee. I always remember him describing the curious detail that the injury didn't hurt at first, because of the adrenaline. He was rushed to hospital where he was told he'd lose the leg. As luck would have it, though, a specialist orthopaedic surgeon, who was travelling with a motor racing event that happened to be nearby, managed to piece the leg back together, an inch shorter than the other one. While he used his orthopaedic shoe for a time, in later years he only wore what we fondly referred to as his Jesus sandals or an array of Hi-Tec Silver Shadow trainers from the town's dusty shoe shop, all in various states of decay, and leaned on a stick instead.

Like me he had taken a while to find a job he could settle on. He gallivanted around the UK and Europe for a time as an amateur rally driver and mechanic. We have a few small trophies of his, but it didn't seem like he won much money: once he had to pawn his watch for the journey home. He eventually bought part of a brewery, splitting it three ways with friends. Together they set about building the business up, from a breezeblock unit in the shadow of the town's historic Hancock brewery.

The tall brick chimney that loomed over them is an icon on the horizon of Wiveliscombe, the small town a couple of miles from the smallholding where my parents settled. The brewery, Exmoor Ales, grew in reputation, and Dad became increasingly involved in campaigning for small businesses and for independent breweries like his. He hit on the idea of setting up a beer and music festival to celebrate the town, and its beers, and in the early 1990s WestFest was born. Each year, as soon as the festival was over, at the end of the August Bank Holiday, he and his fellow organisers would start planning next year's.

Dad told us a palm reader he met during those months of recovery in hospital had looked at the lines on his hands and declared that he wouldn't live past 40. A superstitious and slightly mystical character, and a vulnerable 16-year-old at the time, he took this prophecy as a plain fact. As it happens, the palm reader got their prediction wrong by a decade and, thanks to his heavy smoking and drinking, and stress, six months before his 50th birthday he died suddenly of a heart attack.

My dad was my hero. He was warm and funny, charismatic and everyone in the South West seemed to know him, thanks to the brewery – in the early days he delivered the casks of beer himself in his van – and the festival. At his funeral, the church was full to bursting.

A quarter of a century later I am returning to my home town to inaugurate a street on a new housing estate, which is being named Laker Close in honour of Dad. In Wiveliscombe, or Wivey as locals call it, a tiny town of fewer than 3000 people at the 2011 census, he left such an imprint, in some ways it's like he never left. A group of his friends set up the Jim Laker Fund, which has raised tens of thousands of pounds to support local groups and organisations.

Returning from Cornwall with the shrub, there was a day between my arrival and the inauguration that Barratt Homes had arranged for us. I'd written to them about my book and Barratt's PR people kindly organised the road sign to be made on time for this part of my trip. They sent us a draft running order of proceedings and asked us to write speeches, mine about Dad and my book, my sister Ele's about the Jim Laker Fund, which she is involved with, and their work.

Ele is, if not delighted with her shrub, perhaps slightly amused. 'Will it flower?' she asks, politely, when I show up on her doorstep. It is, admittedly, little more than a few leaves on two leggy stems, but the shrub and I have had lively times together. I grew it from a cutting and I'm quite proud of it.

As we walk the few hundred metres from Ele's house to the building site, I begin to have second thoughts about some of my speech. Remarks that seemed funny during our dry runs, on more sober consideration, with the prospect of recounting them in front of an audience of Dad's old friends, Jim Laker Fund members, my two grown-up nephews and four people from Barratt Homes, plus a photographer for the local paper, seem less wise. I start deleting them from the notes on my phone as we walk. The new estate is on the site of a former abattoir and first to go is a quip about that.

A few months earlier I'd written an article for the *Guardian* on research about new housing locking in car dependency. An investigation by the campaign group Transport for New Homes (TfNH) followed up housebuilder pledges and found walking and cycling links routinely being left unfulfilled in new developments. The charity says that new builds, erected far from other homes and amenities, where planning is easier to obtain, leave residents unable to access their daily needs – anything at all, in fact – without cars. The pandemic left new homeowners isolated and trapped, unable to travel on foot or by bike, when daily exercise or key work was the only permitted reason to leave home. The traffic these developments also inevitably generate increases congestion on local roads, making cycling and walking even more treacherous and unattractive.

One role of Active Travel England is to try and ensure cycling and walking are built in to these new developments, but they have a job on their hands. The current planning system is, in fact, stacked against them. Without boring you to death, land value – or the price builders pay a farmer for a field – is calculated by taking the value of the planned homes, minus the cost to build those homes. If the houses cost £1 million to build, and sell for £2 million, the land is worth £1 million to a developer, so that's what they can pay. Anything that adds to the cost, such as active travel routes to nearby amenities, reduces the value of the land and how much a developer can pay for it without losing their margin. As the landowner understandably wants the highest bid, active travel makes bids less competitive. Even where such things were promised, TfNH found they simply weren't being delivered, or were done so badly as to make them worthless. One cycling and walking path they found ended abruptly in a hedge – literally a path to nowhere – and councils didn't have the staff to follow up and ensure these pledges were actually being met.

As a result, people-friendly features tend to exist primarily on land already owned by the builder, where its value isn't dictated by sales margins. For everyone else, any 'extras' that narrow the margin doom that bid to fail. It creates a race to the bottom on standards and it won't change until things like construction levies, which already exist, provide for cycling and walking routes, or until they are part of the basic standard for new homes. Given there are no senior staff from Barratt to hear me stand on my soapbox, and as they don't in any case control the standards set by government, I delete that bit of my speech too.

Arriving at the site where the sign will go, just three Lakers and three regional Barratt staff left, we then quietly decide there is little point to the speeches. It is a wonderful farce, this big moment we'd nervously prepared for, that trickled out to a few hammy promotional photos. I think Dad would have laughed about it with us.

His faith in Ele and I, his cheerleading us on when we were younger and the fact neither he nor Mum ever made us feel limited by being girls, had a really positive impact. Hanging out in the brewery with him and his colleagues made me confident in male-dominated spaces, from bike shops and the world of cycle journalism to cycling around London, where I assertively claim my space on the road. He enthusiastically encouraged my ideas and taught me how engines work. He shaped the person I've become.

He also imprinted on me the importance of safe driving – and anyone I've berated on the road for putting me or others in danger will have heard his voice through mine. During his rally-driving years he had known highly skilled drivers injured and killed on the open road, he said, because of other drivers' recklessness. He was also possibly the worst person to have as a passenger: when my mum drove, he'd cling on to his seat and make yeeping noises.

He told me, long before I'd ever considered the career, that I should be a journalist, but he never got to see me fulfil his own, rather more positive prophecy. I'm sure I have him to thank for both my obsession with road safety and my work as a journalist and campaigner today. It's hopelessly simplistic thinking, but part of me can't help but feel, if he'd been able to carry on cycling, weaving exercise into his life, he might have stuck around a bit longer.

He was paranoid about us cycling on the roads and insisted we wear helmets, for fear of people behaving badly at the wheel. If the route between us and the nearest hamlet had been safer, instead of a 60mph country lane, perhaps he could have felt safe cycling the two-and-a-half-mile commute between our house and the brewery. Perhaps my work in cycling is in the hope others could be spared losing a parent from a heart attack so young.

In the years after his death, when we were still too young to drive, my sister and I camped out in his house. Without driving licences, and with no pavements or safe paths in the countryside, it was just us, hitchhiking into town and to college, or walking the pitch-black road late at night. That road had long been a source of consternation: we'd lost several cats to the fast, if intermittent, traffic over the years and that had somewhat turned me against motor vehicles. It was so dark at night we literally couldn't see our hands in front of our faces when we left the house until, somewhere up the road, our eyes eventually adjusted.

———

It's threatening rain again when I don my waterproofs and head back to Taunton for a train home to London. NCN3 passes about four miles south of Wiveliscombe and there's no nice way of bridging the gap – just country roads, with the usual fast traffic speeds and blind bends. Many of Britain's country roads are quirky little singletrack lanes like this; Postman Pat-type affairs that meander happily between high hedges, making every vista that pops up in front of you an immediate surprise. Cycling on them in the 1980s, you were unlikely to encounter much traffic, but that's no longer the case.

Sometimes councils have tried to intervene without upsetting traffic, using only tiny signage and blind hope, making the interventions so subtle as to be imperceptible. In the Netherlands, unsurprisingly, they've nailed this by designating two types of road: flow roads and access roads. The former are through roads, on which you'd put a separate cycle route away from traffic. The latter offer no-through routes for motor traffic, allowing people in cars to access homes and businesses, but not cut through on their way elsewhere, making it safe for cycling. The current thinking is that if there's more than a thousand vehicles a day or they're going at more than 35mph you really need to do something about it if you want people to feel safe.

Traffic engineers talk about something called design speed: how fast a road or route allows you to safely travel. These little lanes, which terrify American tourists, come with an optimistic default 60mph speed limit. While people take this as a target, the measured design speed can be far, far lower. Two drivers travelling at 60mph in opposite directions have a combined speed of 120mph, requiring a stopping distance of 400m – which means you need to see each other long before you both slam on the brakes. British lanes rarely allow for that kind of long view. In reality, engineers tell me, some of our most eccentric little lanes come with a design speed of more like 7mph. In south-east England, Surrey Council is trialling long-overdue 20mph speed limits across swathes of its single track lanes, with the ambition to remove what it calls the 'obsolete' 60mph default on all but dual carriageways. Residents have told the council they want lower speed limits because they can't walk to the shops, ride horses or cycle in safety when there's fast traffic about, and because they want rid of the noise from speeding drivers.

New quiet lanes guidance by Active Travel England will set out measures to tackle some of the risks on rural roads, some of them surprising tactics to startle drivers into expecting people walking and cycling in the road – possibly things like sheep painted on the tarmac, new crossings and so on. In Oxfordshire Sustrans 'filtered' a dangerous rural road to through traffic using slightly more conventional bollards and there are historical examples of traffic reduction going back to the 1970s and beyond. You could also, in theory, change the input on satnavs, reducing the predicted travel speed so people no longer try to rush through to shave a few seconds off their journeys. With 90% of our landmass rural, we do need to do something with country roads if we want to help people to cycle and walk more. Using land beyond the hedgerow for new separate cycle routes is another option, but the way we manage land acquisition for cycle routes needs to change for that to work.

After passing a pub in the middle of nowhere with a startlingly large car park, I start to sing Joni Mitchell's 'Big yellow taxi'. I barely break stride to perform an emergency stop over a bridge for two oversized 4x4s coming the other way. It breaks my sign-reading focus, though, as I manage to misinterpret the next NCN arrow. Mid-song, I emerge at a junction where a woman is walking two collies. One of them pulls in my direction. 'Hello!' I say to the woman and 'Hello, friendly dog!' I even bid a cheery greeting to the next pigeon on a telegraph pole, before resuming my song. There is a fantastic view of looming hills under dark blue skies. I never know which hills are which around here, but they look spectacular. I whoosh downhill, stopping to let a driver behind me come past with a friendly wave. At a T-junction at the bottom of that great hill I notice a suspicious absence of NCN signs, realise I'm in the wrong place again and, with no reasonable alternatives available, head back up the hill – in silence.

Another nerdy intervention before we move on: all signs have a designated size and NCN signs are by design small, intended to be read at cycling speed, not driving speed. This makes NCN signs tiny and hard to spot compared to other road signs. These tiny signs often end up swallowed by hedges or they get broken or knocked by passing drivers and, too often, no-one notices, or there's no money to replace them. All over the country, on national speed limit rural roads where cyclists are being encouraged to venture, no-one behind a steering wheel expects to see a cyclist around a blind bend, or can tell any difference between this and any other road on which they're attempting to drive at 60 mph.

Inconspicuous NCN signs make trying to navigate cycle routes a frustrating treasure hunt even by bike, and my tutting and about-turning became a familiar refrain across a summer of NCN exploration. At a T-junction near Hillcommon, outside Taunton, a driver is tailgating a touring cyclist with panniers ahead of me. I watch the cyclist pull over as the car overtakes. He performs a laboured U-turn, huffing in frustration and glancing at a GPS on his handlebars.

'You OK?' I ask.

'Yes, missed the turning.'

'I'm always missing those NCN signs,' I say in sympathy.

Making my way through Taunton on the NCN, a journey of just three miles takes a lengthy 30 minutes. As usual, some signs are missing, weirdly someone installed authentic-looking blue arrows pointing in the wrong direction and someone has plonked a building site right in the way, requiring more tutting and turning.

Small frustrations aside, Taunton has remarkably high cycling rates for the UK – around 10% of commuting trips are cycled. In 2022, when cycling rates across England dropped back after pandemic lockdowns, Somerset West and Taunton bucked the trend. The Active Lives Survey found 11% of people cycled at least once a week in 2021, up from 10.7% in 2020. That's practically Dutch, by British standards.

Taunton is a flat, compact town and there are some decent paths through parks. The NCN pleasantly makes use of these green spaces and I realise to my delight the route takes me right across the campus of my old college.

Because my sister would come home and teach me everything she learned in her first year of primary school, I skipped my own first year, which put me a year ahead throughout my school career. This meant when Dad died, I was 14 years old and at the start of my final school year. It also meant I started college at 15. I moved out of home the following year. My response to this freedom, and the massive upheaval that came before it, was to party instead of studying. In the end I didn't bother turning up to half my A-level exams, because I'd totally failed to revise for them. In effect, I flunked college. I took a series of jobs around that time, as a lorry banksman and equipment painter at a concrete factory, as a waitress, a cleaner and a sales assistant at a DIY store, most of which I was fired from – usually because I stopped turning up, and dealt badly with figures of authority. My mum takes a low-intervention approach in others' lives, which was in some ways a blessing: I won't be told anything and so I got to make my own mistakes. It also meant I could pursue my own way, unhindered.

My sister came to the rescue again when she told me one day in her no-nonsense way that something needed to change: I had to do something with my life. Some friends carried on partying and, though most of them moved on eventually to pursue healthy, productive lives, for some their story ended tragically. The time made for some outrageous experiences and some very close bonds, and the people I knew then were my adopted family when I most needed one. I soon turned away from the party scene and moved to south Wales to retake my A-levels and start my life as an adult, whatever that would hold. However, it feels poignant that the NCN, this thread I am now following in that adult life, runs straight through a place forever frozen in time as a point where I could have taken a very different path.

11

PROGRESS AND FLIPPING
BORIS THE BIRD

In November 2015 I stood on Vauxhall Bridge waiting for Boris Johnson, the then mayor of London, to appear on a bike. The press call didn't entirely go to plan. As Johnson crested the brand-new cycle lane he was there to open, a man riding the other way very decisively flipped him the bird. The photograph became famous: the cyclist riding away from us with his middle finger held high as the now former prime minister, cycle helmet askew, lifted a hand as if receiving deserved plaudits.

This was the first of almost a billion pounds of new cycle routes Boris and his walking and cycling commissioner, Andrew Gilligan, opened during his second and final term as London mayor. As the assembled journalists interviewed Boris for soundbites, he seemed to attract an almost constant barrage of insults from passers-by. One heckle emerged from a passing van. 'What did he say?' I asked, sensing a frisson of excitement among my fellow reporters. 'I think he said he'll see me next Tuesday,' said Boris with a wry smile.

Boris, I realised, really didn't care what people thought of him – and he didn't care to an astounding degree. Having attended a state school, an ordinary college and a non-Oxbridge university, I had never witnessed, close up, the sheer self-belief of some of our upper classes. I'm not saying we need toffs to deliver bike lanes – cycle routes should be as pedestrian a part of the streetscape as, well, pedestrian routes – but instead their delivery is reliant on rhino-skinned individuals defying the status quo. This is not just a problem in the UK, but a pattern repeated the world over, whether in Paris or Copenhagen. Naturally we don't like change – that's why people rail against reallocating road space the world over. However, with things like cycle lanes and low traffic streets, which start with majority support, once we see and experience them for ourselves, even the detractors don't want to go back. This has also been the case, for the large part, in London.

It's an oft-repeated fact that, whatever you think of Boris Johnson, the man was good for cycling, first as London mayor and then as prime minister. In 2016, Boris' final act as London mayor was opening part of the 'longest cross-city cycle route in Europe', an 18-mile, two-way cycle route from Barking in the east to Acton in the west. The removal of a traffic lane on the car-choked Victoria Embankment took a very public struggle with the city's taxi drivers' lobby and bosses at Canary Wharf who, Andrew Gilligan claimed, didn't want their limos held up each day.

Approximately 13% of Londoners were driving into the centre every day, at the time 17% of traffic was delivery vehicles and vast amounts of the city's public space, its roads, were given to private cars. Consultations aren't usually the kind of thing people get excited about, but the East-West and North-South cycle routes became one of Transport for London's biggest public engagement exercises: of a whopping 21,000 respondents, 84% supported the schemes.

Within 24 hours of their opening, I stood with Boris Johnson and Andrew Gilligan on the junction of those routes at Blackfriars Bridge and watched a steady stream of cyclists pass by on the protected cycle routes. Soon they were moving 46% of people in just 30% of the road space and the gridlock that detractors predicted never came. One route, symbolically, runs right past the Houses of Parliament and Buckingham Palace. Within five years it had carried an estimated 11 million cycle journeys; not just people in Lycra, but office workers and tourists on city hire bikes, cargo bike deliveries and, the litmus test for safety, even children cycled there. Of staff working in Westminster 26% now cycle, walk or jog to work, no doubt thanks in part to those safe routes. It had, in the words of Andrew Gilligan, 'changed the face of London.'

My early journalism career spanned Boris' journey from cycle-curious mayor in 2008 to a staunch supporter of high-quality protected cycle routes. I covered his early forays into 'cycle superhighways' – no more than blue paint that disappeared under the nearside wheels of buses and lorries – and his bolder second term of protected main road cycle routes, criss-crossing the city. This second term saw the biggest single investment in cycling the country had ever seen – almost a billion pounds, including in outer London suburbs and town centres. Within a year cycling in outer London areas that received investment increased by 18% and walking 13%, while shop vacancies on low-traffic streets were at an all-time low. People spent 216% more time in pleasant pedestrianised high streets, whether sitting on a bench, stopping at a café or going into shops.

The billion pounds that made this possible was vastly more than what the NCN was founded on. There were hopes, including from Chris Boardman at the time, that this work would pave the way for similar transformations around the country. People would say, you can't build cycle routes or curb traffic in the UK, we aren't the Netherlands, it's too hilly, we have a different culture. This work would prove that theory wrong.

London's subsequent mayor, Sadiq Khan, expanded that early network by five times within his first term alone and further again in his second; work that ramped up even more during the pandemic. I enjoy the fruits of Boris and Sadiq's labours on a weekly basis, when I use the protected cycle route along a dual carriageway running four miles from Stratford in east London to Aldgate on the edge of the City. Even as a confident cyclist unafraid to claim my space on the road, I wouldn't ride there without it – that road, and the Bow Roundabout part-way along it, were certified death traps for cyclists. Now they are filled with cycle delivery riders during the day and cyclists of all stripes commute from the East End to the city at rush hour.

During the pandemic the government, under Boris, funded emergency pop-up lanes and Low Traffic Neighbourhoods (LTNs), which sprouted around the country at pace, including where I live. What were once fairly hostile residential streets, where drivers tried to hurry cyclists out of their way in their rush to elsewhere, are now quiet and safe. Every day, children cycle and scoot to school, and people on mobility scooters avoid the cracked pavements, littered with parked cars, and ride down the middle of the smooth, quiet road.

I can now ride from my door to the Stratford bike lane entirely through LTNs, and from there, via a pandemic-era route, I can connect to the one that runs past Parliament and Buckingham Palace and beyond – 11 miles of cycling entirely on safe routes. Cities like Manchester, Sheffield, Coventry, Cardiff, Glasgow and many more have followed suit, but, you won't be surprised to read, progress is slow. In 2018 councils were encouraged to come up with local cycling and walking infrastructure plans (our friends LCWIPs or 'Elsie Whips'), but with no funds to deliver the routes, progress developing these was – you guessed it – also quite slow.

In June 2022, two years into the pandemic, Chris Boardman was appointed to try and bring up the standard of cycle route delivery across England, with £2 billion of new funding over five years to deliver it, part of which was for the NCN. Boris, then PM, wanted cycling and walking to become the 'natural choice' for short journeys, connecting to public transport, new homes and schools. Across England the proportion of children driven to school had trebled in 40 years to almost half of primary school children and a quarter of secondary. The government would fund more school streets, timed road closures outside the school gates making it safer and easier to walk, cycle and scoot instead.

The plan was to double 'active travel' and avoid a car-led recovery by treating cycling and walking as transport. This shift in how we get about would boost people's health, cut transport emissions, save us money, and make our towns and cities more pleasant places to be. New design guidance, and the new delivery body, Active Travel England, with Chris Boardman at its head, would help ensure this happened.

12

CHRIS BOARDMAN, CHESTER AND THE 'LEAST SHIT OPTION'

On a train into Chester there's a young man vaping surreptitiously in a seat near the bike spaces. A cloud of fragrant smoke erupts as I pass and he offers a nervous smile. I'm nervous too, checking my questions. I'm on my way to meet Chris Boardman. I, like many people, admire Chris. He gets on with things, he has given so much to the cause of everyday cycling and he's a great spokesperson – level-headed, eloquent, likeable and down-to-earth – plus he makes time for interviews.

I also want to ask him about his mum. Carol Boardman died in the summer of 2016 after a driver, recently on their phone, hit her while she was cycling. Chris was already a cycling advocate when she was killed, and admits he struggled to process the event and its horrific irony. After weeks of back-and-forth emails with Sustrans to find a decent-quality route Chris and I can ride that serves every-day journeys, we land on NCN5 running west from Chester – the Millennium Greenway. Chris lives on the Wirral, so it's in his neck of the woods, and I head there on my way home from another cycling trip. However, I have somehow overlooked the fact NCN5 passes within 800m of where the fatal crash happened, at Connah's Quay, but in the end Chris, doing his own research, discovers the OS map's NCN layer for the first time, and its little orange and blue lines. He finds us a circular route that avoids Connah's Quay and motor traffic in general.

Outside Chester station, Chris rides three sides of a long rectangle, the taxi drop-off route, to pull up at the kerb in front of me. When I chuckle, he says in explanation, 'A single photo of me cycling the wrong way or on the pavement and I'd get *Daily Mailed*.' A cycling gotcha is like catnip for some publications.

In 2017, after years of campaigning for safer roads, Chris took the job of cycling and walking commissioner for Greater Manchester, and then, in 2022, the national job for England. He jokes that after his professional cycling career he'd spent 10 years painting himself into a corner, campaigning for facilities to support everyday cycling journeys. When he was offered the chance to deliver those protected cycle routes it wasn't a job he had sought, but he felt he couldn't say no, given how long he'd contested the status quo. With his various business, sporting and punditry successes he doesn't need the money either, but, as he puts it, 'It's a good use of life.' He's also undoubtedly good at it.

'I didn't know what you'd be riding or wearing,' he says, 'so I went in between.' He's got on a dark grey T-shirt made of some technical fabric and black shorts, the loose kind designed for mountain biking. I'm on my way from another trip, so I've been sweating into all my cycling clothes for days, haven't had a chance to wash them and also haven't quite clocked we're riding 15 miles today. It's possibly technical fabric territory, but I've got on slacks and a long-sleeve T-shirt. There's always been a tension around what to wear cycling, but for those in the business of campaigning the ideal standard for a route is one where it's so safe and unhurried you don't need to dress up to use it. Chris calls it 'dressing for the destination, not the journey.' I guess today's ride is somewhere in between.

'Have you looked at the route?' he asks.

'Briefly,' I say. Barely is more like it.

'It's pan flat,' he reassures me after I admit my legs are tired from cycling and walking in the Lake District.

'Cycling in traffic makes me feel cross and frustrated, and I try to avoid getting cross and frustrated,' he says by way of explanation, leading us off the main road and through a delightful, traffic-calmed area neither of us were expecting to find. This, it turns out, is Chester's first 'home zone', installed in 2004 with funding from central government. The initiative helped forge safe outdoor space on streets around the UK, in densely populated areas with little green space. The idea was to allow traffic in and out but not through – only people cycling and walking could do that. The idea predates today's LTNs, though it escaped the backlash seen around the introduction of recent LTNs, as far as I can tell. Another traffic-taming idea that was trialled and then promptly forgotten about.

This is partly a Chris Boardman psychogeographical tour. Chris used to live right here in the middle of Chester and he points out his old flat as we pass. When I bring up something I read in his autobiography, he wonders whether I've ever come across the person who largely wrote it. 'Have you met my wife?' he asks. I haven't. 'She's the brains, though I wouldn't tell her that,' he says, with a smile. They have been together so long that she ended up writing the book – it was, in many ways, their shared history.

They moved house recently. The new house sounds very nice, though he's embarrassed at how well he's done. One or more of his kids ended up moving back in for lockdown; he and his wife have six children and, with grandkids, it amounted to 10 people all eating together each night. 'It was quietly wonderful, on a personal level,' he says.

Chris is a private person and we're soon back on to the subject of his day job, or at least one of them. As well as leading Active Travel England he's chair of Sport England, owns a bike brand, Boardman Bikes, and presents cycle sports for ITV and the BBC.

Years of appearing on TV since he retired from professional sport, he says, was an apprenticeship of sorts for what he's doing now. The TV work, he says, 'was just a massive training course on how to connect with an audience.' You can talk about cycle route specifications until you're blue in the face, but how we use our streets is about people and that's what makes it appealing. The conversation has to start with what people need, not what someone else might think is good for them. 'So it's not that this is good for your health,' he says, 'It's this is how we save money.'

He believes it, too. Cycling and walking touch everything pressing in society: mental and physical wellbeing; economics – both individual and national; the environment. For him it's bigger than kerbs, routes and land acquisition, it's about making our lives better. Like him the bicycle quietly gets on with it – saving the world, one crisis at a time. Thinking about it, that's what appeals to me too.

We head down a ramp to a canal towpath and out to a broad estuary. Unsurprisingly, he rides faster than I normally do, this former Olympic champion. 'This is the River Dee,' he tells me. 'This is on my two-hour loop.' I ask if he means a fake commute, of the sort I took up during the pandemic, before realising this is something to do with exercise. Although he's largely got over an earlier, very successful, obsession with numbers and data, the one that won him an Olympic gold medal and a yellow jersey at the Tour de France among other *palmares*, he still believes in keeping fit.

Chris points out the enormous number of Canada geese, dotted across the estuary mud at low tide. It's pleasing that he also likes to appreciate the view. While we ride and talk, I like to play the game of seeing who recognises Chris. It's a popular cycle route for men in Lycra, out getting some exercise, often in pairs – the kind of people for whom Chris is a hero. Some greet him, after doing a double-take. 'Why would you only say hi when you realise who it is and not bother normally?' he says or unless you're in 'the uniform' of Lycra and a road bike. I feel the same; but then I say hi to everyone while cycling, including tiny dogs.

A pair of men overtake us: Lycra, road bikes. I try not to hit Chris's bike with my panniers as we let them pass. One of the men sees Chris and jokes about me carrying all the luggage, suggesting Chris should take a turn. 'Nice bike,' Chris calls as they cycle away. It's a Boardman. A few more people overtake us. I'm causing us to go slowly, but neither of us particularly cares. It's a relaxing place to ride: no traffic, the estuary laid out beside us, the company of other people on bikes. I'm not surprised he is fond of this stretch of tarmac.

When I ask if he came here during lockdown, he becomes uncharacteristically emotional. 'During the pandemic, cycling along here I was almost in tears, thinking, "This is what I've been talking about: that people will embrace this, given the chance."' Up and down the country, when the world as we knew it was placed on pause, people flocked to quiet, off-road routes like this, seeking green space, fresh air, solace and a chance for outdoor exercise. The bicycle, as it often does, shone in a time of crisis. In 2020, cycling rose 46%, more than in the previous 20 years and the biggest post-war increase. That time gave all of us who work in this world and know about the benefits of walking and cycling a tantalising glimpse at an alternative future.

While some of those shoots of growth survived, inevitably not all did. The pop-up routes installed up and down the country under instruction from Prime Minster Boris Johnson to help people social-distance and exercise in safety met with a mixed response. Some, like the ones in my neighbourhood, were well-loved, improved and made permanent, and some were pulled out at the first whiff of dissent, sometimes after complaints from MPs themselves.

'I worried we were going to lose the growth in cycling if we couldn't keep up,' says Chris. 'Andrew Gilligan [Boris Johnson's cycling advisor] works by force and that requires momentum. There was no way he was going to sustain it across the country and so councils were pulling out schemes after complaints. We've gone backwards since the pandemic; people don't want to do trials any more.' Many councillors were burned by loud, vocal opposition, which had a tendency to turn nasty. Planters intended to block streets to through traffic were vandalised and even set alight, and some politicians, even in Boris' government, cynically turned against schemes they had previously supported. For many local politicians this, and the abuse that often came with it, was too much and they backed down.

In Greater Manchester, Chris said they lined up all the councils when the pandemic began and said: 'We need NHS workers without cars to not be using buses – let's create routes for them to cycle.' He says they got all the leaders on side, apart from one, leaving an essential piece of the puzzle missing, right in the heart of Manchester. With pop-up cycle routes ending abruptly before cyclists had reached their destinations, those cycle journeys didn't feel safe. Soon enough, some of those temporary routes were taken out. I remember at the time interviewing one man who started cycling to work during 2020, only to return to driving because the pop-up lane he'd been using was removed.

After a huge upswing for active travel investment and support during the pandemic it looks like we're entering another trough; yet another repeat of the yo-yo cycle of funding and defunding; belief, fear of the challenge, then paralysis. I ask Chris what gives him hope amid this turmoil. 'Active travel is so robust,' he says. 'It's an easy thing to believe in. You just have to say, "What's the next crisis? OK, we can help," and keep reframing it.' One pressing crisis is the cost of living, and cycling and walking are incredibly cost-effective – if there were safe routes, households could give up one or more vehicle. Each car we own, Chris points out, costs us roughly the same as a family holiday, every year. I know which I'd rather spend my money on.

'It's just a means to an end, cycling and walking . . . to make nicer places, sustainable places to live and cheap transport,' says Chris. We might, he says, be fighting a hundred fires as a society, from a ticking health bomb, the NHS crisis, air pollution to the cost of living, but the important question is which one is going to kill us first. 'In every crisis we've had, active travel has been part of the solution, part of the saviour. It's been the most robust bit that just keeps working throughout. It should be a T-shirt, you know: "The least shit option". Even if you hate it, look at all the problems you've got to face.'

Although they came at a time of enormous limitations, the empty roads during the pandemic showed us the kinds of freedoms traffic-free streets could give us, becoming places to play, to run, walk and cycle in peace and relative safety, not just thoroughfares for motor vehicles. In representative polls, between two thirds and four fifths of people support this agenda. Often it's written into council policy that elected officials stood by in their manifestos. Then the local consultations come around and we disproportionately hear from those on the extreme ends, one side being those motivated by what they fear they might lose – often people with the time and resources to respond and campaign against them. The debate, from there, is held in shouty headlines decrying council overreach. Minority or not, those are the voices politicians listen to. Chris believes the rest of us are quietly getting on with our lives, supporting quieter, cleaner, safer streets without writing angry letters or social media posts, and often not responding to consultations. He wants to represent the majority, not the loudest shouters.

On his bike, clippy shoes attached to his pedals, Chris hurries along the towpath and I scurry after him. On the broad Deeside path we pass a building he wanted to use for his bike brand's headquarters, a beautiful redbrick structure right on the waterfront. Occasionally I have to up my pace again not to lose him, his shoulders rounded, purposefully pressing on.

After years at the cutting edge of cycle sport, first as an athlete then in British Cycling's secretive development department, the grinding slowness of local and now national government were a real gear change. He seems to apply the same problem-solving mindset that has served him so well across a varied career, though he scoffs at calling it a career at all.

One job is to try and make active travel resilient within government, no matter who is in charge. Active Travel England's predecessor, Cycling England, lasted five years, before being dismantled by David Cameron's 'bonfire of the quangos' in 2010. Its replacement didn't appear for more than a decade, leaving cycling floundering. Chris's aim with Active Travel England is to weave cycling and walking into as many departments as possible, reflecting its wide-ranging impact, from regenerating high streets to improving people's health and wellbeing. This should make it resilient to the ebb and flow of politics.

This is a delightful route, low stress and beautiful along the river, leaving us to chat without worrying about passing drivers and whether they have seen us. We tackle the day's one small climb over a wide cycling and walking bridge spanning a huge main road – one of the millennium bridges, I believe. We turn away from the river and on to NCN5, part of Chester's Millennium Greenway. Like all railway paths it's flat, straight and smooth, and surrounded by trees – a calm, green corridor. Chris asks me how I would feel about riding this alone and I say, 'Well . . .' He guesses, 'Not at night?' Bingo.

I tell him barriers can be scary for me as a woman as having to stop makes you feel vulnerable, particularly in the dark. '[That's] the kind of thing councils need to hear,' he says. He brings up Isabelle Clement, the woman in charge of disabled cycling charity Wheels for Wellbeing, who we'll meet in the next chapter. She uses a wheelchair, which she turns into a handcycle for exercise and transport. Chris admires her and her campaigning work, and wants the people who install anti-motorbike barriers to look Isabelle Clement in the eye and explain why she's being excluded from certain spaces.

Chris understands that unless you've experienced something for yourself it's hard to properly get it. He wants the people delivering a new generation of cycling and walking routes to better represent society. I know from covering accessibility in transport, from gender, to race, disability and neurodiversity, that it works poorly for most of us, because people design for those like them and the transport industry is historically so lacking in diversity.

Chris and I stop at a bench to chat. I've always thought part of my interest in road safety and cycling is to do with losing my dad suddenly to a preventable, inactivity-related illness, and to seeing him deal with the lifelong fallout of his injury. The journey I'm on, writing this book, has brought that back into focus and it makes me curious about the impact on Chris of his mum's death and whether he can make sense of it.

When I slightly awkwardly make the comparison, he says it's probably part of it. People ask him if her death motivates his work, sometimes not realising he was already campaigning when the crash happened, but it makes the work more personal. He believes that if we'd had a network of safe cycle routes, separate from motor traffic, his mum would still be alive. 'It kind of makes a point and underscores it,' he says. 'If she'd had safe space, you know, if it had been like

Holland, then that interaction would never have happened. It gives more weight to it, is probably the best way to put it.

'She was riding over there in hi-vis and helmet,' he says, nodding beyond the river. In a moment a driver, who had been texting moments before the collision, ended everything – for her family, her partner of a lifetime, her children and grandchildren, and everyone whose life she touched. The driver will be back behind the wheel in 18 months.

'She would have believed in all of this as well,' Chris says, meaning the drive for safe, protected cycle routes. 'She used to take – here, actually – used to take kids out on bike rides and things for the local club.' On this very path, I try to imagine her riding along, nurturing the next generation of riders, bringing them here where it's safe. 'She spanned the use of it as well,' he adds. 'She did this is my transport, this is my social life – that's how she met my dad – she did the racing thing, then she did the exploring thing. And then it was also transport, going to the shops, so she just did the whole gamut.'

After meeting me, Chris is going to the hospital where she died, just up the road, to formally open some new cycle parking. 'It's the least I can do,' he says. He pauses and we both smile sadly. What else is there to say? A life cut short by a stupid chance encounter. The result of decades of prioritising motor traffic, creating a transport network where one false move can be fatal – and we largely shrug our shoulders and accept it. It's no way to design a transport system – in other areas of life it would be considered negligent.

Just then Andrew Gilligan, Boris Johnson's cycling and walking advisor, phones – his government advisory role continued after Boris left – and Chris gets up to take the call. After he's finished, we press on. The path is tree-lined, flat and peaceful, with the odd reminder of its former use as a railway, where stone road bridges cross above the path.

Part of the problem is basic inertia. In the past, even when councils said they were prioritising cycling and walking, in reality little happened on the ground. Proposals are written, rewritten and forgotten. Leaving councils to deliver their own cycling plans, Chris says, is like 'not only asking turkeys to vote for Christmas, but it's letting them cook the dinner'. Until now, we've funded grand cycling plans that are scaled back when things get difficult, until they are meaningless – and no-one tended to check how public funds were being spent. Rinse and repeat. That's what Chris's team is here to change, a kind of Ofsted for cycling and walking delivery, helping councils do better and reminding them 70% of people actually support this agenda – the 20% we hear from, opposing reduction in motor traffic space, may be loud, but they are a minority.

That doesn't mean not listening to everyone. In Manchester Chris and his team went to community groups, handed them pens and asked them to draw on maps where the holes in the walking and cycling networks were. 'Agreeing the terms of engagement away from the heat of battle,' he calls it. Then they went about tackling those connections, creating a network with crossings as well as protected cycle routes. Neighbouring communities started requesting improvements, too. It wasn't perfect, there was pushback over some LTNs, and it certainly wasn't easy, but they were the kind of conversations we need to have about our neighbourhoods nationwide.

In Ghent, a circulation plan which divided the city into 'segments' that people could drive in and out of but not through, a giant LTN if you like, took three years of consultation and discussion before it was finally introduced. However, 40% of traffic in Ghent was through traffic, which was instantly removed when the plan was implemented. Within a couple of years the city had reached its target of 35% of all journeys being cycled – 13 years ahead of time – while public transport use rose by 10% within a year. Residents delight in the sound of birdsong, where once traffic noise dominated.

It took a while to get things going in Manchester under Chris's tenure as commissioner, too. His explanation: 'You're starting from scratch. I totted it up, they'd spent £80 million quid [on cycling] and didn't have any change in journeys from it. That's just because they'd spent it on stuff that was easier to do rather than what people needed; because there were no standards. They've just got money to keep their staff employed, and just kept developing and developing,

developing and consulting until all the money's gone, so you just have a paper network.

'The best thing they have, which we got sick of talking about, is the Oxford Road corridor, which still has loads of issues.' This three and three-quarter-mile route, one of the first major, high-quality main road cycle routes built outside London, saw a 200% increase in cycling in one year, making one of Europe's busiest bus corridors safe for cycling – and it was funded with bus money, a prime example of joined-up policy thinking making longer journeys possible without needing a car.

It is painstaking work, locally and nationally – risk aversion meets antipathy. Weeks before the pandemic, in early 2020 I got up at the crack of dawn to trek to the Transport Research Laboratory in Berkshire, a research facility testing Chris and his team's 'side road zebras'. These crossings, minus the Belisha beacons, are commonly seen in Europe and cost a fraction of their flashing cousins. Placed at side road junctions, they give pedestrians priority over turning traffic. Three years later, there's still nothing on the ground. Because the DfT is nervous about road changes it will be almost five years since that visit before they are rolled out here.

Transitioning from R&D at the elite end of cycle sport to the grinding bureaucracy of national government is certainly a change of pace, but Chris holds out hope he can recreate some of the magic that delivered Great Britain's medals factory in everyday cycling. He likes targets, so I ask where he would like to see national cycling infrastructure in five years. 'If you go to Manchester now, there's big chunks of [the network] under construction. That's five years after we started, five years after we had £160 million quid, and now it's starting to go in, so in five years I'd like to see England under construction.'

We're back on the narrow towpath, dodging tiny dogs, which I can't help but greet as we pass. We reach a fork, one path leaving the towpath, where Chris goes off to the hospital and I momentarily wobble, before heading off along the canal, ready to catch another train. I wish him good luck as I go and his reply is fitting: 'We'll make our own luck.'

13

GUNG-HO HAND-CYCLING

Isabelle Clement and I are attracting attention – at least Isabelle is. The director of disabled cycling charity Wheels for Wellbeing rides around London on a wheelchair converted to a three-wheeled electric handcycle, and this particular bit of kit is not a common sight. She and I are whizzing along the quiet residential streets of her south London neighbourhood during a heatwave. Our plan is to cycle six-odd miles to the Wandle Trail – one of Isabelle's favourite local stretches of the NCN.

Isabelle is a force of nature. With a tiny budget and handful of staff, she and Wheels for Wellbeing have managed to change the way the UK views who 'active travel' is for, advising local and national government on what inclusive cycle routes look like. She believes most people can cycle, whatever their ability, whether on a regular bike, a tricycle, or a side-by-side tandem cycle, where one person can pilot and do most of the pedalling if needs be. The charity hires out adapted machines from its south London hub to unleash the enormous benefits of cycling for disabled people.

Isabelle has experienced these benefits first-hand: a long-term wheelchair user, when she discovered the handcycle adaptation, in her 30s, it changed her life. It's a simple device, albeit at £5000 an eye-wateringly expensive one. It has one front wheel, stabilised by two tiny wheels, with a sloping frame and a long chain up to a set of handlebars she cranks like pedals. She operates the gears and brakes from the handlebars, much like on a bicycle. The first time Isabelle clipped the device on to her chair, she not only moved around the streets faster, but for the first time she experienced the endorphins from exercise. After years of having to drive the machine in the boot of her car to safe cycling routes to use it, the pandemic produced another first: in 2020 Lambeth council transformed her local streets into LTNs, allowing her to finally cycle from her home in safety.

It's not all smooth sailing, though. I've met Isabelle countless times, have seen her speaking on various stages about disabled cycling, and I've witnessed her manoeuvring around buildings poorly adapted for wheelchair users. I've even been on group rides with her, though I hadn't fully appreciated the wonders – and challenges – of her hand-cycle. Just as we begin our outing today, Isabelle warns me, 'I behave differently to someone on a bicycle. I might have to suddenly stop or swerve to avoid divots or potholes in the road.' She also has to ride in the middle of the street so the camber – which I barely notice on two wheels – doesn't constantly pull her towards the gutter. We ride side by side, me on the inside and her in the middle of the road, cranking the machine forward with her arms. It feels radical in a way, claiming our space in the street.

We set off due south, through residential streets of substantial-sized homes. Today, temperatures will reach 32°C and, while we set off early to avoid the worst of it, by 9.30 a.m. it's already very hot. 'It's all LTNs around here now,' Isabelle says. 'Before the LTNs, I couldn't cycle on these roads.' Before she would have regularly met annoyed drivers who were unaware of why she was in the middle of the road and expected her to get out of their way. It didn't feel safe cycling in those conditions.

In 2020, during the pandemic, councils up and down the country introduced planters on streets to prevent through-running traffic and enable social-distancing while people got out to exercise. While all addresses in LTNs are still accessible by car, reaching them might require a slightly longer drive. The idea is that by making cycling and walking more direct than driving you reduce short car trips and improve safety – and it seems to have worked. According to Lambeth

Council, traffic on streets within the Streatham LTN decreased by 54%, while increasing 13% on boundary roads. It was a net reduction of 5% or 6100 vehicles in the area each day. The measures are now permanent.

However, the changes were not universally welcomed: in the first months, signs were vandalised and even removed by people angry about reduced vehicle access. Isabelle admits, 'It made me worry that people who lived around here felt so violent towards this change.' She was concerned she herself would somehow be a target of aggression.

Change may make people angry, but this is often based on fear, not fact. Analysis of 50 boundary roads across 12 LTNs installed between 2020 and 2022 found that in most cases traffic wasn't displaced on to boundary roads long term. Even if initially there were jams, over time people changed their behaviour and drove less, walking or cycling instead for local trips. This reduced car traffic across the area in 35 of 50 cases. For the remainder, rather than simply going back to the status quo, councils would ideally find ways of reducing any unintended knock-on effects by understanding the kinds of trips people are making and further improving cycling, walking and public transport links in the wider area to provide alternatives. While some people need to drive, Isabelle's contention is, when conditions are right, it's far fewer than you'd think – something she is living proof of. 'I hardly ever drive now,' she says. 'Thanks to low traffic neighbourhoods [LTNs], it means I can do an hour, two hours' cycle ride to go and find nice green spaces for leisure.'

She even cycled to an event at 10 Downing Street the previous week, a 40-minute journey by handcycle. 'Now I wouldn't think of doing anything else, but in the past I've always driven into central London.' Instead of arriving stressed and annoyed by traffic and the challenge of finding a parking space, she reached Number 10 energised – and it only took 15 to 20 minutes longer.

Concerns about traffic being displaced on to other roads are understandable (though currently there is no evidence of strong systematic impact on boundary roads, either way), but it's hard to know which way it will go until the measures are in place, usually

as a trial. Either way councils then need to tackle wider traffic problems, including on main roads, to encourage yet more people out of
cars, but none of it is easy.

We cross a busy road lined with bus stops and four lanes of fairly
dynamic traffic, including lorries, and I worry with Isabelle so low to
the ground drivers will fail to see her. At one point she and the chair
jump slightly, and she makes a startled sound. The tarmac has melted
and formed a rut under the weight of heavy bus traffic, and, having
not seen it until it's too late, she is nearly unseated. That's not to underestimate her strength and capability on the road. Describing herself as
'gung-ho', she confidently manoeuvres the handcycle, leaning into the
corners and adjusting her chair by pushing the rear wheels with her
hands, sometimes performing a three-point turn for a tight corner.

Wheels for Wellbeing campaigns for disabled cyclists, both those
who already cycle, those who would like to and those who don't even
know cycling is an option. As well as producing reports and research
with national and international reach, the charity's inclusive cycling
hubs in south London loan out non-standard cycles so people can
experience cycling for themselves and learn which cycle works for
them.

The charity's national survey, published in 2021, found that for
64% of disabled cyclists cycling is easier than walking – and for 59%
their cycle is their mobility aid. Of 245 survey respondents more
than half (60%) used standard bicycles, 26% tricycles or recumbents,
16.6% cycles and 8.53% tandems. The challenge is to ensure the
environment enables people to cycle, however they do it. 'Cyclists
dismount' signs, steps, barriers and chicanes all hamper people like
Isabelle. Surface is crucial, too.

By 2018, in addition to the thousands of barriers scattered along
the NCN, Sustrans identified 831 miles of routes that were unsuitable for a narrow-tyred hybrid bike to pass comfortably. This renders
all those miles, and by extension many around them, unsuitable for
wheelchair users too. The NCN isn't unique, however: decades of
underinvestment in roads has left many riddled with holes, while
dedicated cycle paths often lack maintenance budgets entirely.

Frequently Isabelle will slow right down or make a wide turn to avoid an imperfection in the road I haven't noticed. It doesn't take much to tip someone out of a wheelchair, she explains – an uneven paving slab can do it. 'As a non-standard cycle rider, danger sits in different places than it does for two-wheeler riders,' she says. 'The danger from cars is often less than the danger from the bad quality of the road surface. It's just endless, the number of imperfections in the road surface, which could tip me out of my handbike and into the path of another vehicle.' Manoeuvring around both other road users and these imperfections means on busier roads she's sometimes left with no choice but to just pull over. With an LTN, even if the road surface is imperfect, Isabelle can negotiate a route in relative comfort, without fear of intimidation.

Isabelle's machine turns heads and a few people make positive comments as we pass. It's no insignificant piece of kit, but despite its clear advantages for health and mobility, there are no straightforward ways to financially support disabled people to purchase equipment like this – stuff that isn't fully electric – in the UK. This supresses awareness of the existence of more active modes of travel for disabled people, and the market that supports its availability and maintenance. It leaves most people with disabilities reliant on expensive or inaccessible transport like private cars and taxis or, where they are accessible, buses and trains. Isabelle and the charity's assertion is that most people can enjoy the freedom and benefits of cycling, but, like her, they just need the right conditions and the right equipment. Changing awareness on this is a long, slow process.

Many of us who cycled more during the pandemic did so thanks to a sudden lack of traffic on the roads – and this was particularly the case for disabled cyclists who are less willing, or able, to share the road with motor traffic. And I'm about to gain a better understanding of how that works in practice. While most people are extra courteous and we get far more space from overtaking drivers than I am accustomed to – I think because they aren't sure what to make of Isabelle – as we leave the safety of the LTN a man drives up behind us and revs his engine aggressively, hurtling past as soon as there is a gap in the parked cars. This kind of behaviour is as hard to fathom as it is common on narrow residential streets that double up as shortcuts for frustrated drivers.

Isabelle's phone is giving us audio directions from a routing app, but it is far too late to warn us of turns. If the route mounts a pavement, particularly if there's a slope involved, Isabelle must first steer herself out into traffic, in the same way a lorry driver would to make a sharp turn, to avoid tipping her chair. We misunderstand the directions and turn down a narrow alley on a housing estate with a particularly tight chicane barrier. Isabelle has to uncouple the handcycle from the chair, manoeuvring the handcycle attachment under the barrier – no mean feat – while she navigates the chicane in her chair. It isn't a cycle route, but it's certainly not wheelchair accessible and Isabelle points out that anyone with a bigger chair, or with their foot rests further forward, wouldn't get through. The process takes a good minute and a lot of energy.

'When we say everyone can cycle, we don't necessarily mean for everyday journeys,' she says, 'and it's because of things like this.' Isabelle's machine has electric assist, but, like any e-cycle, the power doesn't kick in until the wheels are turning. Every time she stops suddenly, there's a physical strain on her upper body – and it happens 'all the time' on most UK cycle routes Isabelle uses.

The start of the Wandle Trail isn't signed and neither is our cycle route through south London, so we're reliant on the app with its far from perfect and sometimes overly complicated or ambiguous instructions. We've taken the shadiest route to avoid the worst of the heat and it's not a route Isabelle knows well. I am constantly worried we'll find something inaccessible: a set of steps or something she won't be able to navigate.

With detours, stops to look at the map, and avoiding rough surfaces, entry and exit pavement paths and crossroads, what should have been a half-hour journey takes an hour. The Wandle Trail is worth the trip, though. It begins off Merton High Street, at Merton Abbey Mills, a complex of brick buildings William Morris bought in 1881 to weave, dye and print his famous cloth patterns. Today it is roasting hot and buzzing with a craft market and eateries with busy outdoor seating. We cross the river Wandle near a working water wheel, and it and the gravel path are thankfully shaded from the sun. It is a real delight to see this beautiful wedge of green, and the water, after our long, hot traverse around south London.

Like seemingly everything for wheelchair users like Isabelle, our visit today required a bit of forethought. Because the path is unsurfaced, it becomes inaccessible for a full two weeks after it rains. I try and imagine how many weeks of a normal year are fully dry for more than two weeks and conclude it's probably not many at all.

Isabelle's machine can do up to 20mph but it needs a smooth surface. On today's ride, there's a brief stretch of tarmac where she can finally stop riding defensively and speed up – between the speed bumps. It's the road to the car park.

Isabelle visibly relaxes. 'I only get it in small chunks: the "Oh wow! This is just amazing"; the feeling when I'll have enough of a stretch of good infrastructure where I can let my brain be relaxed and think about other things and really feel the enjoyment of the ride. When I do, it's just amazing. And I never find that anywhere else. Because you're getting the endorphins as you're moving, there's this sheer joy of being able to move unimpeded when generally, in the rest of your life, it's blinking hard work.'

Back on the dirt, she skilfully manoeuvres the handcycle over a worn-out railway sleeper bridge, snuggled into a dirt bank over a stream. I hold my breath and stand back. If those of us who discover cycling become evangelical for others to enjoy the transformation, Isabelle is even more so. We encounter a man walking with a pronounced limp, who remarks he'd like a handcycle like hers. We stop in the boiling sun as Isabelle patiently gives the man Wheels for Wellbeing's website address and phone number, and tells him about their cycling hubs.

Into Morden Park, the broad dirt path crosses a grove where families play in some water and we are shaded by established trees. Isabelle looks around and says, 'Isn't this wonderful? When I was a child, my father would carry me on his shoulders to parks and then, when I was old enough that I no longer wanted to be carried, I couldn't access places like this.' She says for a long time adventure was out of reach, blocked by a gravel path or steps or a cattle grid or chicane barrier. The handcycle has put greenways and parks back within her grasp, but it hasn't solved everything.

'You can live quite a cosseted life as a disabled person if you're not careful,' she says. 'You can be restricted to driving to a car park somewhere that's quite busy and hope it's somewhere nice, with decent paths.' I struggle to imagine how stifling this would be. And it is despite 20 years of equality legislation.

The benefits of access to nature and physical exercise extend to everyone, and the mental health benefits are huge: research shows physical activity can cut depression rates by 30%. Cycling can also be a low-stress transport option, in the right circumstances. Isabelle says, 'For some people in the middle of a mental health issue getting about can be stressful, but I've heard from people living with mental health issues who find they do not use public transport because that's so stressful, but they get on their cycle: they are in control, they are not around other people, they can really get in the zone. That does amazing stuff for your soul.'

When I ask what an accessible NCN would look like, straight off Isabelle explains: 'It has to be excellent quality: road surface quality. Even if it's a path, it should be tarmacked, should be all-weather.' While it may look more natural in parks like this, compacted gravel becomes rutted and impassable for wheelchair users very quickly. Joint first are camber and angles, and they are not minor issues: Isabelle was once tipped out of her chair on a sloping path that suddenly exited, at a sharp angle, on to a gravel track.

Third is decent path width, so users can pass each other comfortably. Visually impaired users can find narrow sharing paths with cyclists uncomfortable, while for non-standard cycle users stopping and starting to avoid pedestrians can be hard work. Wayfinding is fourth – including accessibility information – and consistency is five. For routes that chuck you on and off pavements, Isabelle says, 'Actually, the time and stress and physical and mental energy that all takes makes the infrastructure that's been put there for cyclists unusable or pointless compared to just staying on the road.

'If it can't be done well, it shouldn't be done at all. I think you're endangering cyclists by just doing a little bit of badly signed, cambered, sharp turn bits of infrastructure. You have to deal with the road: you have to either lower the traffic level or you protect the cyclists. Doing it on the cheap helps no-one. It wastes money, it wastes resources.' The design standards for most of the above already exist, it's about funding improvements to bring the standard of existing routes up.

Disabled people already suffer worse physical and mental health, and financial stability, and everyday life can be beset with challenges, physical and mental. This is no less the case while cycling. A quarter of respondents to Wheels for Wellbeing's 2021 survey said they had experienced abuse or hostility and, astonishingly, were even ticked off by others for being out of the house during the pandemic.

Isabelle says one friend didn't leave the house in two years during the pandemic, except to get vaccinated and for emergency medical care. Once the many disabled people who were shielding emerged from their homes after the first lockdown, they encountered a newly hostile world, and the worsening of entrenched discrimination and inequality. Disabled parking bays at shops and medical centres were given over to social-distancing infrastructure, while some physical distancing and traffic-reduction measures blocked the dropped kerbs wheelchair users needed to cross roads. After a high-profile legal challenge, councils learned to better consult disabled people.

It was like progress on disability equality had rolled back, says Isabelle. 'It was as if disabled people were forgotten, out of sight out of mind, and it took months to get back to the way it was before.' This is on top of general fears disabled cyclists have of being reported to the authorities for seeming 'too active' to be genuinely disabled, threatening their benefits payments. While less than 2% of disabled cyclists have been reported to authorities in this way, a quarter fear this happening. Some even avoid cycling as a result, even when it's their only way of getting around independently. I've spoken to people in this situation, where this fear robs them of joy, physical exercise and independence, in one fell swoop.

Cycling was the safest way of getting around without exposing ourselves to the virus on public transport and for a lot of us, disabled people included, cycling was the only form of exercise when leisure facilities were closed. One survey respondent told Wheels for Wellbeing, 'I had no choice but to cycle because of being clinically extremely vulnerable and not having access to a car. I was told not to use public transport and I didn't feel safe using taxis.' The four-mile journey to hospital for chemotherapy was only possible thanks to a cycle path most of the way, with a few pavements in between. 'I'm happy I was able to cycle as I think it pushed me to be more active,' but, they added, 'it's a total lottery: if I hadn't lived where I did at the time, with access to the cycle path, then I don't know what I would have done.'

Subjectively, drivers seemed more aggressive towards cyclists following lockdowns and speeding rates increased dramatically on quieter roads – which disabled cyclists found particularly off-putting. Isabelle hopes, in her role as non-executive director for Active Travel England, she can start to change the status quo, not for people already cycling, but for those locked out of it – 'putting accessibility and diversity at the front, first and foremost of our work.' As she puts it, if we're not making public space accessible for everyone, we 'might as well give the money to the NHS, to deal with the consequences of people not being active.'

It's lunch time and we stop in Morden Hall Park, a wheelchair-accessible facility with a gorgeous garden and a cool café where we eat sandwiches. A man with Down's syndrome is working there and I think, in my hopelessly idealistic way, of a world where everyone is included. After lunch it's unbearably hot, so we head back. In a couple of hours' travel we've managed to cover just over a mile of the Wandle Trail. More recent changes at a national level, of which Isabelle is a key part, will bring improvements, but it's not happening anywhere near fast enough.

14

THE MYSTERY OF THE COALASH TRIANGLE

Twenty years is a long time to work on a three-mile stretch of cycle route, but that doesn't faze Richard Ackroyd. It's his 64th birthday, a pleasant afternoon, and I cycle from Bath to meet him in Frome, via a delightful two-hour, remarkably flat 30-mile ride almost entirely on former railways. Three miles from Frome the cycle route abruptly ends at a former rail bridge over a country lane. From there it's a series of incredibly stiff hills on narrow country roads. I get off and push. It's impossible.

Richard is the former mayor of Frome and has been trying to get those final three miles connected up for two decades now. We have tea and cake at the Cheese and Grain café and music venue, and walk the riverside path marking the start of Frome's 'Missing Link' – a short section of path that will join to the 17.5-mile Colliers Way rail trail to Dundas and onward to the Two Tunnels route, all the way to Bath. True to the make-do-and-mend spirit of the past 40 years of UK cycle path construction, Richard's group used ground-up stone from a derelict bridge as ballast; its scaffold poles became railings ('Everything's recycled!'). On the edge of town, we reach a field gate marking private land.

Frome Missing Link (which, perhaps aptly, can be shortened to FML) is perhaps emblematic of what happens when we leave the development of a national cycle network to chance and goodwill. Sustrans has to focus its limited resources on projects it can deliver within a reasonable time frame – and this is not one of them. In these cases, it falls to people like Richard and his team of mostly retired men to do the endlessly slow work to make it happen – or it doesn't happen at all.

Without the necessary powers, Richard and his co-conspirators have become adept at negotiations, and working their contacts and skills. We cross a riverside meadow that spans three landowners, patches of gradually darker tarmac marking the striations of past dribs of funding. In the near future it will continue into the next field, linking a pre-school to the town centre and already marked out by 600 saplings, all planted by volunteers. Somewhere beyond that is the Colliers Way.

The future of Frome's Missing Link is now in the hands of various landowners, spread across several fields and alongside a still-working quarry train line. While two of the five kilometres (the metric Richard works in) are either built or in the process of being built, there's a three-kilometre gap in the middle – minus what Richard jokingly calls the Coalash Triangle – 170 metres of disconnected cycle path in a field they tarmacked because of a time limit on getting the work done. Where the Bermuda Triangle lost ships and planes, this one could easily swallow cycling hopes and dreams, but Richard is philosophical.

'You've just got to have a long-term goal,' he says. 'I've come around to thinking that this is just bit by bit, bit by bit, as opportunities arise.' Because the bits around it don't exist yet, for now it goes nowhere. 'You can walk it,' Richard adds brightly. While John Grimshaw is negotiating positively with Network Rail to build beside the railway, the process is glacially slow. The rest is a moveable feast. 'We've had 10 different possible routes,' says Richard – drawn up by a land agent with a feasibility study. 'And then after that, because we couldn't buy a piece of land that we wanted, we also came up with, I suppose, an 11th route, which was an alternative through some farmers' fields.'

'Does it join up with the Coalash Triangle?' I ask.

'Not yet,' says Richard. Each time the route changes, they also need to consult with roughly 20 local stakeholders – from local anglers to the landowners themselves.

'When do you think it'll be done?'

'If we had a million and a half to spend, I think we could make it happen.'

'By when?'

I'm getting ahead of myself. One 150m strip of land has been in negotiations with three generations of farmers over a period of 15 years. The farmer who originally agreed to sell it for an eye-watering £25,000 died unexpectedly. By now Richard and Frome Missing Links had set up a charity to receive donations and grants. After a respectful wait, they approached the son, who didn't like the idea of a cycle route and refused to sell. He then died and the grandson was happy to sell. The snag for the cycle path was that his father passed away intestate, leaving the land tangled up in probate.

'Is that the last 150m of route?' No, of course not.

Even now-prosperous towns like Frome have households locked into unaffordable car ownership for lack of other options, while around 22% of households in England don't have access to a car. We wouldn't think twice as a society in prioritising this missing link if it were a key road or rail connection; it's only overlooked because we don't treat cycling seriously. Sustrans deals with this kind of tangle all the time – the charity has decades of experience doing so – because cycle routes don't have the money or power needed to deliver them.

The following month I join an online meeting of local campaigners and councillors on the border of Cumbria and Lancashire, talking through a 2.5-mile-odd stretch of potential cycle route that would provide a safe, traffic-free alternative to a rural A-road.

Some of the assembled attendees have waited 25 years for the path so far. In two and a half miles of potential path, Sustrans reports, there are seven landowners with differing ideas, including two county councils. One private landowner is dead against using their stretch of disused railway, one that is potentially in a very poor state anyway, taking that option off the table (one less landowner to deal with!).

Other landowners are hesitant about letting the public in, fearing littering and the 'urbanisation of the countryside' or path users trespassing on the rest of their land. Sustrans could ask the councils to use their compulsory purchase powers, if councillors were willing, which they usually aren't – but there's a risk they'd then alienate the other landowners, who talk to each other. An alternative path through town would squash cyclists on a pavement between fast-moving traffic and multiple side roads, which would make it less pleasant and less safe – not least because one council didn't want to widen the narrow footpath to meet current design standards, fearing backlash over its ecological impact.

The NCN, unlike footpaths, bridleways and roads, doesn't even have a legal status. That means in theory someone could build on a bit of NCN or close it if they don't feel like having people traipsing across their property that day. While I understand the rough state of the NCN from riding bits of it and how hard it is for local groups of campaigners to build routes, I'm slightly shocked by these meetings. Although these aren't the first people I've met fighting for a decade or more for something as seemingly simple as a safe cycle path, I'm starting to appreciate how remarkably under-supported our NCN, a piece of national infrastructure with undeniable benefits, is and frankly it's blowing my mind.

15

THANK GOODNESS FOR WALES

It occurred to me, once I started my quest, that much cycling infra-structure in the UK is parasitic, but I hadn't quite appreciated how far this pathology went. It's striking that almost nothing I've seen on my travels to date has been crafted, from scratch, for cycling: rail-way paths were built for trains, pavements for pedestrians, and roads, though originally widened by foot and horse traffic, and tarmacked thanks to lobbying from cyclists, have become dominated by, and subsequently shaped around, motor vehicles. Even when most new off-road routes are forged, they are designed to be shared with pedes-trians. When cycling is one of the most efficient means of conducting humans over the kinds of short journeys we do the most of, a total lack of dedicated provision increasingly seems like a glaring oversight.

Just when I am beginning to despair at the state of the NCN and feeling constantly hemmed in by car traffic, pedestrian traffic, barri-ers, crappy surfaces and random closures, in early July I head to Wales, where things start to look a tiny bit brighter. South Wales, I discover, is home to the closest thing to a network of traffic-free cycle routes that we have in the UK. Yellow lines of off-road routes streak across the Ordnance Survey's NCN layer in wobbly parallel lines, like a paint pot has leaked. Many of these follow former mineral railway tracks along valley floors that once transported passengers and goods from mines to docks, and beyond to Bristol, Shrewsbury, North Wales and the Mersey.

The rest of Wales is rather less crowded. As Dafydd Trystan, chair of Wales' Active Travel Board, puts it when I talk to him on the phone, rolling his Rs delightfully as he goes, this is a country of rurality: 80% of Wales is countryside, and many of its three million inhabitants are scattered across small towns and villages. These places are, like the rest of the UK, largely lacking in cycling connections. Curiously, Wales boasts two cities of fewer than 4000 people – St David's and St Asaph, in the west and north of the country. A brand-new city, Wrexham, named for the Queen Elizabeth II's Platinum Jubilee in 2022, is entirely marooned from the NCN, though as part of its masterplan to expand the network, Sustrans subsequently developed plans for five arms of routes crossing the city.

There are some gems, though. A long-distance route, Lon Las Cymru, NCN8, follows a spectacular but sparsely populated trail 350-odd miles north, from Cardiff Bay via Bannau Brycheiniog (the Brecon Beacons) and Eryri (Snowdonia National Park), to Anglesey. It's supposed to be wonderful and I briefly consider cycling the whole thing, but it is principally an adventure trail that doesn't pass through many towns, and frankly it seems like hard and hilly work.

I set about exploring south Wales instead. I base myself in Cardiff for a week, working some of the time and cycling the rest, and finally start to see what's possible for the future of cycling in the UK. While I've been travelling roughly around the coast, Cardiff is the first city I've spent any substantial time in, London aside. Towns and cities are crucial in cycling journeys because more than 80% of the UK population is urban. These are where most short journeys take place, and where there's the most potential for walking and cycling. Delivering the routes to enable active journeys isn't technically challenging, it just takes some money and an amount of political courage. Cardiff, and Wales more broadly, seem to have this in spades.

Like many cities, Cardiff quietly sped ahead with cycling improvements during the pandemic, rapidly changing the balance of power on city streets away from cars and towards people. The idea was to quickly install widened pavements and pop-up cycle routes across the city centre, many separated from traffic by plastic water-filled boxes, and pencil-like wands bolted to the road. The aim wasn't perfection, it was speed, and many routes would be tweaked, improved and expanded where needed. Routes like these appeared all over the country; they were cheap and quick to put in place, and a rapid response to a public health emergency.

South Wales is a place I called home for several years, first during my second run at A-levels, in Swansea, and then my first go at completing a degree, in Cardiff. After tiring of driving less than three miles to university in my rusting Mark 2 Ford Fiesta, I attempted the journey on my flatmate Sadie's old mountain bike. Scouring a city map, I cobbled together a route from residential roads and housing estate cut-throughs, and a brief stretch of the gorgeous Taff Trail along the eponymous river it traces, before mounting the pavement on the busy dual carriageway of Western Avenue.

Cardiff, I'm told, suffers an epidemic of cycle theft, so I leave my nice bike in the Airbnb and use the public cycle hire scheme around town, releasing bikes from their docking stations using an app and riding them to cafés around the city centre to work.

On Saturday a local cycle campaigner, Hamish, meets me near where I'm staying in the north of the city to show me what has happened since I left Cardiff two decades ago. Hamish is a passionate advocate – one of the many remarkable and generous people who give up their time to promote cycling in its various forms. He waits for me in a nearby park on his electric cargo bike. It looks like a regular cycle but for its long, rear pannier rack, designed for carrying things like shopping or children.

It is another very hot morning in a scorching week in July and we stand in the shade of a large tree at the edge of the park while Hamish shows me the colour-coded, hand-highlighted map he produced specially for today's tour. We set off across the suburbs before ducking through an underpass beneath the roar of my old friend, the ever-hostile Western Avenue. From there we start to see the city's new cycling vision take shape.

Hamish's printed map of Cardiff City Council's planned cycle network looks strikingly like plans made in London a decade ago that transformed the city and conjured millions of cycle journeys, seemingly out of nowhere, by suddenly making cycling feel safe. Cardiff's routes are numbered C1, C2, C3 and C4, in a similar way to London's. Since the pandemic there's a new three-mile route running east–west across the city centre, reclaimed from a lane on a multi-lane arterial road (buses claim another lane). Here a blue dotted line, representing an as-yet unbuilt route, heads east towards Newport, disappearing enticingly off the map.

A wide, two-way cycle route, which snakes through a supermarket car park and off in two directions through trees and parkland, towards the city centre, is convincingly the beginning of a network of bicycle roads, complete with miniaturised road markings, including pedestrian crossings and a separate pavement beside it. No inconvenient shared space here. This path is easily the best UK cycling-as-transport route I've seen outside London

From there a series of impressive main-road cycle routes head away and into the city. Some of these are finished articles, kerb-protected with new bus stops and wide pavements, others are still little more than pairs of plastic wands bolted to the tarmac. In places we see the stubs of future routes to be extended later. Slowly these are turning places only the fearless would cycle into somewhere you see students and tourists on hire bikes.

We ride alongside the imposing stone walls of Cardiff Castle, where the city council closed Castle Street to through traffic in July 2020 for a year, abruptly replacing three lanes of almost constant traffic with 240 al fresco dining spaces. The move cut air pollution dramatically, enabled businesses in the nearby arcades to stay open during pandemic restrictions on indoor dining, and turned the dual carriageway that cut off one of the world's most impressive castles into a public square.

However, in a consultation 53.8% of people wanted it reopened to traffic. Some, Hamish says with a note of irony, opposed pedestrianisation on the grounds a lack of cars negatively changed the character of the almost 2000-year-old street. It's amazing how quickly we forget – for most of its history that street would have bustled, and its businesses thrived, on foot traffic.

Many, of course, viewed motor traffic as essential for the city's success and just 33.8% wanted to keep it as a public square. In the end, there was a compromise: a new bus gate was installed on Westgate Street, one lane was reopened on Castle Street to private traffic – and the cycle lane stayed.

The City Council was busy during the pandemic. Hamish takes us north to Wellfield Road in Roath, with its independent eateries and shops. What is now a two-way cycle route, separated from the road by more wands, started off as the city's first Covid experiment in expanded people space. When lockdown started, the pavement was too narrow for people to keep two metres apart, and the council plonked planters and large red and white Lego blocks filled with water in former parking spaces and loading bays up and down the street, to aid social-distancing. They weathered cries it would ruin trade and vandalisation by those opposed to the changes – someone even came along in the night and sawed one of the saplings in a planter in half.

Today the temporary red and white blocks have been replaced by newly expanded pavement space the colour and surface texture of golden sand. Between the potted birches are new seating areas for restaurants and cafés, protected from the now one-way street by the bike lane. The council reintroduced parking on one side of the street and expanded pavements on the other side, and local businesses added their own touches: one restaurant owner placed planters with olive trees next to their new outdoor seating. Some local people are still coming to terms with the changes, and local news outlets have reported people tripping over the black and white feet anchoring the wands to the road.

Research from cities like New York and London has shown improving pedestrian and cycle space can boost retail spend by up to 30%, with high street visitors who walk spending up to 40% more, and visiting twice as much, as drivers over a month. While some customers doubtless drive, research repeatedly shows business owners overestimate the proportion of car-borne visitors and underestimate those who walk and cycle. In fact, customers who walk, cycle and take public transport spend the most in urban shops. Still, it takes a while for people to believe this for themselves; another reason trials like this are so crucial. As with countless initiatives that came before, concerns around the changes on Wellfield Road soon died down and life carried on.

The cycle lane abruptly finishes and Hamish and I gaze out at a broad crossroads, acres of tarmac devoid of cycle space, but even here, out of the city centre, there are plans to extend the route further north and east. Once the routes are made permanent, there are fancy improvements in the pipeline. Some new cycle routes Hamish shows me are in the process of being fitted with 'rain gardens'. These are kerb-enclosed areas of soil and gravel, planted with drought- and deluge-tolerant plants and trees. Such is the impetus to reduce the volumes of rainfall regularly flooding Cardiff's overloaded drainage system that the rain gardens are often finished first, before the cycle lanes.

With climate change comes heavy rain and heatwaves, and impermeable tarmac and paving exacerbates both, by storing heat in the summer, and by rapidly funnelling rainfall into drains and sewers that can overflow during storms. To see life inserted into what is a traditionally lifeless environment is inspiring. By soaking up water, and cooling the street, these planting areas aren't only health and transport measures, but part of the city's climate change mitigation programme.

It's almost midday by the time we're finished exploring the new routes. Eventually, the city's network will reach a grid density of 500m, with a safe route every 250m or so in central areas, meeting Welsh legislation requirements – at which point perhaps Cardiff will perhaps resemble a city like Rotterdam. The eventual goal is that routes will be 'continuous and cohesive, linking all key destinations within the locality as a complete journey so that cyclists can travel seamlessly on good quality infrastructure.' In other words, a network.

I follow Hamish to an inclusive cycling centre in Bute Park, where people of all abilities can try out different cycles, in a similar way to Wheels for Wellbeing's London hub. We're here for Hamish's cargo bike meetup. There is just one member this week, a young man with a toddler, looking to meet other parents who've ditched a family car for a cargo bike. The child sits shaded under a sun hat in the cargo box at the front of his machine, and he and Hamish chat about becoming accustomed to ferrying their kids and shopping by pedal power. The rapidly growing network of safe routes makes this possible, along with the city's programme of school streets – the name for timed closures to cars of roads outside school gates during pick-up and drop-off time.

We three adults and one toddler head out again towards Grangetown, Cardiff's first rain garden – or SuDS (Sustainable Drainage Systems) project. This is a place that does a lot with a few tweaks. Each year 108 planting beds across just 12 Victorian streets, small areas of shrubs, trees, day lilies and the soil they stand in soak up and evaporate roughly a quarter of a Millennium Stadium's worth of water annually, instead of directing water into Cardiff's ageing combined sewer system. According to research, these shade-creating areas can reduce the impact of heatwaves by up to 12°C . Installed in 2016 by Cardiff Council, Welsh Water and Natural Resources Wales, this area, a stone's throw from the stadium and the river, was the beginning of a great big experiment, now being rolled out at speed. Not only is it doing a lot functionally, it transforms this low-income area into a beautiful oasis.

The next day I head for the Cardiff Bay Trail. This was a place I last saw in 2016, reporting on completion of the first stage of the country's plan to revolutionise cycling. New Welsh legislation, the Active Travel Act, passed in 2013, perhaps coining the phrase 'active travel', required councils to map existing walking and cycling routes, and then set about improving and connecting them, while design standards defined what routes would look like. It was out with shared footways in busy areas, in with wide, accessible paths. What's more, everyday people could contribute their ideas to these maps. The UK had never seen anything like it, a seemingly nerdy bit of paperwork that had the potential to change transport in Wales and beyond.

By 2016 the mapping work was done, but as I stood with the Welsh Minister for Public Health, civil servants and campaigners beside a heaving Cardiff Bay Trail to celebrate this achievement, the excitement was somewhat tempered. There were early signs of progress unravelling – councils had ignored routes that were poor quality or too rural – and with no dedicated funding, in most cases improvements weren't possible anyway.

The Cardiff Bay Trail has since been removed from the NCN due to inaccessible barriers and path widths. Finding myself with time to kill one hot afternoon, though, I decide to cycle it anyway, for old times' sake. I ride from the Millennium Centre, Wales' national arts venue, past the Senedd, through a busy pedestrian area and out across the barrage, which helps keep the sea out of Cardiff Bay. The water is pretty, but it's essentially a strip of tarmac atop some boulders and entirely without shade until you reach the early 2000s-era waterside apartments on the other side of the barrage.

There a pedestrian and cycle bridge lifts up like a long, thin lid to let a ship through on the river Ely far below. I'm first to arrive and about 20 people wait on foot and bikes behind me. It queasily reminds me of a recurring dream of being lifted high in the air on a flimsy structure that breaks when I am impossibly far above the ground, sending me plummeting to earth. When the paired gates slowly reopen they do so on the right-hand side first and all those waiting on the right proceed. The folks on the opposite side spread out across the bridge, leaving just enough space for me to cycle between them and the right-hand barrier.

Then a man on a mobility scooter appears in the gap, yelling at me to stay left. As there are people walking towards me on every other part of the bridge, I simply slow right down and brace for impact. Thankfully he only tears a bolt off my right pannier when he hits me and, shocked as I am, I can't help sympathising with him. At least I can dismount and lift the bike when faced with an interminable number of barriers, and I guess I'm the softest one he's encountered in a while. Once the shock has subsided, the incident mainly serves to remind me how poorly our public space caters for disabled people. I'd probably be angry too, faced with constant barriers and inaccessible places, all despite years of legislation outlawing it.

Almost a decade after the Active Travel Act, the body tasked with coordinating, advising and scrutinising councils' cycling efforts, Wales' Active Travel Board acknowledged that local authorities had been given a 'mammoth task without sufficient resources or clear direction' to deliver and, ultimately, the Act had 'slipped into oblivion.' Without a standard approach to monitoring, almost none of the required cycling and walking improvements in new housing and business developments had happened, representing countless missed opportunities to help people walk and cycle, and locking in car dependency for the coming decades. Highways authorities had effectively broken the law by failing to upgrade roads for cycling and walking when they carried out road improvements, not necessarily out of pigheadedness, but simply because they had always designed for car journeys, not for cycling.

Thankfully this wasn't the end of the story. Cycling ticked boxes for several of Wales' key goals, including those in the Wellbeing of Future Generations Act, legislating that authorities should leave Wales and its people in a better state than they found it. Health was, at the time, 48% of the Welsh government's total budget, its single biggest spend, with much of the nation's ill-health due to inactivity. The government recognises cycling and walking routes create cheap, easy opportunities for everyday exercise. With cars accounting for 55% of Wales' transport emissions, they would also help meet environmental goals – once again, there is very little that more cycling and walking doesn't improve.

Thanks to this legislation Wales is also changing the way we value road investment, part of whose supposed economic gain comes from a nonsensical calculation, adding up hundreds of thousands of individual 30-second time-savings for drivers when you widen a road – time you can't do anything with. Its new appraisal tool includes social and environmental factors, not just economics, returning the human element to transport. It rebalances transport's value in terms of things people can use: things like clean air, quieter neighbourhoods and access to affordable means of travel.

In 2018 former Sustrans Cymru director, Lee Waters, became Wales' Deputy Minister for Economy and Transport and, in 2021, with Climate Change Minister, Julie James, announced a freeze on new roadbuilding. In 2023 that became an effective ban, unless the roads improved walking, cycling and public transport provision. Under a new administration keen on delivering on active travel, cycling and walking funding ramped up from £12 million in 2016 to £70 million in 2022 – an almost 600% increase.

This translates to more than £22 per person per year – a huge sum for the UK; more than the £1 per head in England after the 2023 budget cuts, although less than Scotland's £58 per head. There was a lot of ground to make up, though: as the Active Travel Board pointed out at the time, the sum total spent on active travel in two decades of devolution was equal to the widening of five miles of the A465.

Dafydd Trystan, chair of Wales' Active Travel board, is in charge of overseeing this funding. He describes himself as 'like Chris Boardman, without the money or the power, or the Olympic Gold medal.' Despite the budget increases, thanks to decades of underfunding and an incredibly small team of staff, Wales is effectively delivering cycling and walking routes on a shoestring.

Interviewing him for an article, Dafydd had piqued my interest by telling me his greatest desire – the satisfaction of which would allow him to 'die happy' – is a cycle route between two Welsh cities and I wanted to see the vision for myself. The idea of intercity cycle routes to replace car journeys is not so fanciful as it might seem. Two of Wales' three biggest cities, Cardiff (362,750 people) and Newport (151,500), lie just 15 miles apart, along the flat south coast. Thanks to the vagaries of traffic, a journey on the M4 from Newport to Cardiff can take anything from 20 minutes to more than an hour at peak times. A dedicated cycle route that's direct, separate from pedestrians and motor traffic, and given priority at side roads without unnecessary stops, could whisk you there in a similar time – given an electric bike or a fairly fit rider. The route doesn't exist yet, but, and this is the bit that got me jumping up and down with excitement, there is every indication it will.

In June 2019 the First Minister of Wales, Mark Drakeford, announced the Senedd wouldn't be proceeding with what many felt was an essential piece of infrastructure: a proposed M4 relief road intended to ease congestion around Newport. Every time the Brynglas tunnels are blocked, motorway traffic is pushed on to local roads and, while some called the problem 'a foot on the windpipe of the Welsh economy' and road expansion the answer, others, like Drakeford, saw it differently.

The time – and the £1.2 billion – needed to deliver the M4 relief road would have an 'unacceptable impact on our other priorities in areas such as public transport, health, education and housing,' he said. He also put 'significant weight' on the environmental and ecological impact of the road. It would be incompatible with meeting the 95% reduction in carbon emissions needed by 2050, as part of net-zero goals.

In November 2020 the Welsh government's Burns Commission produced a report recommending a 'network of alternatives' to a relief road, with public transport and active travel at its heart. They recommended a tripling of rail stations between the Severn crossing and Cardiff from three to nine, and a new network of rapid bus and cycle corridors across Newport and Cardiff. These would be developed as an integrated, interconnected transport network, with Newport a major focus of this work. This was radical stuff for the UK, but it makes practical sense: cycle routes can expand the catchment area of public transport interchanges from a radius of just over half a mile – around a 20-minute walk – to 3 miles.

Unlike the relief road, the vast majority of bus and cycling improvements, the resulting report said, could be delivered within five years and the rest within ten, at a fraction of the cost – between £600 million and £800 million. Learning from Cardiff, some cycle routes could be delivered on a trial basis and improved later.

A Cardiff-Newport cycle route, eventually extending west towards Swansea, would be a commuter cycle corridor, with spurs – side roads – into towns and cities along the way. The 'cheek-to-cheek' proximity of bus and rail stations to cycling and walking paths, and secure, convenient cycle parking, would mean more people could easily reach stations along the route without needing a car. This meant, in theory, journeys along that route could be done entirely car free.

To glimpse the possibility of this vision, if not to see the finished route, Dafydd Trystan meets me on the vast pedestrian plaza outside Cardiff Central Station on yet another scorching July day. Dafydd's plan for us is to cycle to Newport and back, on the route that, when built, will allow him to die happy. An ebullient, almost boyish, stockily-built man, he's wearing shorts and a T-shirt, with a baseball cap to protect his head from the sun.

He bids a cheery hello to almost everyone we pass, some of whom he apparently knows personally, but I quickly realise you underestimate Dafydd Trystan at your peril. He's steely and indefatigable, and where he can't persuade, he will push. Unable to find the data himself, he wrote to schools across Wales to find out two thirds of primary children lived within a three-mile catchment area – or walking and cycling distance – making the case for better facilities enabling them to travel actively.

Some of it happens through doggedness: his efforts to ensure that active travel be built into new schools, limiting car parking spaces, took two years of effort before he finally happened to meet the right person, who said, 'That seems like a good idea,' and made it happen. In his 'day-day job' he's registrar of the Coleg Cymraeg, planning and developing Welsh provision across universities and colleges in Wales. He's also chair of Ysgol Hamadryad – Wales' first active travel primary school by design, where 'consistently, whatever the weather, 90%+ of children travel actively to school.'

From the train station we head out of town on the new cross-city cycle route on Newport Road – the start of the future intercity route to Cardiff. There's little shade and we joke Dafydd can make the traffic lights change, sparing us from a roasting, using a secret device in his glasses.

The plan is for not one but two intercity routes, one to shadow the thundering A48 with its heavy lorry traffic, the other to improve the partially complete NCN88, following quiet backstreets and country lanes, which will eventually stretch from Newport, through Cardiff and Bridgend, to Margam Park. We mainly follow the latter route, Dafydd's personal preference.

Over 15 miles Dafydd leads me via a series of residential streets, a stretch of scary main road with high-speed traffic, a gravel path and a narrow wooden causeway through pretty wetland, tarmacked cycle paths, some country roads and, yes, some pavements, to Newport. It's pretty much flat all the way, though there is a headwind. Handily, Dafydd is also an ultra-distance runner with an uncanny knack for pacing runners to within a few seconds' accuracy and he acts as a human windbreak for much of our ride.

This route isn't complicated, it just needs the back streets to be filtered to through traffic and given priority over roads that it crosses on the way, and a few off-road paths upgraded. Then there's the technically easy, but perennially controversial, issue of removing a few stretches of car parking in built-up areas to give cyclists space. Dafydd wants to challenge the norm of having cars parked along every street. It's about changing the culture, he says, and we laugh at how easy it is to say and how difficult to deliver. Grangetown's rain gardens, he says, represent 'a model of taking out parking and making it more cycling friendly,' one they can follow elsewhere.

At Newport Station Dafydd is excited to see a new cycling and walking bridge taking shape – a great double-arch winding up and over the roof of the station with a ramp and stairs. It connects a substantial residential area with the town centre – and it cost about £8 million of Wales' annual £75 million active travel budget.

Dafydd believes, 'If you can build momentum with things like that, you can drive demand' for more active travel routes. One walking or cycling trip to the shops made possible by a new bridge might become a longer trip if there's a safe, pleasant, convenient route. It also shows what's possible elsewhere.

After lunch in Newport's newly revamped and rather lovely indoor-market-turned-food-court, we stop for an ice cream by the river. As we rest in the shade, Dafydd explains that spending the rest of the money is a surprisingly tricky undertaking in a fledgling cycling nation. 'We haven't had enough bids that we've been sufficiently confident in supporting,' he says. The board is sensibly developing a pipeline of projects, so if there's a problem with delivering one route – which is not uncommon – there are backup options to save the money being clawed back at the end of the financial year.

On the way back to Cardiff we pause beside the A48. It's heaving with gigantic trucks and crossing it at a series of traffic lights is painfully slow. Details are still being ironed out, but Dafydd shows me some very basic plans for a roadside cycle path, very close to the traffic lanes. I have flashbacks to the day I cycled 16 miles of pavement paths around Port Talbot: a computer-generated image shows a blue cycle lane alongside a grey road with a narrow strip of grass as a buffer – and as many such computer-generated images do, it looks laughably uninviting. Ideally, they'd use land away from the road, tucked behind a nice thick hedge, so it's enjoyable to use as well as being direct.

There are other options. Where roads are noisy, dirty and dangerous, railways can be pleasant, tree-lined, level corridors, sometimes with unused land alongside. It's not a new idea to use this resource for cycling: Belgium has developed some of its growing network of cycle routes using rail-side land and plans to create many more, particularly around the Brussels capital region. Similar to Belgium, Britain has one body, Network Rail, which owns much of our railways, making it, in theory, far easier to develop routes than working with multiple councils and having to dig up busy road junctions.

In Warsaw, Poland, most cycle routes follow the main roads, which are managed centrally by the city – one exception being a road parallel to the six-lane Aleje Jerozolimskie, which instead follows a side road, Nowogrodzka – a more pleasant route and a shorter distance, end-to-end, with fewer junctions to navigate along the way. There's no magic bullet to inserting new infrastructure into built-up areas, but there are plenty of ideas from around the world that work.

Replacing motorway trips with cycling is, on the face of it, laughable, but the point of intercity routes isn't that everyone rides from one city centre to another, but that trips along the route corridor are accessible by cycle, and connected to other routes and modes of transport along the way. As we cycle from Cardiff to Newport and back, Dafydd regularly points out major employers whose staff could commute by cycle were there a proper route.

Surrounding Copenhagen in Denmark is a network of 120 miles of cycle routes, connecting not just the suburbs but surrounding towns. Understanding the potential for longer-distance cycle commutes in the capital region in 2008, the city and national government dedicated more than €134 million to develop 'cycle superhighways'. By 2017, with national government contributing up to half of the cost, there were five superhighways and the following year local municipalities joined forces to expand the network further. They had become 'one of the most profitable infrastructure investments in Denmark' in socioeconomic terms.

By 2019 the more than 100 miles of superhighways were carrying 248,500 miles of cycling journeys a day, with a single weekday peak of 29,000 cyclists. Half of users are women and 14% previously used a car. What's more, cycling trips were surprisingly competitive over longer distances: analysis measured journey times along one seven-mile section of route, representing the average cycle superhighway trip length, and found ebike trips were just five minutes slower than driving and regular cycle trips 12 minutes slower.

Practical and enjoyable though these routes no doubt are, their added mental and physical health benefits represent the bulk of their benefit to society – reduced costs for medical treatment and sick leave effectively doubled the initial investment needed to build them. Even power-assisted cycling, e-cycling, offers substantial health benefits, particularly for someone who didn't cycle before. In

10 years, cycling within the city region had grown from 29% to 34% of all commuter journeys.

The recommendations report, produced by Wales' Burns Commission, noticed this, and other European successes. 'In the Netherlands,' it said, 'the RijnWaalpad superhighway was built in 2015 to connect two towns around 10 miles apart (broadly comparable to the distance between Cardiff and Newport) and, thanks to good design, cyclists only have to give way to motor traffic twice.'

Dutch engineers call these convenient cycle routes 'keep on going routes', because their benefit comes not from users being fast, but because they don't lose time constantly stopping. The route in question, between Arnhem and Nijmegen, was built specifically to take pressure – and cyclists – off the trunk road. I cycled it in 2017, both ways – to the Museum of Dutch Life to see beautiful old windmills and a musical parade on a summer's night. You barely need to stop the whole way.

Now, between 1000 and 2000 riders use it daily, its designer's only regret that officials insisted it was built beside the trunk road, albeit with a wide strip of grass between the two, instead of somewhere behind a hedge, where it would be quieter. Its designer, Sjors van Duren, a planner who has helped develop 50 miles of routes in the Arnhem–Nijmegen region, explains it's common for cycling trips to replace even trunk road trips, most of which are no more than 10 to 15 miles in length. However, it takes regional co-operation of the type we're starting to see in metro mayoral regions in England and, hopefully, in south Wales.

For a cycling bridge Sjors developed in Cuijk, he said, 'We proved that having 1000 to 2000 cyclists a day on that bridge would improve traffic flow on a motorway bridge three miles downstream.' The bridge was a missing link in the seven-mile MaasWaalpad, a 'keep going route' spanning four municipalities and three provinces, and, because it was of regional importance, it involved the national government, the national road body and the rail body. Enterprisingly, Sjors, working as a consultant, began with some seed money and went to each province in turn, drumming up contributions from each province like the pied piper of cycling investment until the full project was coordinated and funded. It just took someone to believe in it and to rally calls for support – albeit someone with considerable charm and persuasive skills.

I was surprised when he told me that, despite decades of cycling being the norm, drivers in the Netherlands still oppose new cycle routes and voice concerns about loss of driving space. Either way, he points out, 'We're not different humans in the Netherlands than in the UK.' The difference is the Dutch don't baulk at these very normal concerns – the Boris Johnson rhino-hide approach, if you will, is normal there. Cycle routes are part of their strategic long-term transport plans. They are the right thing to invest in – and boy do people use them once they're built.

Back in Wales, it is now being suggested further similar routes could be developed and extended, including one linking Barry to Cardiff, a journey of 10 miles. An ebike trial, which tracked people's use of a set of loaned electric bikes, found people were regularly riding the 10 miles between Bridgend and Cardiff. It's needed: at present, the route west of Llanelli features one incredibly good set of traffic-free cycle routes between small towns along the coast to Kidwelly, part of a £35 million Millennium Park, opened by the late Queen in 2000.

This route, intended for everyday journeys and tourism, has little signposts telling users how far it is to each town and even a Tellytubbyland-like bridge, a charming grassy hillock, taking the cycle route over a railway. The remainder of the way, it's 16 miles of inventively awkward pavements along some of South Wales' worst trunk roads, the kind of place almost no-one would choose to cycle. I found it dangerous, inconvenient and more than a little shocking: it's certainly not an experience I will soon forget. It is my sincere hope the Newport–Cardiff route represents a new era for intercity cycling in the UK.

Wales also pioneered changes to archaic rights of way rules that effectively ban cycling on almost 80% of the country's footpaths, bridleways and byways. Campaigners at Cycling UK want to see access reform where rules, created long before the bicycle was invented, are changed, presuming access on most of these paths. Many of them run in and around towns, ancient footpaths following the flattest and most direct routes to nearby destinations, making them perfect potential traffic-free paths today. However, the pre-pandemic momentum to lift those restrictions was substantially slowed by 2021, leaving campaigners frustrated. With Wales suffering some of the worst physical activity levels globally, they argued, increasing access to the outdoors was crucial, as well as the paths' potential contribution to Wales' £481 million outdoor industry. The same changes could happen in England, where the same archaic restrictions endure, and indeed in 2023 English Labour promised to reform access, if elected.

There's still plenty to do in Cardiff itself. Towards the end of my time in the city I stay at a friend's house in the west, a lower-income area utterly dominated by motor vehicles and entirely devoid of safe cycle routes. Accustomed to living in a relatively cycle-friendly part of London it's a shocking reality check. I brave a horrifying dual carriageway a few times, constantly worried I'll be mown down, before trying to concoct a safe route into town away from traffic.

This is much harder than I imagined, with the only way to cross the railway and river headed into town via a single main road bridge – a great big bottleneck. I cycle into a brand-new housing estate with no cycle lanes, but plenty of car parking – a wasted opportunity. I lift the heavy city hire bike up the steep, narrow steps of a railway footbridge, I wander around local streets and scour maps until I find a way through a large park in a residential area that would cut off one of the worst bits of road. There are a series of anti-motorbike barriers there, though, one of which forces you into a metal pen, like a large kissing gate. In the daytime it is inconvenient. At night in an unlit carpark behind a deserted rugby club building it feels like a human trap. On one journey through the park I notice an ingenious motorbike rider has somehow gotten through the barriers anyway and is happily enjoying some laps of the grass.

In spite of the inherited problems from decades of car-centric planning, I leave Wales feeling hopeful: it seems like the start of a blueprint for a positive future. It's a nation walking the talk on decarbonising transport, acting on health and inequality, and putting its money where its mouth is. During my visit Wales passes a law for default 20mph speed limits on certain roads and, in early 2023, the effective roadbuilding ban. Cardiff's boldness in trialling new temporary lanes rapidly is inspiring. Some of those routes were removed after lockdown, some improved and others were made permanent – but without the experimentation there was no way of knowing what would work and what wouldn't. They made an academic idea real, and people took to it, for the most part.

I saw some historic bad routes, but the legislation and leadership, and now the funding, puts Wales miles in front of England. They're a decade ahead of us in mapping and expanding their network, something England is only starting as I write this. The comparison becomes starker: weeks after Wales voted to end most new roadbuilding, England cut funding for cycling and walking to one twentieth of Wales' levels, a laughable £1 per head per year, while ploughing ahead with its environmentally ruinous – and I'd argue pointless – roadbuilding programme. The difference is so stark it honestly makes me want to move to Wales, where my tax money would go to something I believe in.

16

LAKER IN THE LAKES

The romantic poets have a lot to answer for. Wordsworth, who popu-
larised the Lakes in the late 19th century, was among those who
railed against the arrival of steam trains: noisy, dirty machines which
he worried would spoil the area's peace. His poems and writings at
the time inspired a national debate about who the Lakes belonged to
and what they were for, while early tourists, the so-called 'Lakers' –
my people, I like to think – helped popularise the area in prose and
painting. A century later Dr Beeching's axe removed all but one of the
branch lines and slowly, with few other means of getting about, like
many of our most beloved landscapes, the Lakes filled up with cars.
Today, more than 85% of the roughly 20 million annual visitors bring
their own vehicles, worsening car traffic and 'fly parking' in farmers'
gateways and verges across the region as visitors try to access places
of beauty.

You'd be forgiven for thinking if there's anywhere we should let
off the hook, a place you probably need a car, it's the Lake District:
it's rural and hilly to boot. But, like many places in the UK, a lot of
everyday journeys by tourists and locals are very short. In Kendal, a
key hub for tourism and jobs, 40% of commutes are less than three
miles, which you could cycle in 20 minutes, and 27% are less than one
and a quarter miles, which you could walk in 25. This is a place where
18% of residents have no access to a car. Although tourist trip data
is patchy, journeys from accommodation to the shops and back, to

restaurants and local attractions, tend to be short. The reason people don't cycle or walk more for practical journeys isn't purely because of hills and distance – ebikes could solve those problems, with purchase subsidies or financing to help more people use them – it's because there's no real provision for riding a bike.

Perhaps unwisely, I'm visiting the Lakes on the August Bank Holiday with a non-electric bike. I'm spending the long weekend with a friend and her family in a holiday cottage – or at least catching up with them in the evenings. During the daytime Sustrans has kindly lined up rendezvous across Cumbria with local volunteers, cyclists and staff over three days, and on the first morning network development project officer, Dave Shuttle, meets me at Penrith station with his car.

By chance my friends chose a place with a surprisingly flat, very quiet lane running seven miles to Grange-over-Sands Station, with only a short section of busy road for me to cycle each day. A dispute is in full swing between train drivers and rail operators over reliance on overtime working, and to navigate an array of suddenly cancelled trains I find myself running out of the cottage door, toast in one hand, to cycle to an earlier train or otherwise rapidly tweaking the day's plans.

Dave Shuttle is a rangy young man who's worked for Sustrans for less than a year. He was previously a cycle guide and loves to be outdoors on his bike, so the current job suits him perfectly. Without irony we throw our wheels in the boot and park the car on the outskirts of Keswick. We're headed for a fabulously successful cycling and walking route, with one of its more unusual users.

Like the Camel Trail in Cornwall, the newly upgraded Keswick to Threlkeld cycling and walking path, NCN7, has quickly become one of the Lakes' most popular tourist destinations. While the start of the path may be tucked incongruously behind a gym building in Keswick, there is no missing Peter Knowles. In his yellow cycling jersey Peter, a fit-looking man in semi-retirement, sits in a large, low-rider tricycle. It's like a grown-up go-kart, with hefty wheels and what look like Tibetan prayer flags flapping from a pole at the back.

An energetic and enthusiastic man with bright blue eyes peeking out under a grey baseball cap, when we arrive he's raring to go.

With its electric assist, his Ice Trike, a machine which set him back a mind-boggling (but still cheaper than most cars) £10,000 kept Peter cycling since he developed arthritis in his left hand. His swollen thumb sticks out at an awkward angle and the upright seating position, with handles positioned like arm rests for steering, keeps the weight off his hands. Peter is part of a group of local non-standard cycle users who ride together when they can and try to encourage others to do so. They're about inclusion and accessibility, and so is the route we're here to see.

The shared-use tarmac path, on a former rail branch line, may travel just three miles between two fairly small towns, but as one of the only traffic-free paths in the area with a decent surface, which also happens to be flat with beautiful scenery, it's incredibly popular. The Keswick to Threlkeld path crosses the meandering River Greta six times, treating users to views across the Greta Gorge. Today, after months of dry weather, the river babbles quietly over tumbled rocks, but on 5 December 2015 Storm Desmond, a cyclone, brought 70mph winds and lashed nearby Honister Pass with over a foot of rain in just 24 hours.

The river rose to engulf the valley floor, the force of the water destroying two substantial metal railway bridges, folding one of them like a tin can under a boot. The lost bridges severed the famous C2C or Sea to Sea route, of which it is a part, and local businesses sorely felt the loss of passing walking and cycling trade: one pub owner reportedly offered up £30,000 of their own money, in cash, to get the route reopened. The repair bill to renovate the path was rather higher, though, at £8 million, which was eventually gathered from various sources, including National Highway and European Regional Development Funds. Exactly five years after the storm, on 5 December 2020, the route with two new bridges, a newly cleared railway tunnel and a fresh new surface, reopened.

The path is so popular it could already do with being wider: with Peter's hefty tricycle we have to ride single file to pass others. We ride a short distance and sit at a picnic bench by a newly reopened railway tunnel, eating lunch with the great east–west road, the A66, passing incongruously, but surprisingly quietly, above us on towering concrete stilts. A near-continuous stream of walkers and cyclists emerge from and disappear into the tunnel as we eat.

The rail tunnel was filled with rubble after the branch line closed and for many years the cycle path skirted it via a wooden walkway, held over the river on its own stilts, which sounds precarious – yet another of Sustrans' ingenious low-cost workarounds. Refurbishments included the tunnel's clearance and resurfacing, just as the walkway was nearing the end of its life. After lunch we emerge from the tunnel ourselves. We greet the broad river, which splits at a rocky island where great tree trunks are piled up like driftwood against a stand of living trees. Steep pine-covered hillsides rise up on either side.

One crucial part of the route's upgrade almost didn't happen: when word got out the new path would be tarmacked, all hell broke loose. Peter was among those who thought tarmac would ruin the route's character. The 'national treasure' nature of places like the Lakes means when any change is proposed, the debate quickly goes national. Lake District National Park (LDNP) staff were subject to a flurry of angry correspondence and abuse, from local people heavily invested in the area all the way to anyone who had visited Keswick once. National papers ran hyperbolic headlines claiming the LDNP was turning the Lakes into a theme park, with the suggestion this was the thin end of the wedge, the start of the asphalting of the entire park – when clearly it wasn't. While concerns were well-meaning, for anyone involved it was a painful battle, based on a fundamental misunderstanding of their motivations.

When I speak to the Lakes' lead sustainable transport strategy advisor, Emma Moody, about this time I can hear the emotion in her voice. 'They kind of assume that you're going to be tarmacking paths up to the top of the fells and covering the Lake District in tarmac,' she says. 'It was really, really, really unpleasant.' After the route reopened, though, the decision was vindicated: usership more than doubled from 110,000 to 256,000 a year. The tarmac threw the doors open to people previously locked out of this space. As if to underline this, we pass a woman in a mobility scooter, apparently travelling with several generations of her family. Unlike Peter's machine her mobility scooter, with its small wheels, is emphatically not designed for rough terrain.

While the route's success, and personal messages of thanks from disabled users, proved them right, the experience has made the LDNP hesitant to similarly improve paths elsewhere in the park. Although no-one in the world would advocate dirt surfaces for roads now, the national conversation about active paths like this effectively keeps cycle routes in the past, a time when access to the wild required money, physical strength and confidence.

I can't help but feel angry reading those headlines, knowing if these well-meaning people had won the argument the woman with the mobility scooter, and many users like her, would be off the path, out of sight and out of mind. That is surely not what we want our green spaces to do.

Contrary to the concerns of tarmac detractors, the path isn't filled with road cyclists going at speed. It's a mix of ages and activities, dog walking, wheeling and cycling in family groups. Peter has the luxury of avoiding the path at peak times, as a self-employed, semi-retired person, and in general road cyclists tend to stick to the roads where they don't need to dodge strolling dogs. If there were more of these paths across the Lakes, and the country, it wouldn't be so crowded, and nor would so many people need to drive each day to visit it; ideally they could cycle there.

Midway along Peter leaves us, and Dave and I stand by the path and watch him navigate two awkward field gates before scaling an incredibly steep winding country lane, pedalling into the distance. Dave and I drive off, passing a few C2C cyclists on their big adventure, fit over-50s with road bikes and panniers. Two have stopped in a lay-by and I notice their NCN-branded jerseys, blue with a red numbered square in the middle, like the signs, and it reminds me how much people love these routes, for all their flaws.

We meet the A591. Running along one side of Thirlmere reservoir, it's one of the worst congested roads in the Lakes – or one of the most popular roads in Britain, if you're in the satnav business. In the local dialect it's often 'thranged', the past participle of throng. Across the reservoir Dave points out a road that's on the NCN, the quiet, parallel alternative to the busy A-road. It was closed by a landslip, but nobody bothered to tell Sustrans about the blockage. They only found out when people started emailing them, politely.

We stop in a lay-by, retrieve our bikes from the boot again and make a dash between thundering vehicles. We pass 'road closed' signs and a temporary yellow gate, held up by concrete blocks, to stop drivers from attempting to get through, finding the way blocked and having to reverse back up the narrow lane. There's enough room to cycle and walk around the barrier – instantly creating a quiet lane. Dave tells me this landslip represents an interesting experiment on the NCN – an enforced traffic filter, saying, 'We'd like to do much more of this.'

The little road is delightful: it spans the reservoir dam, above whose mossy brick parapet we see a huge expanse of water, stretched out pearlescent under a patchwork of clouds. We bank left at the foot of a wooded hillside, tracing the shore, and the reservoir blinks through the trees. Partway down, the trees part to reveal the mighty Helvellyn mountain on the opposite shore, its huge rock-strewn, green flank flecked golden by the dappled sun. It rivals the Keswick-Threlkeld route for beauty.

With a couple of concrete blocks and a few gates, you could radically improve the transport and leisure cycling options in rural communities by prioritising some roads for through traffic and making others safe for cycling and walking trips. It's a similar idea to an LTN, levelling the playing field so cars don't dominate every road. It's also a low-cost way of making active travel possible: a protected cycle track costs roughly £1 million per kilometre; one or two filters like this, a few thousand. Months later, Sustrans tells me it is in talks to filter this road, but by the following summer the new Cumberland Council had proposed applying for a permanent closure order.

While Sustrans and the council attempted to assure the public this was merely a formality, and promised it would reopen, campaigners feared permanent closure in fact meant permanent closure. While Sustrans trustingly assented to the proposals, campaigning charity Cycling UK asked why, when temporary road closure orders were commonplace during roadworks that overran, the council was applying for permanent closure instead. There seemed no answer to this question and an earlier FOI had revealed the council had no plans in place to reopen the route. Concerned local users raised an 8000-strong petition and within a week, more than a thousand had written to their MP, copying in Cycling UK, protesting. Once again it seemed like a crucial cycle route was falling through the administrative cracks. When Storm Desmond destroyed part of the A591 in 2015, that vital local road reopened in five months. Two years after a 2021 landslip closed a vital part of the National Cycle Network, that road is still blocked, with no certainty over its reopening and no safe alternative route. It didn't seem like Sustrans, or the NCN's, finest hour.

Sustrans and the Lake District National Park are slowly gathering the necessary millions to resurface bridleways and reclaim bits of road space along the north–south A591 corridor either side of the reservoir, as well as connecting two NCN routes across the east–west A66, but it's very slow going. Dave says someone in Sustrans has a dream to build a 21-mile cycle path to relieve the busiest bit of the A591 north–south all the way between Keswick and Windermere. The piece de resistance would be a Lake Garda-style boardwalk* on Windermere itself. However, while its Italian counterpart has become a tourist attraction in its own right and internationally famous, the British version remains a pipedream, with no feasibility study and no plan for funding it.

Like all councils, Cumbria is short of money. In 2014 it stopped subsidising bus services at a time when local authorities lost 27% of

---

*The Lake Garda path is a raised cycle lane on the lake shore. The first seven and a half miles, opened in 2018, were such a success, the path is being extended to stretch 87 miles around the lake.

their government funding in just three years. The LDNP receives about 3% of the upkeep cost for its 1850 miles of footpaths, which inevitably degrade over time under tourists' feet and weather, rendering them ever less accessible. This is a problem nationwide: countless UK walking trails are degrading because authorities lack the meagre funds to repair them.

Repeatedly a visitor tax and congestion charge has been mooted for the park, although it is usually shot down by businesses concerned it will drive away visitors. For £1 per visitor – a price the 20 million people who visit the Lakes annually, who care about the environment, would surely pay – transport alternatives to the car could be funded very quickly. In the Black Forest in Germany, and French resorts, visitor taxes fund things like free buses, and well-maintained footpaths and cycle paths. In Danish national parks, busy tourist hub towns like Kendal have on-road protected cycle routes as standard.

The UK is peculiar in believing preserving an environment means letting motor vehicles run amok, while defunding the alternatives. In early 2023 Manchester 'blazed a trail' by introducing its own tourist tax and shortly after St Ives in Cornwall announced it was considering the same. The Welsh government, too, started looking at gifting its councils powers to introduce visitor levies. It is surely a matter of time before the idea spreads – and in some places it can't come soon enough.

While cycling, walking and public transport languish in poverty, bedevilled by stop-start funding that makes long-term strategic planning and investment impossible, road widening continues apace, thanks to taxpayer largesse, but with little clear benefit. In October 2022 the DfT and NH admitted its planned £1.49 billion splurge on widening the A66 represented 'poor value for money', with the benefit to cost ratio (BCR) so low it would actually lose us money (earning back just 90p for each £1 invested). In the same breath they announced road widening would go ahead anyway.

While NH insists it can only build cycle routes if the BCR stacks up, this and countless examples like it underline that this isn't the case when it comes to roads themselves. In fact, analysis by the Transport Action Network found £16 billion of our roadbuilding projects represented poor or low value for money, the scrapping of which could halve the current budget deficit or, indeed, almost fund the £18 billion needed to enable half of all trips under five miles to be walked or cycled by 2030. We are on roadbuilding autopilot.

The reasoning for pressing ahead was that widening the road – the same one running on stilts high above the Greta Gorge – is essential for freight traffic. At the same time, though, NH doesn't collect granular data on who uses its roads, why and how far they are driving on specific sections, so to an extent this is all guesswork. It's a phenomenon known as predict and provide, a self-fulfilling prophecy, because you build roads that grow traffic. Time will tell how much general traffic this road scheme, like all the others before it, will generate – and to what degree it will fail to solve the problems it set out to solve.

It's surely worth considering what else we could get for the cost of that one road-widening scheme alone. One option might be 186 Keswick to Threlkeld-type route improvements, giving local children the option to cycle to school in safety and independence. We could easily deliver Kendal's planned walking and cycling network – which otherwise wouldn't be built for another decade due to lack of funds – and countless other urban networks across the region. Another is to build a route akin to the fabulously popular Lake Garda path, extending beyond Windermere to Kendal, relieving congestion on the region's most thranged road, while benefiting tourists and locals. With the loose change from that, you could build up to 45 more 20-mile-long strategic cycle routes.

Any of these options, and indeed a combination of all of them, would easily achieve five times the value for money of the road widening project, while genuinely helping cut congestion, save people money, improve health and dramatically reduce transport carbon emissions. Around the world, even in the Netherlands, cycle route BCRs end up artificially downgraded because, compared directly with roads, they wind up so high people don't believe them.

Ultimately, this is not about rationality though: we invest in what we value and the car is still winning.

On a topographical map the Lakes are 'bordered by mountain, marsh and sea – the [Scottish] border hills, the Pennines, the Solway and Morecambe Bay.' From the south, centuries of travellers met Morecambe Bay first, home to the UK's largest mud flats, where the rivers Kent, Keer, Lune and Wyre all wind up. Before the first turnpike road was built in 1820 travellers embarked on a dangerous adventure, crossing at low tide, led by carters, who knew how not to succumb to the estuary's notoriously dangerous quicksands and disorienting mists. Still, plenty of people perished on this crossing. Even after the railway arrived in 1857, great coaches of travellers would take the short cut, traversing the sands and sometimes getting bogged down under their sheer weight.

Headed north, they would cross the treacherous Duddon Sands next, before the triple estuary of the Esk, the Mite and the Irt at Ravenglass. While the turnpikes headed inland at each estuary, making for solid ground, rail engineers, who came later with presumably superior building prowess, constructed bridges that made shortcuts across all three. Following those lines would make for a level, straight cycle route too, in theory, but Network Rail, like rail bodies the world over, is reluctant to permit anything like a cycle crossing to be attached to their ageing bridges.

Nowadays cyclists, like drivers, go the long way round. Aspirations for a cycle route skirting the Lakes have been kicked around since the 1980s when Cumbria County Council founded the Cumbria Cycleway, a 260-mile fully signed orbital cycle route looping around the Lakes from Carlisle, via Appleby, to Kirkby Lonsdale in the east, before following the coast road back. This route also travelled through the Lakes' most populated areas.

This trailblazing idea, the first route of its kind in the UK, came with council-produced maps and leaflets with suggested accommodation along the way for long-distance riders, or day rides with train stations at either end. However, within 20 years, as the roads became busier, the route, little more than signs and paper maps, faded away.

Jonathan Powell is a local campaigner and barrister, in his early 60s, who lives near the Duddon crossing. He collects me and Sustrans' Paul Bruffell from Foxfield Station on my second day in the Lakes. Jonathan is well-spoken, eloquent and drily funny, and his turns of phrase occasionally have me howling with laughter. His mission is to see the Cumbria Cycleway revitalised. He drives us, our bikes and his large dog, Kurt, to Duddon.

Jonathan believes there would be 'very obvious economic gains through tourism' in revitalising it, drawing people away from the honeypot areas in the central lakes and providing a beautiful, largely flat route at sea level, with links into the National Park. It would be, he believes, 'of world class significance'.

The local roads are now treacherous; narrow, winding and heavily trafficked, few are more intimidating than on the approach to Duddon estuary. A confluence of roads meets here on a narrow stone bridge, with traffic lights at each end to let vehicles through single file. This includes a steady stream of 40-tonne HGVs, appearing roughly once every minute. On the way Jonathan pauses in his dialogue to point out the Old Man of Coniston, shortly before someone performs a danger-ous overtake, almost colliding with a lorry in the opposite lane.

The NCN and the England Coast Path should converge here, but there's no pavement and it's rightly considered unsafe for foot traf-fic, so the walking route effectively disappears, replaced by a 'land bridge' – PR speak for a train. For cyclists, part way across the bridge there's a raised embankment along the estuary, heading back out to the coast northward, but, as Jonathan shows us, it's been given the 'Somme treatment' by local fishermen. We make a dash between traf-fic to a gate, bedecked with barbed wire to prevent would-be cyclists intruding on this fishing spot. We stand in the gateway, trying to make ourselves heard over the procession of lorries. That one user of this path can summarily bar a safe cycle route seems bizarre in the extreme. Jonathan believes turning the path into a byway would solve the issue. In 2006 the council commissioned a cycle network plan for the area around Millom and Haverigg, a town and village on the estuary, to improve active travel on this corner of the coast, but like the Cumbria Cycleway, and countless plans like it up and down the country, it was forgotten. The idea was reinvented at least once, but without funding it has never been realised.

Adrianne, a local councillor, is a rare cyclist in the area and an even rarer female cyclist, who dresses in hi-vis and covers herself in lights to face the roads – what Jonathan describes as 'a Yuletide approach' to clothing. She takes us to one very short route that was developed locally, on a farm track near Green Road station, surfaced with coarse gravel and potholes. She says local police were once sent there after someone complained about cyclists using what was technically a footpath. The one place it's safe to cycle and you're forced to endure the double humiliation of a physical jolting and fear of arrest. The constant uphill struggle is exhausting second hand, and I don't know how people like Adrianne and Jonathan stick at a cause like this without totally losing hope.

Paul and I say goodbye to Jonathan and Adrianne, and catch a train north to meet Mick Shaw, a local man who's working on the next estuary crossing north, on the Esk River. Mick is a tall, jovial man with grey hair and a youthful zeal for life. With one knee in a heavy-duty looking strap due to a recent skiing injury that's awaiting surgery, he meets us at Ravenglass Station and apologises for travelling by electric car, not bike. In fact, he doesn't cycle around here for fear of the traffic, but he'd like to.

He and a tiny group of locals have commissioned the design of their own bridge that would save cyclists travelling along the coast a six-mile (more than half an hour) detour, involving another narrow road bridge and a steep climb over Muncaster Fell. Near the station, where the railway crosses the estuary, Mick points to each of the three river mouths. It's an incredibly beautiful spot, the low tide creating an infinity of pale sands, washed out pastel colours, almost glutinous in texture, bordered by sharply luminous grasses.

However, with the rail bridge not an option for cycling – there's only a very narrow footpath on one side of it – Mick's eyes are focused upstream. We lock up our bikes at Ravenglass Station and Mick drives us to the site of what he hopes will be 'the world's longest single cable footbridge'. A former physicist and entrepreneur, with a lifelong love of bridges, Mick tells me he's pursuing a boyhood dream. First, though, it's a tale as old as the NCN – he'll need a lot of money and access to land.

He drives us to a point, just west of the hamlet of Newbiggin, where he hopes the bridge may go. The structure they want is an elegant curved walkway, 240m (two and a half football pitches) long and 2m wide, suspended by a single cable, anchored to one mast on each bank. He hopes the wow factor will help attract the estimated £8 million needed, not to mention acceptance in the two world heritage sites and site of special scientific interest it spans. The compromise is, it's very narrow, because every 10 square feet of bridge add £10,000 to the price tag. They had a pledge from a previous cycling minister, in a previous government, to match-fund anything they raise, but they have to raise it first.

Thanks to the hallowed status of the area necessitating something fabulous and pricey, and the vagaries of landowner permissions, the bridge and its cheerleaders are painted into a corner. While the owners of Muncaster Castle are happy to place a bridge anywhere on their land north of the River Esk, permissions to the south are harder to come by. One farmer withdrew support after seeing the futuristic bridge design. The next landowners along the riverfront initially assented, but then there was a horrifically ironic family trag-edy. Mick points out the spot where their 14-year-old boy descended an off-road track on his bicycle, emerging on to the main road where he collided fatally with a driver. The family is in limbo and under-standably unable to think about cycle routes.

We scale the hill by car to meet the bridge's great supporters, at Muncaster Castle. On the way, at the narrow road bridge crossing the Esk, Mick brakes suddenly when another driver appears over the brow. There isn't enough width for both to pass safely – another horrific bit of road. When we arrive at the castle, Mick waves at a man in a shirt and fleecy green gilet, who I assume is a gardener. He walks over to us, a kind-looking man with grey hair and beard. He is carrying a jacket potato with cheese and beans on a plate, a reject from the kitchen, he explains, which he's been contemplating eating for some time, between tasks. 'I knew if I heated it up, you'd arrive,' he says. This, it turns out, is Peter Frost-Pennington.

Peter leads us, with his plate, across a yard behind an old stable building, explaining he can offer us sandwiches for lunch from the visitors' refectory. It turns out this is his wife's family's castle, he was the local vet and the two fell in love – a fairy story. As we eat our sandwiches Peter apologises about the noise from the hand dryers in the visitor loos, a few feet away. 'We've just finished filming a toilet scene', he explains, gesturing to the doors behind us. His wife and the owner of a Liverpool nightclub have swapped jobs for a reality television programme, and today one of the castle's toilets got blocked and the nightclub owner had to help unblock it, in her designer clothes.

Muncaster Castle, a tourist attraction in itself, sits on a block of land in the landscape where the mountain range of Scafell Pike tumbles down to the sea. It's a mile and a half from a narrow-gauge railway, another popular tourist attraction, but it's up a steep hill, putting it just out of reach for tourists. Peter believes the cycling and walking bridge would be a huge boost for the whole area, not just for the castle. He says, 'I remember sitting in Whitehaven Civic Hall after foot and mouth in 2001, and they were saying, the next big thing is going to be cycling. I said, "You are nuts – cycling is never gonna take off in Cumbria. Have you seen our hills and how busy our roads are?" And then of course, that was before Bradley Wiggins in the Olympics . . . and then electric bikes.'

He and his wife and grown-up kids cycle together, some on ebikes, and he'd love to see an ebike network here. He tried to do it himself, renting out the bikes at the castle, but it was in the early days of ebikes, under-14s can't ride them by law, and it needed to be part of a joined-up, planned network to function. Safe cycle routes, like the one that would connect the bridge, could help tourists cycle more, ebikes or not, as well as local people – from children cycling to school to workers at the Sellafield nuclear site.

In 2013 the UK government funded an ebike hire scheme trial to help shift some of these short visitor trips out of cars. While the scheme, which loaned ebikes to accommodation providers for tourist use, proved popular, it was short-lived and when technical support ended it did, too – another trial that fizzled out. Those behind it, which included Isobel Stoddart of the early NCN days, believe it would have continued, only a lack of ongoing support to businesses, who aren't experts in bike maintenance, meant the initiative eventually failed. She says being able to try an ebike at campsites, hotels and B&Bs where people were staying was 'transformative – everybody came away with a smile on their face, regardless of whether they were novices or lapsed cyclists.'

Holidaymakers said after trying ebikes that they were tempted to buy one when they returned home. However, even though they're far cheaper than a car, the cost is still daunting and, unlike in Europe, there are no purchase subsidies to help people switch to ebikes. According to a 2019 analysis, an ebike grant in the UK could be more than twice as effective at cutting CO_2, per pound spent, as existing electric car grants. In France, ebike grants had a massive impact, increasing how much recipients cycled each year on average by seven times, from 200km to 1400km. People reduced their driving distances by 660km and CO_2 output by 200kg each. Almost a third of users said they wouldn't have bought an ebike without the grant. It also made cycling more equitable: while men make most cycling trips in France, ebike take-up was almost gender-equal (48% of grant beneficiaries were women).

Research by the University of Leeds found ebikes could cut England's transport emissions by half. In rural and semi-rural places like the Lakes, ebikes are at their most powerful. Researchers predicted people in those busy areas around the Lakes could, in theory at least, ride 20 to 30 miles per day – if there were safe routes. That adds up to between 4000 and 7000 car miles replaced per person per year. It is an academic assessment and while most people won't cycle that far, many will gladly do less, given the access to suitable, affordable bikes and safe routes. In European countries ebike purchase subsidies have enabled people to ditch their cars.

A call comes through Peter's walkie-talkie; he needs to leave us and head for his bird of prey show and then he starts filming for the reality programme again at 2.30 p.m. It's almost 2 p.m. now and goodness knows how he fits everything in.

After lunch, en route to watch the vultures and kites in action, we walk past the front of the castle, a magnificent red sandstone lump on an enormous promontory of land high above the River Esk with monumental views over the Esk Estuary and beyond. Peter picks up a discarded juice carton from the floor and carries it until he finds a bin, talking the whole time. Mick hobbles behind us. 'If you weren't with me, I'd be walking at double the pace,' Peter says. 'You have to cover a lot of ground in this job.'

From the front of the castle we look down over the Esk River Valley and across to the Sca Fell Pike. 'For hundreds of years,' Peter says, 'my wife's ancestors puzzled over where to build a bridge. The road used to go over there,' he says, pointing to the Roman ford crossing to the west, just upstream of the Eskmeals Viaduct. Eventually, the bridge was built even further upstream, to the east, and the road now ducks behind Muncaster, losing the family their strategic position.

The bridge is understandably a long-held dream for Peter and, he says, until he met Mick, 'I was a voice shouting in the wilderness' – he'd been trying to get the county council to do a feasibility study for a crossing of the Esk for ages. 'I got so frustrated.' The two of them held consultation events in two different parishes about a potential crossing. They realised they needed to sell the idea to locals that 'even if they hate tourists' the connection will improve their lives, giving them access to this beautiful place. Peter says, 'The result of the consultation was, I don't think we had any negativity, and we had "Just get on and do it." I'm thinking, "Well what do you mean just get on and do it? It's just us!"'

He learned from financing the castle's upkeep that initiative is crucial. 'We've no revenue support, but we have been very good at getting grants,' says Peter. 'We stood up and said, "Hey, we're gonna do this" – and that gives confidence to grant funders.' The council, sadly, were less enthusiastic. 'I thought, let's embarrass them into supporting us and do as much of the work for them as we can, free of charge, which is where we are now. I hope we're at the stage where it's probably getting beyond us as just a couple of individuals with some supporters in the local area.' He knows funding will be a major, major problem, but hopes it means more that the idea is being driven by local people. Mick adds: 'Maybe it's intractable, but if we fail, we'll have tried blooming hard not to fail. And hopefully eventually something will happen.'

A local business sells ice cream at the castle – including sea buckthorn flavour, made from a plant that grows on the Drigg Dunes. Peter wants other businesses to benefit from the cycling visitors new routes would attract. He points to the Scotland 500, an on-road route that generated a £22 million annual tourist boost in Scotland within its first three years, supporting 180 full-time equivalent jobs.

Mick drives Paul and I back to Ravenglass, where we carry our bikes up the coast by train. As if the waters of Cumbria hadn't thrown enough spanners in the works, at Sellafield the NCN has managed to fall into the surf.

———

As Icarus flew too close to the sun, the NCN at Sellafield, it seems, got too close to the beach. Caught between the fence of a nuclear power station and the sea, erosion eventually did for the path, which had to be closed permanently for safety reasons.

In 2021 Sellafield employed 10,581 people and on a busy day up to 8000 of those employees are on site. Although Sellafield still has its own train station, there now aren't cycle routes in any direction that are tempting or convenient enough to help all but the hardy to cycle. As a result, locals know to avoid the traffic tides at each shift change.

Izzy is one of those hardy few: once or twice a week she crosses the power plant's threshold with her Lycra and her road bike, ready to ride the 17 miles home. Izzy took up cycling after her divorce 'to feel normal again'; as well as allowing her, a young single mum, to fit exercise in before and after work, and to find a community of fellow road cyclists at weekends.

Beyond the landslip, the NCN used to travel south and east as far as Kendal, 41 miles away as the crow flies, but the combined effects of busy roads and erosion meant the route was de-designated, leaving nothing north of Barrow-in-Furness. Replacing the seafront section was deemed unviable because of cost and landowner issues, so Sustrans is hoping to knit together public rights of way to make an alternative route inland.

Paul and I get off the train at Sellafield with our bikes and wait for Izzy. She emerges from behind the power plant's great fences in the hot afternoon sun, ready to ride home. Although her commute north traces the extant NCN, its maddening combination of shared pavements, off-road paths and quiet lanes adds two miles to the journey, and significant time stopping, starting and slowing down. The only people Izzy knows who use the NCN here are travelling very short distances: over longer stretches it doesn't make sense. 'It is very indirect and you get a lot of dog walkers,' she says.

Izzy shows us the start of her journey from the power station. As we pedal our way along the road – the one rammed with traffic at every shift change – I notice an odd-looking path, which cuts across the pavement through some industrial-grade bollards that look like they'd survive a tank collision. Beyond them is a debris-coated strip of tarmac behind a crash barrier. I think I know what I'm looking at: this is the NCN, notionally serving cycling trips north of one of Cumbria's largest employers. After crossing the main road beside the power station, the ongoing pavement path is blocked, inexplicably, by a barrage of traffic cones. Unsurprisingly, Izzy didn't know this was even a cycle route.

Still on the road, we turn right at a narrow lane where the NCN crosses beneath the main road. Izzy doesn't use this bit either – reaching it involves waiting in the middle of a busy main road to turn right, only to be sent on to a rough, unlit path through isolated fields.

'When I have gone on the cycle path, I've had punctures because of brambles,' she says. 'If you're commuting in winter, it's pitch black and so if you were to have a puncture or any issue, it's isolated and dark, it's not somewhere I'd choose to put myself. So I only use a short stretch to Thorn Hill, which is kind of a shortcut, but the rest of it I head on the road and it's similar for most people.'

She and I cycle a short way, under the road, and after seeing it I wouldn't fancy it at night either – but nor is the road much better. 'It's either really fast-moving traffic or you're trying to filter between long, long, long tailbacks,' says Izzy. Filtering is the term used for riding through traffic, along the centre of the road – recommended by cycle instructors as drivers are more likely to see you on their offside. On a busy road, though, it means you risk playing chicken with oncoming traffic. 'You're in the middle of the lane, with cars coming the other way. It's not the nicest place to cycle,' says Izzy.

Resolving these concerns shouldn't depend on a route being in an urban area, but without funding, in huge swathes of the country only the fit and the brave cycle for transport. Large employers like Sellafield can generate a town's worth of journeys every day, but like most parts of the country, there are few alternatives to the car.

Sellafield the employer supplies showers, bike sheds and lockers for the hardy few cycling in, and they are trialling ebikes for staff to get around the substantial site, which stretches a mile by a mile and a half. What lies beyond the gates is up to the council, though, and the charity cobbling together safe cycle routes from a patchwork of differently bothered landowners. Paul and I wave Izzy off, and walk back to the station, because Paul's Brompton bike has acquired a puncture.

Reflecting later, I think if intelligent, eloquent, energetic and enterprising people like Jonathan, Peter and Mick, and countless others like them up and down the country, can't make something happen that would have such irrefutable benefits, there is something very wrong. Their efforts are formidable, and testament to a belief in a cause that could without doubt improve transport and leisure options in the area. They aren't alone, and in a decade of writing about cycling and transport I've met countless others engaged in decades-long battles against bureaucracy. The odds are stacked against them: disinterest, paralysis or obstruction by a system set in a car-centric culture that blindly pursues roadbuilding at the expense of all else.

Like other Lakers before me, I realise I'm offering my verdict based on a few days' travel in the area, some interviews and some research, albeit with a lot of experience in this field. However, it seems to me that just as Wordsworth and his counterparts campaigned against the railways in the hopes of preserving a beloved landscape, we make the same mistake today. By preserving the existing transport veins, we embalm the patient, instead of allowing it to adapt to the world around it. We're subjecting it to transport sclerosis.

All of this could change relatively easily. Rural councils often cover vast swathes of land with little funds. If the NCN were considered a strategic network, by law the Secretary of State could commandeer land for new, safe, traffic-free routes, as they can for roads, via compulsory purchase order powers. They could commission bridges and protected cycle routes along and across road corridors. They could fund long-term development of routes nationwide. We don't do these things, because we don't see cycling as a means of transport. It's simply a matter of priorities and no matter how much people like Mick, Peter and Jonathan try, until that changes nothing substantial will change.

17

CALEDONIAN PEOPLE POWER

I'm off to Scotland on a dead electric bike. By the time the power cuts out for the last time, halfway up the traffic sewer of Euston Road, mid-afternoon, one Friday in August, it is far too late to turn back. A summer's worth of abuse on the NCN has finally caught up with it.

In Glasgow, hotel staff kindly let me stow Lily, the dead ebike, in a conference room and as I shut the glass door on her I wonder how I'll get about without my own wheels. We're in the midst of a heat-wave and one Scotsman in the lift clutches lunch delivered to him in a paper bag (by bike I notice), because he can't bear to leave the hotel's air conditioning. It's about 29°C outside. I've come for more than a week to see Glasgow's new bridges, travel around and meet Scotland's active nation ambassador, but before the end of the week I'll end up serendipitously meeting some people busy challenging the status quo and expectations of who cycling is for, too.

The Celtic countries seem to be winning the human-powered transport race as I see it and Glasgow, like Cardiff, is at the pointy end. In 2018 the Scottish government doubled its active travel spending to £80 million. The plan is that by 2024 10% of Scotland's devolved transport spend will go to cycling and walking, not just in cities but in rural areas. There's also, rather boldly, the target to cut car journeys by 20% by 2030.

Most of the shortest trips take place in towns and cities, and Glasgow has a plan to help people travel actively for more of those trips. The following morning, looking for coffee on Sauchiehall Street, my phone rings. It's Paul Kane at the City Council's press office, proudly telling me Glasgow's £115 million 'Avenues' programme – a strategic plan to reclaim 17 city streets for walking and cycling – is 'bigger than Greater Manchester's Bee Network', the city's much-lauded plan for a thousand miles of cycling and walking links. He wants to make sure I don't underestimate Glasgow's efforts.

Coincidentally, the transformation of Sauchiehall Street was the first part of an experiment to encourage shoppers back to shops after the financial crash of 2008, that later enabled Glaswegians and their visitors to social-distance during the pandemic. The entire street was pedestrianised, with trees and seating, and there's even a bike lane people constantly wander into, dodged by delivery riders and commuters on bikes. The Avenues programme will see more of the same across 17 city centre streets.

Having de-designated around a third of its NCN in 2020, much of it fast, narrow, busy, rural roads, Scotland as a nation also seems to have cracked the way it manages its NCN. It is, as Sustrans former CEO Malcolm Shepherd put it, 'quite extraordinary', adding, 'If you're looking for examples of ways things are working for the future, you can look no further than Scotland.'

Scotland is, he explains, using 'what was always the model we had in mind for the future of the NCN.' This was, 'Where government would recognise a) the need and b) their responsibility for funding it.' Here, Sustrans Scotland is used 'as an agent to do a lot of the construction, to manage the whole programme and to work with partner local authorities and others to actually construct, maintain and market the National Cycle Network.

'That really is the way we could and should be working,' he believes. It's a sensible investment: one report estimated for every £1 spent on paths in Scotland, there were £7 worth of returns, in economic, health, environmental and social benefits. The outdoor industry here is huge and the NCN is worth £345 million in cycle tourism and leisure cycling alone.

For now, myself and three Sustrans Scotland employees I've arranged to meet up with are headed to a very expensive bridge to see what this joined-up way of working, and the funding, gets you. Claire Daly is Sustrans Scotland's head of communications, with a gentle Irish accent and a passion for music; Michael is a reserved young engineer who rediscovered cycling recently, since joining Sustrans; and Alex works in fundraising. We pick up city hire bikes from outside Queen Street Station and Michael leads us nervously through Glasgow's American-style street grid and across the most potholed pavement I've ever seen, more hole than pavement, and on to a rough cobbled path beside a metro station. This is a cycle route, apparently. Only then do we start to see some of Glasgow's progress.

Glasgow is criss-crossed by highways, railways and waterways, the kinds of things that can cause long detours for cyclists and walkers, and to cope with this there are now dedicated bridges being hoisted into position across the city to improve access. We cycle a refurbished underpass beneath the M8, with improved sightlines and colourful sculptures where once you might have anticipated a mugging.

From there a recently installed cycle lane on the busy Garscube Road travels three quarters of a mile, complete with planted borders, to (currently) end by to the Forth and Clyde Canal, where an accessible zig-zag ramp, three metres wide, scales a hefty bank up to the towpath. On the way up there's more new planted grasses, trees and huge stone lettering, and even a big metal slide, which we try out, for the purposes of research. Crossing the canal is a brand-new walking and cycling bridge to a new nature reserve, part of a wider £8.8 million project with Sustrans, Scottish Canals and Glasgow City Council, connecting the Panmure Gate and Woodside communities.

Standing between the new bridge and the ramp, Michael comes to life, announcing, 'This is my favourite project in Scotland!' The element of joy, the slide, matters to him. 'If you don't make it fun, what's the point?' he says, adding, 'There were three families the last time I was here, with about eight kids, running up and sliding down the slide.'

This isn't the bridge we're here to see, though, and we continue along the canal towpath (NCN754) and weave through some residential streets in Maryhill in the north east of the city. I know we're there when I spot contractors' vans parked on the pavement. This is a live construction site, we are told, and we're handed wellies, hi-vis tabards, hard hats and rubberised gloves, into which we sweat fiercely. It's 27 °C, but it feels hotter.

The site is all bare, baked earth and we walk past diggers and a long hump of concrete, like a modern-day barrow, whose purpose becomes clear later. The Lord Provost of the Council, Jacqueline McLaren, is leaving as we arrive, one of a stream of visitors checking out progress today. As we pass I remind site management about the dangers of pavement parking; as a journalist I don't need to be popular, just irritatingly righteous, apparently.

In honesty I'd been expecting a humpbacked stone thing over a canal, something small – although the £13.7 million price tag should have given me pause. In fact, the Stockingfield Bridge is a 395-foot-long construction of white metal, spanning the T-junction of a canal, in a wooded valley. The bridge heads off in multiple directions, from a circular viewing platform, topped off by a giant spike like a slanting knitting needle. On the platform you have to turn 360 degrees to take it all in. Homes and stone industrial buildings peek through the trees, as if awaiting the big unveiling.

This canal has separated two communities for more than a hundred years. The only crossing, a tunnel, is so narrow you can barely fit one vehicle through at once, and it's terrifying to walk or cycle through for that reason. One local resident has photographed progress each day, from the same position, and there's hopes it will be part of an exhibition one day, a long timelapse perhaps.

The project is about much more than just steel and earth, though, awe-inspiring as they are, and two artists, Louise Nolan and Nichol Wheatley, are tasked with introducing artwork with the local community. Nichol, visibly excited about the project, with flawless manners and spades of self-deprecation, jokingly says, 'They couldn't get anybody good so they got me.'

Louise, a ceramicist, grew up here in Maryhill and is passionate about bringing people together. She's described as 'one of the most connected folk in the area'. She explains the concrete barrow, currently in the middle of the construction site near the bridge, will be a Beithir, a mythological Scottish creature. Described as 'the largest and most deadly kind of serpent', it's a water-dwelling dragon with a sting that could kill you unless you reach a body of water, say a canal, in time.

While the artists tell me they believe the Kelpies sculpture, the giant mythical horse heads mounted beside the M9 at Falkirk, amounted to art imposed on the community, this project represents art by and from the community. It also solves a separate problem: with limited funding and with 10,800 cubic feet of excavated earth on their hands from the bridge works, some lateral thinking was needed – and so the barrow-like Beithir was born.

While Nichol works on the Beithir, Louise's role is working her contacts and talent in various artworks around the site. She's also making a lot of ceramic tiles. Louise believes art can claim a space for the community – giving it meaning, and preserving local history and stories. The artists are working with 400 local people – anyone from care home residents to school children – decorating 38,000-odd mosaic tiles for benches, the concrete base of the metal spike and the Beithir itself.

There are also eight artworks selected from 14 submissions, including one in sheet metal, from a group of disabled artists called 'Possil-bility', a pun on Possilpark where they are based. Nichol says their work 'celebrates the role of active travel and disabled people participating in active travel in a community. You don't see disabled people celebrated in sculptural form generally across artwork,' he says.

There's a 'river of names' by artist Anoushka Havinden, listing the names of people, places, events and things, from around Glasgow, etched in stone alongside the canal. Artist David Galbraith is burying a derelict car in the site – posing some logistical headaches. 'We're trying not to talk too much about it because we're still struggling with a few issues there,' says Nichol.

Scottish Canals sees its waterways as linear parks, in this case incorporating active travel and reuniting three communities, Ruchill,

Gilshochill and Maryhill, severed for generations by the canals. Reclaiming spaces like this isn't just about ideology and creativity, though, it can be about personal safety. Louise lives close to the bridge and during the pandemic she walked here, for respite, but she found the canal side intimidating: it was a place men came to drink and be rowdy.

While a common policing response is to clear seating and greenery to improve natural surveillance, and discourage people from gathering, this work is doing the opposite: inviting people in, so it feels welcoming and safe. Louise hopes the communal creation of artwork, as well as the new linear park treatment, and walking and cycling routes, will return the space to the whole community.

The bridge isn't open for a few weeks yet, but we are allowed to walk on it. A man cycles underneath us on the towpath. 'An eyesore and a bloody waste of money,' he yells. Seizing a heckling opportunity, I call out: 'Bah humbug'. Unconvinced, he flips me the Vicky and narrowly avoids swerving into the canal.

Balfour Beatty's Ally Johnston invites us to delight in bridge engineering. The 120m-long bridge, he says, features a 60m clear span, between supporting pillars; its 3.5m wide segments arrived on the backs of lorries. When the last piece was lowered into place, there was 4mm to spare, the exact width needed to weld it into place. There's some mystery, too: until 500 people come and walk on it, for all they know it could end up wobbling, like London's Millennium Bridge. (Months later, when it finally opens, it doesn't wobble.)

It's our turn to make tiles. In a portacabin Louise hands us soft, dark grey clay to decorate. I walk outside and squash a triangular tile three times on to NextBike's flying bicycle logo, a triad formation, and the spokes on to another tile, making something more abstract and oily with road grime. Claire prints a key fob, her family crest. Michael whimsically carves penguins into another, perhaps dreaming of cooler weather.

Among the already fired tiles in pinks, yellows, reds, greens and blues, arranged on tables and trays, there are carved shapes and printed photos and adverts from local people and businesses, as well as what Louise terms 'Scottish kitsch' – animals depicted on tartan backgrounds. Each one means something to the maker. To be weatherproof the tiles are fired twice: once at 100°C, then at 1200° for the glaze.

Louise pours a lot of love into her work and the people it encompasses. Before we get back on our hire bikes to go, she admits, 'I get really emotional about this project – it's members of the community creating it.'

I leave the bridge with a sense of wonder and hope. It seems to me that unlike roads, cycling and walking routes can bring people together in a place, rather than rushing them through; celebrating history, local culture and the diversity of society. It's something Sustrans' CEO Xavier Brice has spoken of before and that John Grimshaw, when he founded the NCN, sought to achieve with his benches and sculptures, and communal work camps.

The network was made by people and that work continues, in projects like this. For the first time I understand it's about so much more than engineering, important though that is: it's about making space for people to thrive. It's about joy, too – the possibility for whimsical encounters and, as Caroline Levitt, John Grimshaw's Greenways and Cycleroutes Ltd colleague, puts it, delight. This is something public space often lacks, particularly when it's dominated by traffic, when your primary objective becomes simply negotiating moving vehicles and staying safe.

These routes are also about a sustainable future. As if to underline the fact, that evening the third heatwave of the summer is announced, an amber weather warning issued and an official drought is declared in the south of England. In the pub over dinner the television news is dominated by images of dead grass and half-empty reservoirs. Perhaps the Beithir represents climate change, too. Reminding us that our proximity to, and preservation of, water has perhaps never been so important.

I exchange messages with Louise months later, just as my tiles are about to be installed on the Beithir. I'm thrilled that a tiny piece of something I, a passerby at a moment in time, created will outlive me on the back of a wild Scottish waterbeast, on a cycling and walking route bringing people together in Glasgow.

My sister is in town, by chance, meeting some friends, and I join them for brunch. In Kelvingrove, we happen upon an enormously wide street closed for the day, it turns out, for line painting. A man sitting outside a bar says, 'This is the only time you'll see this street without traffic!' In the middle of the road a small boy on a bike is being pushed along by a woman, with another boy trotting alongside. She lets go of the saddle and follows along, arms outstretched, as he wobbles and pedals. 'First time?' I call as we pass. 'Yes,' she says. Me, my sister and her friends cheer as he goes and he looks delighted. They go up and down the street, the woman calling out to the boy to pedal, and he wobbles, but he's getting more confident. Traffic-free streets bring freedom and delight, part #257.

We drink afternoon cocktails and walk in the park, and later Ele and her partner leave for Somerset. I wander the leafy streets of now-gentrified Kelvingrove, all colourful planters, a riot of verdant plant life. Then I'm in the city's bloated arterial roads and through a bleak, shadeless industrial estate to Dales Cycles, where I left the ebike, in the hope they could fix it. The Avenues programme will eventually transform the wide road it sits on, Dobbie's Loan, with a protected bike lane and trees. There's a university building on one side and what look like halls of residence on the other, and two unfeasibly wide lanes of traffic between. It's eerily empty of cars, but it's the kind of place you're nervous to cross anyway – especially after a couple of cocktails. I wonder how all those students get on.

Though the bike shop closed 12 minutes ago, I spot a staff member on the street, who bangs on the door for me and the bike is released. They couldn't fix it, Jim explains, and my best bet is to order a new part and have it sent to Edinburgh, where I'm headed in a few days. The cocktails wearing off, I wheel it back to the hotel, mildly deflated. In the evening it rains, the first precipitation I've seen in months, and I crack open the window of my tenth-floor hotel room and sniff the air.

I'm exhausted from my travels, cramming in work alongside it, and the constant heat. The next day, after a few hours' work, I head out into the rain, to inspect three more of the prospective Avenues, near the river. These are, like many Glasgow city streets, very wide and drivers drive at speed. I bumble around for a bit, staring at pavement cycle paths in need of some 21st-century treatment and trying to keep hold of my portable mug, which feels oddly heavy in my hand and sloshes tea on to my shoe as I attempt to cross a dual carriageway.

Months later a young woman is killed in a collision with a lorry, while cycling on the road, metres from that junction. With the collision investigation ongoing, her parents start a campaign calling for rapid investment in safe routes so other families don't suffer the same heartbreak.

From too much heat to too much rain, and half the trains are cancelled. I engage in a lengthy conversation at Queen Street Station about the two-hours' advanced notice train operators require to carry a bike on board. The woman at the ticket counter tells me I can check the train report when it comes in to see whether there's a space on board. 'What in the name of god is a train report?' I ask politely, without the blasphemy although with all the implied weariness. The answer is confusing and someone is shouting really loudly from the other end of a walkie-talkie on the counter beside her. She keeps turning the volume down, but it's never enough. I learn that without two hours' notice I'll need to approach a member of staff at the barriers before the train leaves and ask them if there is any space – the train report is for them to know and for me to sniff out like a human Scooby-Doo dragging a dead pink ebike, apparently.

With as much information as I can handle, and at least a chance of reaching my destination at some point that day, I take the 12 or so tickets all of this complexity requires, in a complementary wallet, and wheel the ebike out past the 15 people who have meanwhile backed up in the queue, in a line that snakes out of the ticket office.

While bizarre and frustrating, this is not an unusual experience. Like anyone who has tried to travel with a bike on British trains, I have a beef with the railways. I'll be honest, it easily escalates, via mild anxiety, to a quietly bubbling rage. Cycling and train travel should be the perfect transport combo: you ride to the station, you bung your bike on board, you get out and cycle at the other end. At one time this was a simple thing to do in the UK: in their heyday you could fit up to 50 bikes on British Rail trains. Now you're lucky to get eight on and it often involves a fight. In my year travelling around the country, I spent £1000 on train tickets and with it literally hours on the phone booking free bike spaces – up to 45 minutes for one single space. I even had to run away from station staff at one point, as they tried to stop me boarding a perfectly serviceable train waiting at an adjacent platform.

Headed for a weekend cycling the glorious north Wales coast, NCN5, Claire and I accidentally starred in our own slapstick sketch: all it was missing was some comedy pursuit music. At Euston Station we hadn't made it to the ticket barrier in the two or so minutes between the platform being announced and the imposed cut-off for boarding with a bike, so station staff refused to let us through on to the platform. The train was right beside us at that point, so failing in negotiations we decided, simultaneously, to duck past them and leg it. After the calls of 'Stop', 'No' and 'Please don't do this' faded behind us, we made it on to the train with at least two minutes to spare. We managed to save our weekend's cycling plans and considerable cost, but spent the first five minutes of the journey paranoid we would be arrested by British Transport Police or at least ejected from the train.

While this was an extreme example, after a decade or more of UK train travel, the extent to which our train service makes people with bikes feel like criminals still astounds me. I've wrestled bikes on to hooks in hanging closets that would be impossible for a lot of people, including those with non-standard cycles, to use. I've had to make impromptu announcements to carriages full of people to get baggage or buggies moved from cycle spaces, feeling simultaneously guilty and embarrassed.

As MP Fabian Hamilton put it in a meeting of the All-Party Parliamentary Group for Walking and Cycling, travelling with a bicycle on UK trains is 'a nightmare'. The booking systems are different for each rail operator, the cycle carriage rules are overly bureaucratic and their interpretation at times wilfully obstructive and arbitrary.

Happily, things are changing: UK government policy is actively seeking to increase capacity on services, though rolling stock isn't replaced more than once a decade, leaving us stuck with the meat hooks and no non-standard cycle provision on most British trains. Easier bicycle space booking processes are improving, too, thanks to those policies (no more 45-minute phone calls to book one bike space!).

Cycle-rail travel makes enormous and increasing sense, though. Tourist spots in Europe saw up to 200% increases in cycle tourism during the pandemic, while the Eurovelo network carried 31% more trips than usual, post-lockdown. According to one survey, 32% of holidaying cyclists use trains – and cycle tourism is linked to half a million jobs across the EU, more than the steel and cruise industries combined. It may be inconvenient for rail operators to wait for cyclists to unload and load at stations, and they might not like giving up profitable seating space for bikes, but trains are part of a wider transport system and if we have a hope of cutting carbon from transport they need to get on board. Scotrail and Transport for Wales recognise the benefits for the economy and carbon emissions, and are, unsurprisingly, leading the way with more cycle space on leisure routes.

Meanwhile, some rail staff are absolutely lovely. One train staff member helped me unhook the pink ebike from the meat hook before I missed my stop, in spite of company rules forbidding it. A ticket office staff member at Grange-over-Sands also finagled the awkward booking system to reserve me a bicycle space, emerging from his office triumphant to deliver not only the paper tickets I needed as I waited on the platform, but a rubber band so I could attach the requisite ticket to my bike. I wish them and their colleagues well in striking for better working conditions.

In the time until there's likely to be a functioning train we can get on, me and the dead ebike, in a last-ditch effort before we head to the wilderness, crawl our way across town to find someone recommended as the person who might finally be able to fix Lily.

One problem with Glasgow's grid street system, I notice, is that if you cycle slowly, as someone riding uphill on a 25kg bike with panniers tends to, you just make it to each set of lights before it turns red. It then takes what feels like a good two minutes for the light phase to come back around in your favour, after the opposing traffic gets the green signal, then the pedestrians. A youngish man is, surprisingly, walking a polecat on a lead and I feel like, in a race between us across town, my money would be on the polecat. At one point I hear a little boy waiting on the pavement say, 'Why does it take so long?' as we all stand around watching sod-all traffic moving along an empty road. No-one wants to risk a bus driver rounding a corner at speed and mowing them down, so they wait. It's like being in an awkward lift situation.

I tell one bus driver, 'The line's back there, mate,' after he creeps slowly into my space at the bike box, presumably anticipating our turn at green. Even with the best intentions, and at slow speeds, no-one wants a city bus bearing down on their back wheel – ever. To his credit, at the next three red lights, he keeps stoically back.

A few metres past the end of the nice bike lane by the zig-zag ramp with a slide resides the genius of ebike modifications, aka Kinetics Glasgow. There's a handwritten sign saying, 'No repairs, try Ebike Love,' which is a couple of doors down. I know from emailing them last week Ebike Love staff are on holiday, so I summon courage and knock. A tall man with dark curly hair and a kindly manner answers the door, and introduces himself as Ben. To my relief, and against all odds, he agrees to look at my bike and invites me in. I instantly know I'm in the right place: the workshop is full of bulky, heavy-duty cast-iron machinery in muted greens, greys and blues. There are reels of wire, bits of bike and even a 3D printer, an extractor hood and tools hung on every wall. I don't doubt he uses all of it.

Before I know it, he's got the bike up on a stand, levitating. He removes the battery and opens it up – a few screws and a strip of plastic tape – revealing a surprisingly flimsy arrangement. Three rows of AA-size batteries are taped together, with four tiny prongs connecting the power supply to the motor via a couple of thin wires. I'm amazed this fragile setup has powered me so far and survived so long; it looks like something from a light household appliance. There's not much Ben can do to beef it up, though he moves the prongs a little, adjusts the mount, sprays some cleaner on everything and pops it back into place. After a false start the screen display comes to life and no amount of rattling can stop it.

It is only a few days ago a similarly gifted engineer, Mike Burrows, died. I knew Mike as a legend, through the Lotus bike he built that Chris Boardman rode to Olympic Gold in 1992 in Barcelona, but he was a pioneer of recumbent cycles and leftfield machines, as well as transforming the standard road bicycle itself. I only met Mike once – he taught me how to set off on a recumbent bike on a demo track at a bike show: 'Keep on your toes, like a boxer.' He seemed kind and begrudgingly let me take a photo of us while exclaiming, 'Oh no, not a selfie.' I spot Mike's book about cycling technology, *Bicycle Design*, on Ben's bookshelf. I mention him and Ben admits Mike didn't approve of him retrofitting electric motors on cargo bikes and recumbents. A purist, and a man who didn't suffer fools, he will be much missed. I thank Ben profusely, give him twice what he tries to charge me, leg it back to the station and mercifully secure a space for me and the bike on a train to Aviemore.

I spend two days gallivanting up and down NCN7 on the ebike from Aviemore, south to Pitlochry then north to Inverness. I squeeze a record 60 miles out of the 50-mile range battery on the first day by turning the assist down and using my leg muscles more. South of Aviemore I stand by the road to look at some of Scotland's ludicrously gorgeous scenery: massive hills looming either side of a valley in bloom with heather and a rugged river tumbling over rocks through the centre. I'm cycling through a postcard; they just leave these views lying around.

I'm experiencing a kind of guilt I get once I've been on the road for a while – that I'm being selfish, somehow – that someone else should be here to enjoy it with me. It's a bit of loneliness too, but it's self-inflicted: I head off at the last minute, on my own, through bad planning usually, and while I love doing my own thing, at times I long for company.

After some delightful off-road trails and my first close overtake by a Highlands driver, I'm overtaken by two road cyclists. I catch them again at a pretty humpbacked bridge where a delightful stream tumbles dramatically over great big rocks. I assume they have had a mechanical, for why else would road cyclists, men who primarily value speed, stop? But, no, they are just enjoying the scenery.

I stop at the bridge, too. They introduce themselves as Greg and Norton, two young teachers from Preston. They've taken a train to Aviemore and are cycling back over six days. Greg is in training for his latest Ironman event – 'It's like a cult,' he jokes and he even has the logo tattooed on the back of one leg – while Norton's along just to enjoy the ride. They suggest we cycle together – a bit of an ask for them, given how fit they look and the fact my maximum speed on the flat is just 15.5mph.

Norton is forever pointing things out. 'Look at this floodplain . . .' he says. 'See those small birds flying around the stream . . .' He knows the names and character of all of these things, it seems, and how they fit into the wider ecosystem. He insists we stop for bilberries, small wild blueberries which we pluck from hedges at the side of the road, or whortleberries as I know them. They are sweet and delicious. Bilberries like acidic soil, he explains, and shade, so they only grow in places like this. This is my kind of cycling.

Norton says something at one point, another exclamation of delight at the natural world, but his words are carried away by the wind. I say 'What?' and Greg replies, 'I just let him get on with it. He's enjoying himself.' Greg and Norton are both Teach First graduates and have stayed in their respective posts five years. The kids must love them; they're very entertaining company, Greg a grounded foil to Norton's fierce intelligence and equally fierce judgement of others.

They make up games as we ride – see how many times you can clap your hands crossing each bridge – and are constantly joking.

On the flat they naturally accelerate away. Under some trees, they pull over for a pee. I'm bursting, too, but can't go in a hedge in company, so I ride ahead, leaving my bike in the gateway of the Highland Folk Museum so they'll see it. As I dash across the car park, I see Greg and Norton ride past. I shout 'I'm just using the loo,' but when I come out, they are gone. I feel a bit crestfallen and hope they didn't think I was ditching them. They have 100 miles to cover today so who could blame them for pushing on. In a way it's a nice way to part, no goodbyes. They've lifted my mood, anyway.

From there, NCN7 traces the valley floors between great majestic Highland hills, to the Pass of Drumochter – the highest point on both the Scottish NCN and the rail network. It shadows the A9, the road artery to the north of Scotland, and the railway; the flattest route north. I'm amazed to find out here in the wild the cycle route has a separate, narrow tarmac path, sheltered from the road by a grassy bank. If only the whole NCN was like this. This is one of General Wade's military roads, constructed by the British government in the mid-18th century to control the Highlands during the Jacobite rebellion. Some of these became A-roads, others are just dirt tracks. Others, like this one, now carry bits of the NCN.

This dedicated cycle path feels extravagant in such a rural area. However, even somewhere as sparsely populated as this, everyday cycling journeys are possible – not to mention the sheer bliss of a cycling holiday. In the 52 miles between Dalwhinnie and Grantown-on-Spey, there are nine settlements, most of which the NCN passes, an average of five and three-quarter miles apart – less than a 30-minute ride. Many UK settlements are similarly clustered, even in rural areas, at the kinds of distances children could cycle to friends' homes, to sporting and social activities, and school if there were safe routes. Long before cars, market towns were traditionally situated less than a day's walk from surrounding settlements. In an area like Aviemore that people move to for the outdoor life, where the gap between earnings and housing costs for local workers is already substantial, cycling for transport makes enormous sense financially.

As always, it's when you reach those settlements, where most trips start and finish, things fall apart: off-road routes give up and shove cyclists on to busy roads or inconvenient shared pavements, and suddenly cycling is far less appealing – or even possible – for many people. There was a plan back in 2017 for a protected cycle route along the main road through Aviemore. In the intervening years a new primary school was built, but the proposed cycle lane still hasn't appeared. Now there are wider transport plans being mooted for the town, including cycling links, but nothing on the ground yet. For now the NCN weaves around the back streets, keeping away from the main road, and with it most of the shops and businesses.

I stop at Dalwhinnie Distillery to buy a small bottle of whisky. It seems rude not to. Outside the gift shop my phone rings. It's someone from a regional BBC radio show, wanting me to come on and talk about something in the news. A transport minister has bizarrely told the *Daily Mail* cyclists can 'easily' exceed 20mph and never be caught, and equally bizarrely suggested registration plates, speed limits and insurance for cyclists will do anything substantial to make our roads safer. Every time this happens it momentarily turns some of the public against people on bikes, and news outlets want someone to come on and defend the perceived lawless behaviour of anyone who cycles.

I turn down the researcher, because I'm on the closest thing I get to a holiday, but also because I'm exhausted. This kind of thing happens several times a year and each time it does I get these calls. It would only take for the government minister to check their department's road collision statistics, and the most common cause of death and injury on our roads, to come up with any number of better ideas to try and tackle road danger.

Sometimes I take on these tasks, often badly paid or for free, not to defend anyone's dangerous or lawbreaking behaviour, but to put the matter in context. I, like Andy Cox and all those working to improve road safety, would welcome a debate on tackling the cause of most of the 1600 deaths on our roads each year in the UK, but that call hasn't come yet. Unfortunately, it's easier to pick on a minority road user than to challenge your audience with the more widespread problem of speeding, say, or distracted driving.

There are unintended consequences to perpetuating these lazy stereotypes, though: each time this kind of 'scofflaw cyclist' narrative hits the headlines, regular cyclists become extra-vigilant on the roads in the following days, because we know some people out there will see the headlines, take umbrage at anyone on two wheels and decide us cyclists need teaching a lesson. They might overtake us too close, say, or try to bully us out of their way on a narrow residential road because, well, we probably deserve a little scare.

I shake the feeling loose and return to my adventure. Thankfully it continues, traffic-free for now. The scenery remains ludicrously beautiful and the off-road cycle path carrying me through it is delightful. Even better, there's a sign warning explorers there are no refreshments available for the next 30 miles and the weather up here can be extreme. This is very pleasing stuff: me and the pink ebike are off into the wild.

I've packed sandwiches and a thermos of tea, and I have a water bladder with a sippy straw, the kind mountain bikers use, and a spare bottle too. What follows is an ecstatic couple of hours' riding, stopping, taking photos and basically having one of the most beautiful rides of my life; my joy and wonder levels are off the scale.

Blair Atholl and Pitlochry are wonderful: more stunning hillsides, the broad, rocky river and the odd castle – but you need your wits about you. The town roads seem to have been gradually replaced with bigger roads alongside them, bypassing the houses and shops. While in European countries like the Netherlands those town roads would be filtered so people can only use the big road to drive through the area, in the UK we haven't quite got the hang of this yet.

The new main roads are sometimes less than 100m away from the original, running parallel. No-one would design a high street today, places we hope people will want to spend time, as a long-distance through route for fast-moving traffic. It only happens when we haven't actively managed traffic levels. My stress levels, dealing with high-speed overtakes, are lightened slightly by chuckling at a conspiracy theorist's scrawls on road signs about the earth being flat. After fish and chips in Pitlochry and wine just off the NCN in a pub by the beautiful river, I head back to Aviemore on the train.

North of Aviemore the NCN is mostly on roads and it's beautiful, but much less relaxing, because of the very fast traffic. Speed limits here, even the supposed 30mph limit through towns, are optional it seems. There is a parallel off-road path somewhere in the forest, I'm later told, but it's not part of the NCN and there's no route signage that I recognise. I still haven't worked out the OS map's extra layers. I have little patience with apps, more than a little stubbornness on the topic of technology and I can't bring myself to check. I've got along OK so far.

Drivers go by at ludicrous speeds, even in 30mph zones. I hurtle down massive hills on huge, wide 60mph roads, clocking 34mph on my own speedo, when someone overtakes, making me almost leap from my seat. I stop to eat a Tunnock's tea cake and drink some tea from my thermos cup while two chickens peck about in the layby. While peeing in a hedge I notice some military grade ants going about their days, massive red and black things, and I pray none get in my pants.

I calculate that by leaving early I could ride to Inverness and make it back to Aviemore for 2.30 p.m. to meet Lee Craigie and the chap from the Cairngorms on a train I believe is still running, despite today's train strikes. When I arrive at Inverness in plenty of time, though, I discover, in fact, no trains are running today. I run about, panicking that Scotland's active nation ambassador is currently driving across the Cairngorms to Aviemore to meet me as planned and I won't be there. I call my B&B hoping I can persuade the proprietor to make a 60-mile round trip to rescue me. He suggests the bus.

I know from previous attempts that no UK bus driver will take a bike on board – the two are like oil and water. Still, it's worth a try to avoid a substantial taxi fee. To my astonishment there is a bus driver who will take the bike on board and fate makes a beeline towards him, at Inverness bus station.

When I realise it's a regular bus, not a coach with a luggage store underneath, I ask him where the bike will go. 'I hadn't thought of that,' he says. He strikes me as the kind of man who has surpassed frustration about how the world is run and achieved a Zen-like belief things will probably work out in the end. Still disbelieving, after checking there are no wheelchair or buggy users who'll need the space, I roll the bike on board.

We bump along back to Aviemore, me gripping the bike as it tilts and jostles against its kickstand, pretty much along the road I just cycled. I get to relive most of my journey and thank the transport gods for Scotland's bus service, and in particular this fast-driving bus angel who has come to my rescue. I'm also glad not to be sharing the road with him while I'm on my bike.

It strikes me, and Colin, the man from the Cairngorms I speak to later, that buses could so easily be part of an active travel network: this is the second time in a week I've been stranded by trains and rescued by the Scottish bus service. If the two transport modes connected, if buses routinely carried bikes, people could cycle part of their journeys and catch a bus when they get tired, have a mechanical, need to be somewhere quickly or, as is likely in these parts, the weather suddenly turns.

In some remote areas, like the Faroe Islands, I'm told, bus drivers don't quibble about taking bikes on board, it's just part of a can-do approach to travel. In my experience, we generally get the opposite. One icy night in April I was stranded on Dartmoor, tired and desperate to get to my hotel, only to be told by a bus driver he could lose his job if he let me on board the largely empty bus; the insurance wouldn't permit it.

Buses in the Cairngorms National Park used to carry bikes on racks attached to one end of the vehicle but, like in the Lake District, the trial petered out. In May 2023 the 'Aviemore Adventurer' started carrying leisure cyclists to mountain bike trails at Glenmore and Cairngorm Mountain up to 11 times a day – until further notice. While it starts early – before 6 a.m. – the service doesn't run past 6 p.m. I can't help but wonder how fragile services like this are though and that, by tentatively trialling them, treating them like a novelty or an optional extra rather than a feasible part of a strategic sustainable transport network as they are overseas, you're dooming them to fail.

Trials can be really useful in understanding how best to deliver a service, but they need to be done with the understanding that they can't simply be removed if drivers don't like the extra effort or the service doesn't make money. It should be a necessary part of a green transport network or it won't work. In the UK we have a handful of bike-bus services, but they are the exception, not the rule. The Cairngorms' Heritage Horizons project is looking at ways to improve active travel and public transport, among other things, in the UK's largest national park by 2030, but it's still in its early stages, discussing different possibilities with residents. Some buses on three Border Buses routes, meanwhile, offer two to four cycle-specific spaces, though they are shared with wheelchair users, who take priority.

To my mind, things like this don't need to be used all day, every day, to be valuable: just knowing you can get back home if you need to, with your bike on public transport, should be enough. Wheelchair users rightly expect to be able to travel, though bus services that require them to duke it out with pushchairs are far from ideal. Why not make space for people with cycles, too, not as another user to fight for the same space, but with carrying space outside the bus, say?

18

THE DREAM TEAM

It turns out Lee Craigie, Scotland's active nation ambassador, started her storied cycling career on the NCN. Lee was a professional mountain biker who later became an advocate for women in outdoor sports and all-round inspiration for female adventurers with the Adventure Syndicate. As a teen she would pick up paper cycle route maps, produced by cycle campaign group, Spokes,* at Dales bike shop on Dobbies Loan, take a train out of Glasgow and cycle back.

Lee and I meet in a café above an outdoor kit shop in Aviemore – thankfully the angel bus driver got me back in time. Lee tells me, 'As a kid, it was the NCN that got me into bikes. I couldn't map read, I didn't have a smartphone, but I knew that these little routes linked up and so I could go and get lost, but I could follow them back.

'I grew up just outside Glasgow and then I moved into the city centre when I was 15, and from there there's just a whole network of routes and I had a little map, the Spokes map, with the NCN on it, and I'd get a train somewhere and then I'd follow the NCN home using this little printed map. Who knows, I probably wouldn't have done that if it hadn't been for those networks.'

It makes me think: I was desperate to get out on a bike when I was younger, but the one flat, off-road riverside path was bookended

---

*Spokes was founded by Dave du Feu, another early NCN and Sustrans pioneer.

by roads and you never went beyond those ends. Perhaps that traffic-free forest track near me planted a seed that this was something I could do, though. It seems like whether you have freedom to cycle as a kid really depends on whether you have a safe route to do so: it's a lottery.

A reminder that Scotland is investing more than any other UK nation in cycling: £58 per person per year, versus £1 a year in England, £28 in Wales and around £7 in Northern Ireland. However, delivery varies widely between councils. Glasgow is the poster child for active travel, while Edinburgh seems paralysed into inaction by a vocal backlash to street changes. A network of 'active freeways', rural cycle routes akin to a national cycle network, was announced and then not acted upon. Lee Craigie was appointed, first as active nation commissioner, to identify what an active travel strategy would look like for Scotland, and now as active nation ambassador, to help promote that future.

Lee lives the lifestyle, cycling between meetings almost no matter the distance. She only drove today because she has a new puppy and the puppy sitter fell through. It may not be a coincidence that Lee has some of the most innovative thoughts on active travel I've come across, including that we should come up with a more fun name for it.

I insist Lee brings her puppy into the café and the dog quickly plonks herself in the middle of the restaurant, inspiring the waitress to crouch down to stroke her. The happiness the dog brings everyone reminds me of something Lee has said in the past about bringing joy to active travel and I ask her about it.

The national work Lee does is only part-time; she also works with kids as a psychologist and on Adventure Syndicate stuff and other projects. She believes we need to give youngsters the freedom to get around and have adventures. She's at her lyrical best on this subject of what we call it.

'You'll say that to a kid and they're like "what?" How are you supposed to change behaviour if you call it active travel? We need to stop talking about it like that. We need to talk about this is an adventure, like every day is an adventure. You know, when I was 14, [I was like] "Right, I'm gonna go and get lost. I'm gonna have an adventure."

And it was just using active travel infrastructure, exploring what was out there. We don't think of it in those terms, which is such a waste.

'I think that's got to be part of the rebrand for cycling, because, for girls in particular, cycling is such an incredible tool for female emancipation. It always has been throughout history. And for our young people, especially our young girls, to not have that experience, I think is a sin. You know it's an incredible tool for us all to get some freedom, and not just the people that ride a bike, but the people that breathe our air, they benefit from the freedom of a bicycle.'

She says during the Independence campaign, Nicola Sturgeon compared Scotland with other nations, with similar populations, and there's another thing countries like Iceland, the Netherlands, Belgium, have in common: 'All of these countries have an NCN. They all promote active travel, but we're way behind,' she says.

There's a sense of frustration that, despite the talk, there's still a belief in governments that cycling and walking won't get us to net zero. It will, she says, if we can integrate walking and cycling and public transport. We just need what she calls 'permissive language' to start talking about something as if it can and will happen, rather than constantly finding reasons we can't do it, like carrying bikes on buses.

Cycling everywhere is not just about a principle for Lee, it gives her thinking time. A lot of her ideas and creativity come on the bike, and it's time well spent, because it strikes me she has some of the best ideas going about the way we get about and how we see that as a society.

She, like me, concludes the NCN is a national piece of infrastructure, only it isn't prioritised in the same way as the roads. 'The NCN feels like such an incredible resource that historically hasn't been invested in in the way that our trunk roads network has', Lee says, adding 'it's really important that it's given the same status, the same financial investment and included in the big strategic projects review that Transport Scotland are doing; that it's considered the same as the trunk roads.'

Scottish plans for active freeways, interurban high-quality routes, seem to have been placed on the back burner, however, and things are moving very slowly, if they're moving at all. Having worked with the Scottish government for a few years, I ask her what, given all the clear benefits of movement, is holding us back. She says, 'I think at a political level we really fear pissing off the electorate, because [politicians] still assume that people want to drive their cars everywhere, and people will always want to drive their cars everywhere until somebody is bold and says, "Well you can't."'

It's only when we try something new, Lee believes, that we'll see there are better alternatives – but even at national government level, despite the policies, that message hasn't sunk in yet. In Scotland, 10% of the transport budget is now committed to active travel and it's rising, but there's a big culture change needed so deeds match words. Scotland, Lee points out, has committed to no more new roadbuilding, with the funds diverted to active travel, but is still adding a traffic lane to the A9 and A96. 'If we were bold, we would have said, "Actually, we don't need to do that." All we're going to do is make that road faster and encourage more people to use it instead of investing in public transport and infrastructure.'

She believes this is simply down to fear, outdated thinking and bold leadership. For this we need pressure both from the top down and the bottom up to make it happen. 'We need to be making a noise about this stuff to say, "Your electorate wants this. It's what we want. We will not throw you over if you let us do this."' For whatever reason, people aren't making that noise in defence of cycling and walking. As Lee puts it: 'The status quo argument is always so much more powerful and loud than the change one.' Her clarion call is, 'Make a noise, go to your MP and say, "This is what I want."'

Lee wants to see a young person's panel to feed into the debate about the future of how we move, so that consultations aren't simply populated with the same people with the time, resources and confidence to have their say. There need to be new ways of reaching those young people, too. Lee also wants work culture to change, so we can incorporate movement into our lives – a whole-systems approach, she calls it. This is in terms of joined-up thinking around how we move, which impacts health and wellbeing, as well as transport and tourism. In an era when girls drop sports in their teens, the bicycle could continue to support them to move, if the conditions were right.

On an organisational level she feels a need to shift our thinking, too. In an echo of the four-day week movement, instead of having to account for each minute of the day, squashing as much in as possible, Lee wants people to have reflection time, and time for health and wellbeing, of the kind that she gets in her part-time role. 'It's all overcomeable if we just think a little bit outside the box [and] prioritise our health and our wellbeing over narrow concepts of what time is worth.'

Even nurses and active schools co-ordinators Lee has worked with are sucked into this way of doing things. Instead of being role models, they are fighting against the same status quo we all are. 'These are people that are employed to promote health – and yet they need to drive between schools or drive between patients, because they just are not given the time. Instead of accounting for this time, they should be accounting for their health and wellbeing, and their motivation for being at work and their productivity while at work, which is all positively impacted by being active themselves. We don't think like that and that's a shame.

I love Lee's radical thinking. Increasingly employers recognise the importance of employee wellbeing and that productivity doesn't necessarily come just from long hours. With a climate crisis and an inactivity crisis looming, the argument that we need to keep working to consume, burning ourselves out and living sedentary lives, no longer holds water.

I leave our conversation inspired and determined to keep weaving activity into my days. My conversation with Lee also underlines everything I've heard in Scotland so far: that how we get around is about people. At times I've hurried about the NCN over a summer, trying to get the miles done, to ride from one end of something to another, and in Scotland I've been stopped in my tracks, so to speak, in the very place where some of the best routes, the best projects I've seen so far are. I've been shown that people make these routes what they are. Perhaps it's something about being outside, in the open, the physicality of moving under our own steam, how liberating that is and how levelling. On a bike, or walking or wheeling, we are just people. It's what I keep hearing from those working in this space: done well, transport and travel bring us together and can make our lives so much better.

Cycling could be a great leveller: you don't need much money, any specialist equipment or a fancy bike to do it. The people currently cycling on Britain's roads only give the impression you do, because they're the sporty, confident, often wealthier ones who are brave enough to mix it with traffic.

Active travel academic Professor Rachel Aldred points out women are less willing to share with traffic, or to use circuitous backstreet routes that introduce long detours. They need direct, safe routes. Because we don't have many of those in the UK, for every one woman cycling there are currently three men. The pandemic quite suddenly emptied the roads of traffic and, hey presto, people got on their bikes in droves. One group the quiet roads and new safe cycle routes benefited was women – around the world the proportions of women cycling grew in response to a drop in traffic and billions of pounds' investment in cycling.

Most transport planners are men, which means they (unwittingly) design transport for people like them: other men. Thanks to gender norms, men are more likely to commute from residential areas to town and city centres, women to make shorter, local journeys in succession: to school, to healthcare, to shops (known in transport lingo as trip chaining). Most public transport, and many cycle superhighways, cater badly for these local trips and, on top of that, women are historically less likely to have access to cars than men, meaning networks of safe cycling routes, joining protected bike lanes and LTNs, are a gender equality issue. Safe, direct cycle routes also particularly benefit people with disabilities and older people, who are more likely to be badly injured on the roads. In cycle-friendly countries like the Netherlands that provide a cycling network, more than half of bike trips are taken by women.

Helping people cycle is not just about concrete and bollards, though. When you mainly see fit, able-bodied white men cycling it can make everyone else think it isn't for them. Fast, confident people in Lycra can be intimidating for newer riders – I've met plenty of women for whom 'other cyclists' put them off riding – and if you don't see someone who looks like you, it's hard to start cycling, and keep at it. Near me in east London a Muslim women's cycle group called Cycle Sisters has increased the numbers of women in hijabs riding around Waltham Forest's new protected bike lanes, through its community rides and events. Groups like this offer everything from advice on cycling in modest clothing to bicycle maintenance, to a supportive social network that helps women keep riding. They also help challenge norms by being visibly out and about, making cycling seem more accessible to everyone.

In Glasgow, Shgufta Anwar is Women on Wheels' founding director – Glasgow's equivalent organisation. When I meet Shgufta and her friend and colleague, Mahnoor Sultan-Campbell, they have been in Queens Park all day helping women learn to cycle. With their fleet of about 20 bikes and a dozen-plus staff, they have presided over a day of led rides, maintenance sessions and chats. Now they are sitting, in their matching bicycle print hijabs, and resting their legs. I missed the park activities, because of a fire on a train line – I'd hired a bike beside Loch Lomond and had to catch a bus back – but am glad I made it for the evening event.

In the church that serves as Women on Wheels' base in Govanhill, south Glasgow, one room is set up with rows of chairs, and a young woman in a hijab is unpacking huge pots of food, saucepans of curries and plates of samosa and spring rolls, and pastries. More women, some mothers and daughters, are arriving from the park.

After eight or so years working with charities to get more women on bikes, Shgufta founded her own organisation at the beginning of 2022, with the express purpose of creating a space that's diverse and welcoming for women. At some point she realised that while her charity day job left her feeling 'totally depleted', with Women on Wheels, 'I had boundless energy and that made me realise actually, this was the right thing to do.'

With no funding and no premises, the charity was little more than a board and an idea, but women were already contacting Shgufta excitedly about learning to ride or regaining their confidence on bikes. 'I thought actually, I can't sit around waiting for funding,' she says, so she started the first sessions with volunteers, borrowing bikes from another charity, while launching a crowd funder. The money got them the Govanhill space. People got together in support, though, bringing food along and volunteering their time, and within days they were leading rides three times a week. Now they have around 20 different funders, 10 of which Shgufta rattles off as we talk, including local and national government grants, community sports grants, lottery funds and contributions from the odd cycling brand.

Within a year of getting the keys to their space, more than 300 women have joined them on beginner lessons, led rides, cycle maintenance courses and multi-day cycle touring adventures further afield, and women travel from as far as Clackmannanshire, 35 miles away, to join in. Every month's events are usually fully booked within a day. Although it's aimed at all women, more than half of the charity's board are Muslim women and they are based in Govanhill, where one third of people are from ethnic minority backgrounds, so the participants are really diverse: half are white Scots and the other half from ethnic minorities.

Mahnoor and Shgufta work with joy, creativity and substantial levels of energy – plus a refusal to accept the status quo or anything standing in their way. Events like today's are arranged with women's needs in mind. There's no pressure to get on a bike and some people come to Women on Wheels' social events long before they touch a bicycle. Women often make friends and end up joining in, though. Shgufta says, 'We wanted to give women time for themselves. We decided not to bring kids' bikes to these sessions because otherwise women put the kids first and let them cycle, because that's what they're used to doing.'

Within a few months they launched family events, too, though, so kids and female family members can join in. One member was cycling with her six-year-old in a bike seat, and they taught the child to cycle so they could go further together. Shgufta loves seeing the women graduate from hesitant cyclists to volunteers and even board members. 'It's really fantastic to see women grow like that,' she says.

Mahnoor (or Bajji Mahnoor as the group respectfully calls her, meaning older sister) only learned to cycle fairly recently – and now she teaches cycle maintenance and leads rides. She has a dry sense of humour, with a joie de vivre, and she's brimming with fun. She's sitting on a plastic chair propping open the door of the room in the church, resting her aching legs. I mill about self-consciously, asking questions.

Mahnoor says growing up in Pakistan she wasn't allowed to ride a bike. 'I was 40 when I learned,' she says, 'and after I learned people were like, "Can you teach me?" I was like the Pied Piper on bikes,' she jokes.

Mahnoor loves maps, and because she's so good at finding and planning these rides her nickname in the group is Bajji Satnav. She likes turning on all the cycling layers of the Ordnance Survey app, which is useful in cities as it shows you on- and off-road cycle routes. You can select which surfaces or conditions you're willing to ride in and she uses this information to plot routes for Women on Wheels' rides. I detect a youthful sense of adventure. Mahnoor discovered a Glasgow cycle lane recently that wasn't on any of the map layers. She was determined to solve the mystery. 'I said to hubby, "We'll have to drive there one day with the bikes and see where it goes."'

Like many women of colour, Aneela McKenna has become an advocate for greater ethnic and gender diversity in cycling, both of which it is sorely lacking. Aneela is known for her work in mountain biking, initially as a guide, and increasingly for speaking and inspiring others, pressing for change – and even appearing on cycling magazine covers, representing women of colour to a wider audience.

She's travelled from her Borders home and is speaking about her cycling experiences tonight, in the hope of inspiring others.

Before she is due to speak, I tell Aneela about the cyclist flipping me the V-sign at Stockingfield Bridge, because I think it's a funny story. She delivers her conclusion in deadpan Glaswegian: 'Sounds like a prick.' I quickly realise Aneela is not the kind of person to let others dictate terms. She is petite and one delicate-looking wrist is visibly off due to a recent break that's keeping her temporarily away from the bike, but she has a fire in her eyes and a punk attitude. She built her own mountain bike from scratch during one of the lockdowns and shared a video of the process online to inspire others. She also works as a consultant in the outdoor industry, advising companies on how to be more inclusive. This includes tackling toxic comments on social media. 'If something's a bit racist, it's racist,' she says.

Wanting to make our small group feel comfortable, Aneela suggests we sit around in a circle instead of rows facing the front. She wants to hear about people's experiences cycling. One young woman in a hijab quietly speaks about how Women on Wheels has helped build her cycling confidence.

She says, 'I was so scared to get on a bike and go on the road myself, but in the group there was no pressure to do anything; you could just get on your bike and go. It was my third time trying to ride a bicycle. It was good.'

'Did you ride on the road?' Aneela asks. Sharing roads with motor traffic can be the most challenging bit of cycling.

'A wee bit, yeah.'

Aneela starts to talk about how she got into cycling as an adult. She says, 'I didn't know how to cycle. I grew up in Glasgow and Kelvingrove Park was my green space. My mum was just trying to integrate, so learning to cycle wasn't part of that.' It was only later she discovered cycling for herself.

Aneela adds, 'People need to see more people like themselves to feel cycling is for them. It means making sure white institutions are talking about inclusion. Women have created these spaces because they've been excluded in the first place.'

Aneela looks around the room and says, 'We've all experienced discrimination, it's what you do with it that counts.' It stops me in my tracks a little, but she's right. In 2018 Aneela suffered a mental breakdown following discrimination at work. She says it made her who she is today and helped her do what she's doing now. 'Discrimination breeds community,' she says.

We watch a short film featuring Lee Craigie about cycling adventures in the gorgeous wild places of Scotland helping her overcome challenges in life.

Afterwards, Aneela says, 'We should push ourselves on our bikes, because it transfers into our everyday lives. You've got that resilience, it builds that. After her breakdown, she explains, 'I took myself off to the Hebrides for a month with my bike and bags, and just rode my bike on my own.'

It's hard to hear about these experiences and I'm in awe of Aneela, Shgufta and Mahnoor, and all of these women, breaking out of the boxes people put them in and creating their own narrative in the most difficult of circumstances. It seems trite to call it inspiring, but, wow!

Aneela's eyes suddenly become bright while she's talking and she asks in a louder voice, 'Who wants to share their experience?' or 'What does cycling do for us?' The answer from the group seems to be: freedom, joy, companionship. 'I can throw away my worries on my bike,' says one woman. Others: 'It gives you a high', 'You just feel better afterwards', 'It sets you up for the day.' A lot of women said they couldn't cycle on roads or outside parks until joining the group rides.

One young women, Sue, used to sneak out of home at 5 a.m. to go cycling because her parents told her she couldn't go out alone. As an adult she got a job, with no way to get there, so a friend said, 'Why not cycle?' She says, 'It was seven miles, which I thought was too far, but my friend taught me some basic maintenance and I taught myself some more.' After that, there was no stopping her.

Another woman went on a Lake District trip with the group. She couldn't cycle with traffic and she couldn't manage hills, so she got off and pushed when she was out of her comfort zone. She says, 'There were all these really cool Muslim women and it was the dream team, they were picking us up, feeding us and taking us somewhere safe at the end of the day. These groups made me do more than I would otherwise.'

She quietly explains she gave her bike away when she was pregnant, thinking, 'I'll never cycle again.' She says it as if having a child were tantamount to the end of freedom and autonomy. When she did replace it, she bought a little girl's bike with leopard print, in purple. 'I get in the habit of leaving the bike outside, because I'm too scared to cycle,' she says – as if half hoping someone will take away the fear by stealing it. The women agree she deserves an adult bike. Mahnoor says, 'Come cycling with us, we'll look after you.'

Another woman says, 'When I was learning I was thinking, "If I fall off who's going to look after me and the kids?"' Women on Wheels took off the pedals so she could learn to balance first, giving her the confidence to finally pedal it on her own.

Without getting too nerdy, there are two types of funding for cycling: capital and revenue. While capital is about the physical stuff, concrete and kerbs, revenue is about people, anything from behaviour change programmes to staff who deliver the routes. This is the kind of stuff that teaches people to cycle and shows them the routes, like the crucial work Women on Wheels does. It helps people access bikes. It also trains staff to have the crucial conversations about the changes, from giving residents input on projects, to heading off some of the inevitable misinformation around cycling and walking schemes. Capital funding is sometimes seen as the exciting bit, but without people, making it a success is much harder.

Part of the battle with some women, Shgufta says, is what's in their heads – their own doubts, often from what others have told them they can and can't do. Many women arrive believing they can't cycle and while some pick up all the skills in a single session, for others it takes weeks and weeks of confidence-building before self-belief finally propels them forward.

Having a like-minded group of people to cycle with is key. I know from experience all-male groups, or even mixed groups, can be intimidating when you're learning cycling skills. Women and gender-variant ride groups, maintenance groups, skills sessions and social clubs create spaces where women and non-binary folks can learn in comfort, away from the bravado that can make us self-conscious and nervous of asking questions and making mistakes. One woman sums it up: 'You need a supportive female group.'

Representation is part of making women feel they belong in cycling and Aneela is indignant that so little sports coverage is of women – because if you can't see it you can't be it. In 2018 women's sport was 4 to 10% of coverage combined, though by 2022 it had risen to 15%, according to one analysis. Then there's the practical skills themselves. 'Women always say the biggest barrier is fixing a puncture. Learning that can empower you so much,' she says.

The inadequacy of train services looms large. Sue once had a panic attack on a train platform, because she planned a cycling trip only to be told when she got to the station she couldn't travel with her bike; all the first-come, first-served spaces were taken. Shgufta, once told she could only take two bikes on the train when she was there with her two children, quipped, 'So what do you want me to do: leave one child on the platform or put them on the train alone?' Bicycle carriage policies can seem cruelly arbitrary and add additional layers of stress and uncertainty to a journey: another woman was ejected from a train by a conductor with two kids and their bikes, only to have the next train conductor let them on.

When Aneela asks what everyone will do to challenge themselves on the bike, Mahnoor announces she wants to plan her very first multi-day cycle tour. It's clearly a big deal for her and there's a sense now she's said it out loud, she'll do it. She says, 'I've been thinking of doing a week-long trip, possibly with hubby joining me for breakfast and dinner, but probably just me cycling.' The group is excited for her and supportive.

We clear away the chairs and wheel the bikes into a room in the church to be stored. When I get outside, laden with leftover chickpea curry, samosas and spring rolls, Mahnoor is still in the car park. She'd left the building some minutes ago. When I ask if she's OK she calmly explains her bike was stolen while we were inside. It was on the back of her car on a rack, which she normally locks, but she was so busy unloading the bikes from a van earlier and so tired from an already long day, she forgot.

I look around the corner of the building, in case for any reason it's there, and peer up and down the street, wondering how the thief would feel knowing they were stealing from someone who dedicated so much energy and time today and so many other days to helping others. Perhaps they wouldn't care, perhaps they were desperate. It's a horrible feeling, still. The others come out and are as horrified as I am. Everyone is sad, everyone knows what it feels like, most of us have experienced cycle theft. 'I thought it would be safe in the car park,' Mahnoor says.

I feel a longing for my own community, for what these women have together. For many of them safe cycle routes are key – cycling with traffic is terrifying when you're only just learning to ride. If you're then cycling with children your tolerance for risk and for sharing with traffic is further reduced. But for diverse groups of people, including women from ethnic minorities, to feel welcome on these new bike routes, groups like Women on Wheels are crucial. These groups offer support when things go wrong, keep each other motivated to learn and provide social networks and friendships that enrich each other's lives. They commiserate the setbacks and make each other stronger. The more diverse people you see out on the roads on bikes the more people will think this is something for them. It's not so much, 'Build it and they will come' as 'Build communities and they will come.'

19

NED BOULTING ON HELMETS AND
A HELTER-SKELTER OF HISTORY

Sports commentator and author Ned Boulting is a magnet for
information. When I arrive, puffing, at the top of the hill beside
the Greenwich Observatory, Ned's interest is piqued by a statue of a
man with an excellent cape. This, he tells me, is General Wolfe, the
man who won Quebec back from the French. The statue was a gift
from Canada.

It's the end of September, the second gloves day of the year, but
I'm sweating. Ned said I might need to push my bike on some of the
ascent to our meeting point, so I determinedly cycled it. I'm maxed
out by the top. Ned says, 'but we're a good climb up, look how high
you are.'

It's a famous viewpoint, looking across the Thames towards the
towers of Canary Wharf and the City. 'I love this view,' he says. 'It's the
best view in London in my opinion.' He points across at the skyscrap-
ers. 'I've been in London for 25 years, which is a good stretch, and it
used to be just 1 Canada Square, then came the HSBC building in the
early 1990s, by Norman Foster, then Citibank I think. The four on
the left, after the gap, have been built in the last few years, during the
pandemic. I think they're just flats.'

We cycle back down the hill, and meander around the pretty back
streets of Greenwich. The information continues to flow. He points

out the library where he goes to write his books. The plan is to ride Quietway 1, one of his favourite routes and the way he cycles from home in south London into the city centre.

There's a brand-new cycle route opened at Greenwich that I found by accident on the way, so we have two routes to choose from. It's one of an increasing number of impressive new cycle routes popping up across the city in the last decade or so, whose progress has accelerated in recent years: it's wide and long, a two-way track protected from traffic by a solid kerb. We opt for Ned's favourite route, the Quietway. 'This isn't part of it,' says Ned, accidentally leading us on to a main road.

It's a sunny morning and both of us are happy to be out on the bike, out for a ride in London, just because. Low-traffic routes like the Quietway, largely free from the harassment and stress of sharing with often impatient drivers, just make it 10 times better.

These quietways, begun under Boris Johnson's tenure, are designed to provide priority cycle routes using back streets. They are common in the Netherlands and, while they're sometimes seen as 'second tier' routes, in some cases they could become a primary cycle route through a neighbourhood and further afield. They use things like traffic filters – bollards in the roads, essentially, to filter out through-car traffic – to make walking and cycling safer and more pleasant. There are some new protected lanes and existing cycling cut-throughs through housing estates have been widened, often formed by generations of Londoners using the most direct, backstreet route into town.

By upgrading these informal routes, several boroughs working together create a coherent network of paths into and across the city. Delivery has been patchy, because not all boroughs were willing to take difficult decisions to reduce motor vehicle access. Part of this route still serves as a motor traffic rat run, for one, but for the large part it is delightful. All it needed were a few bits of kerb and some bollards.

It's lucky Ned is with me, because it's not always obvious where the route goes. There are signs, but you need to look out for them. Where a route like this in the Netherlands would be a mini-road, with one surface leading you obviously through back streets and between houses, this switches suddenly between road and pavement and little cut-throughs. It's not intuitive, but it works.

We traverse hidden and beautiful corners of the city, new and old. We cross Deptford Creek on a structure Ned tells me is called the Ha'penny Bridge. It is dainty-looking, with a wire threaded into a metal hatch in the ground where there's probably a lifting mechanism. Everywhere your eye roves, there is something arresting. We stop and peer down into the broad creek. It's low tide and old timey-looking ships are beached on vast expanses of shining mud. Beyond a rail bridge, to the other side is the Trinity Laban Conservatoire of Music and Dance, which I've never seen from this angle. It's a unique, pale cube of a building with a colour wash on the outside, which, reflected in the shining creek, looks like a petrol spill. 'I love this part of London,' Ned says, as we pedal away.

'Is this where the football place is?' I ask, as we enter a path that looks like it could have been a former rail line. Ned laughs. 'You mean Millwall? That's a way up', he says, explaining you emphasise the second syllable. Ned was a football commentator for some years, before falling out of love with the sport, its toxic politics and the increasing inaccessibility of its players – and moving to cycling. His rediscovery of cycling predated mine by a few years – his via the sport, mine via using the bike as transport – but our realisation of what the bicycle could do in everyday life eventually met in the middle.

In 2003 ITV sent Ned to cover the Tour de France. He loved the complexity of the sport: '178 players, each with different motivations' – a puzzle that, once you work it out, is richly and permanently rewarding. He loves languages – it's what he studied at university, he speaks German fluently – and the language of cycling is French. However, in 2012 the language of cycling was increasingly spoken in the UK, too. During the London Olympics, and for several years of the Tour de France, Britain was at the pinnacle of cycle sport, helped behind the scenes by Chris Boardman and an innovative programme pushing the boundaries in technology; the science of marginal gains. Ned rode that wave as a reporter and he, like thousands of other Brits in the following years, came away from the Tour and bought his first adult bicycle. It was the start of a homecoming of sorts – and simultaneously a revelation.

'There's very few things that almost everybody in this country can share,' he says, 'but here's one: the moment – they might have been three years old, or five years old – when they were riding a bike with their parents or their sibling in the park. They suddenly realised that that guiding hand was no longer holding the saddle, and they were actually riding the bike themselves unsupported. I can remember that moment. You can remember that moment.' Ned has tried this with others too – everyone remembers that moment.

'It sounds trivial, but it's not, it's formative, almost like a Freudian step in the separation of the child and the parents – and a bicycle enables that. It's extraordinarily powerful.' When we rediscover it, we wonder why we ever lost it – this gift of freedom, this very pure joy that exists atop a bicycle. It's one the car industry promises, with its slick and ever-present advertising, beguilingly comfortable cockpits and easy access to power, but, on freedom and joy, cars rarely deliver. The bicycle, humble in essence with, for the most part, few frills and gadgets, does the opposite: it delivers freedom and exhilaration by the armful, even on a gentle potter through the neighbourhood (cars permitting).

Ned recalls, after years of driving, his rediscovery of the bicycle. He says: 'Like the vast majority of the population in this country, I just forgot about it, and moved into adulthood and put my childish toys away – and the bicycle, for whatever reason, was one of those childish toys. It took being sent to go and cover the Tour de France by ITV in 2003 to reconnect me in any way at all with the bicycle. So, in a rather infantile manner, I came back from covering my first Tour de France and went to Halfords and bought a bike. I mean, it was that simple. And then, of course, I went through all the strange phases of misunderstanding what cycling is all about.'

For some time, he wouldn't ride a mile and a half to the station without wearing Lycra and clip-in shoes. 'Bit by bit,' he recalls, that relationship with the bicycle changed; now he almost never dons stretchy fabrics. 'I've completely redefined and re-understood my relationship with the bike and returned, actually, to something much closer to that four-year-old in the park. That's what it feels like now. So, it's genuinely come full circle, via a very convoluted path.'

Now, anything that offers the excuse for a bike ride gives an 'almost inexplicable' sense of joy and satisfaction; one that anyone who cycles will instantly recognise. An excuse to ride the bike becomes the best part of the morning and it's one he relishes. 'I can't articulate why it matters so much, but it gives me so much pleasure and the slower I go and the more frequently I do these little journeys, the more I get out of it. I almost never go for long rides out into the countryside that take four or five hours and test me physically. Almost all of my cycling is literally just bimbling around town. It's very curious.

'You can ride to get exercise, you can ride with a sense of purpose, because you need to drop something off in Deptford. Or you can simply, like we're doing today, go for a ride for no reason other than it's just great fun and a nice way to talk, and all that sort of thing. Isn't that great?' It is great.

There's some beautiful graffiti – artwork, really – on a railway bridge structure we pass and Ned explains, 'We're into the hipster heart of Deptford. The high street here has been voted the 33rd most authentic high street in the world, because of the lack of concessions.' After almost falling off at a junction for no apparent reason, I ask, 'By design?' 'I don't think so,' he says. 'I think it was just because of poverty.'

The difficulty of co-ordinating London boroughs meant most of London's Quietway programme was a flop – while several main road cycle routes were finished by Boris' second term, no quietways were. Quietway 1 (which was project managed by Sustrans for TfL), although slow, was the success story, but it's far from perfect and still defers to motor traffic in places. At one point, on a pavement path, we pass the entrance to a dump, which not only smells but intro-duces large lorries across the path. There are signs Ned dislikes: the passive-aggressive 'Considerate cycling welcome' in a park; the one that says 'Pedestrians and cyclists beware vehicles crossing', but, so far as he can tell, drivers, who could do far more harm in that scenario, are not warned to watch out for pedestrians and cyclists.

Ned's journey back to the bike led, circuitously, to thoughts of advocacy. He remembers jogging with Chris Boardman, during their Tours de France coverage, and hearing Chris make arguments about cycle safety that were totally counterintuitive. They were like another language to be understood and Ned saw an opportunity to make a contribution to this debate. 'The first time I had the helmet conversation with Chris, I came at it like probably 95% of the population: "What are you talking about, you bloody idiot? Why would you suggest that you don't have to wear a helmet? Of course, you should wear a helmet."'

He remembers Chris patiently explaining the impact of mandatory helmet laws in Australia. There were unintended consequences: the changes introduced inconvenience and new perceptions of danger, and fewer people rode bikes as a result. The government may have reduced head injuries, but by putting people off an easy form of exercise, it raised their risk of heart attacks and diseases like diabetes and cancer. From a public health perspective, it was poor policy. Chris often pointed out people were more likely to suffer a head injury in the bath – or inside a car – than on a bike, and only one of those activities regularly attracts calls for mandatory helmets.

Recalls Ned, 'I think I was so excited by listening to him launch these very patient, slightly counterintuitive arguments that seemed to make so much sense when you actually sat back and thought about it. I wanted a bit of that.'

We often hear stories of 'helmet saved my life' and for Ned it's true. At one point we emerge on to a pavement to cross a main road – one of the route's compromises – only for Ned to narrowly miss a man who suddenly emerges from behind a building, cycling along the pavement. Both come to a dead stop. The man, clearly philosophical, looks nonplussed and we continue.

'That was really close,' says Ned. 'That would have been interesting for your book.' I joke he might have woken up believing he'd won the Tour de France again. He recounts in his book, *How I Won the Yellow Jumper*, coming round in hospital with a bad concussion after crashing his bike and believing he'd won that year's race. His helmet had cracked in two.

The experience left him immersed in one of cycling's more interesting contradictions; the helmet debate is a lively one. 'I am living proof of that argument that it can only happen once and that a helmet can save your life, because it arguably did in my case, but I also see a bigger picture beyond that.' He says since the crash he's changed the way he approaches decision-making around cycling, including the wearing of helmets. 'There are times when I know I'll be pushing on a bit and I'll wear a helmet,' he says, and other times, like today, he's riding slower and he won't. He acknowledges it's a hard one to explain, but that there is a rationale. I am the same; sometimes I'll wear one simply out of superstition; I'll get the heebie-jeebies and put one on, just in case, but the fact that it's my choice is crucial.

Now, as we roll along, he recalls the experience of concussion. 'It was really weird, because although I didn't really think I'd won the Tour de France, I thought I'd done pretty well, like top 10.' We laugh, because that meant not only had he forgotten a few hours, but that he'd potentially forgotten an entire sporting career, involving years of training and dedication. He tells me the memory loss was surreal. His partner Cath kept explaining, many times over a period of hours, what had happened: 'You had a bicycle accident and you hit your head,' and he could repeat the information, but each time he would feel it slipping through his fingers, unable to hold on to it. 'It was scary. I kept wondering will I ever work again?' As in, will his brain ever work again. 'I could remember anything longer term – Cath, everything about the kids – but the short-term memory had gone.'

There's nothing wrong with his memory now, though, and he stops intermittently to point out places of interest and their history. There's a pub, the Lord Clyde, painted letters on the side saying it was the home of 'Maloney's fight factory', the owner of which, the then Frank Maloney, managed boxing legend Lennox Lewis, taking him to one of his two world heavyweight titles. Ned tells me Maloney later underwent gender reassignment treatment and re-named herself Kellie. London is full of human history, remarkable stories and a ride can be an exploration. The building was sold recently, probably for flats.

We finally reach the path alongside Millwall stadium, forged by Sustrans from a former wasteland; it's now a wide, flat path on an embankment. There's a surprise warning here: someone has daubed in paint on the asphalt: 'Beware robbery and theft on this route.' Ned isn't surprised: he won't use the route at night for fear of muggings. It's tucked away and, like many tucked-away paths, a target for unscrupulous criminals. I read in the news that week that people have been robbed of their bikes at knifepoint. Others I speak to tell me they won't cycle on it at night either.

There are shouts coming from a training facility on site – the sound of football. As well as being out of bounds at night, this section is closed during matches to stop people getting illicit peeks of the game. One alternative route is the Old Kent Road – a terrifying prospect – or, eventually, the new protected cycle route I discovered this morning to the north of here, as yet unfinished. It highlights the importance of a network – alternatives, contingencies, just like you'd have with roads.

Three quarters of our way into the city, we stop at a café on the route, which opened in 2016, the year the cycle route opened, replacing an empty shop. Ned recently shared a clip on social media of scores of everyday cyclists, in a kind of peloton, rolling across the junction outside the café. It was a mirror of his day job, people moving in unison on bicycles, but for entirely different purposes. These aren't necessarily cyclists, per se – people who define themselves using the bicycle – they are people who happen to use bikes to get somewhere, to access the city. We sit outside the café and watch the daily spectacle. Even today, mid-morning on a weekday, there's a steady flow of cycle traffic.

'On the one hand, they're two completely different expressions of the same thing – of riding a bike,' Ned says, but on the other, they are connected in the same way his bike is geometrically like a racing bike, but used for entirely different purposes. He acknowledges that while the Tour de France is 'a carbon nightmare' – tens of thousands of people driving across France every summer for a month, and the helicopters – it's also 'the greatest global shop window imaginable for the Victorian invention that is the bicycle.

'You only need to see how Bradley Wiggins' success in 2012 drove bike sales of all descriptions in this country and actually awakened this active travel revolution in London to some extent, to see how those dots can be joined. It requires careful thinking about, but there are strange connections between the expression of elite sport and everyday utilitarian cycling that shouldn't be underestimated.'

I knew about Ned before I met him, through his work commentating on the Tour de France and reading his books about his journey into the world of sport cycling. When a mutual friend, Adam Tranter, suggested we three start a podcast together, I didn't expect Ned to say yes. For him, though, it was a natural progression of some of his musings. 'I leaped at the chance; it matters hugely to me.'

It's a frustration, though, in many ways. We've been recording *Streets Ahead* roughly once a month, for several years now. Ned is our anchor, so to speak, the professional broadcaster who questions our assumptions and keeps our jargon in check. 'I do feel like most of the time I'm just shrieking into the echo chamber and getting a lot of shrieks back. We've spoken about this so many times Laura; breaking that cycle of talking only to the initiated.'

The pace of change in everyday cycling can feel glacial, then there is a leap forward. I've been talking about this subject for a decade: you can just talk to those who agree with you or you can have the same conversations again and again with those who disagree. Sometimes people simply haven't thought about it before, and the leap between scepticism and support is not that great.

I, like others in my position, am asked to appear on radio and TV shows to repeatedly defend cycling or cyclists' behaviour. To explain why mandatory helmets aren't the answer to preventing road deaths, say. Why forcing cyclists to wear bright clothes isn't going to help them be seen if drivers aren't looking for them. Why number plates for bikes would only have the same impact helmets would, making cycling harder, restricting access to a cheap form of transport for those who can least afford the alternatives and destroying the health gains.

Cyclists are mistaken for a homogenous group, in the way pedestrians or motorists aren't, but Ned's video of a different kind of peloton cut through the noise. It was seen hundreds of thousands of times on Twitter. It was just people on bikes, there was nothing you could reasonably object to, but clips like Ned's show that people who cycle are as varied as people are.

In the right conditions, and increasingly in London, change is happening, as if by itself. Ned says, 'The mini peloton of people who sweep past this junction day by day is growing of its own volition simply because more and more people are using it, and they're coming home and they're dumping their bike in the hallway and they're saying to their friends, "You know, you could just cycle in," and it's just happening. It's a word-of-mouth thing that's just getting out. And so maybe, ultimately, the answer isn't people shouting about it from the rooftops, it's about quietly building the opportunities for people to discover it for themselves. The one thing that I've really kind of concluded of late is that it's going to need immense patience.

'Because the last thing we want here is a peloton of Bradley Wiggins wannabes. That would ruin it to some extent and miss the point massively, but there are connections and I sit right in the middle of those connections sometimes. I feel sometimes quite conflicted, but sometimes quite enlightened by the way that the two Venn diagrams do overlap.'

The route has some more wonders to offer; it passes newbuild flats on a street shaded by established trees, industrial units and neighbourhood centres with picturesque London pubs and miniature parks. Growing numbers of cyclists collect, congregating on the city centre, as we pass block after block of dense flats and council housing. There are neat little cut-throughs with a bollard, some kerbs and some smooth tarmac, transforming streets into havens for cyclists and walkers. Then we're into the well-heeled neighbourhoods of Borough, through an awkward chicane gateway the residents fought to keep – just accessible with a handcycle, at low speeds. There's a leafy square and we stop near Borough High Street. It's a lovely place to end the ride.

Ned's off to find some Edwardian shirt garters for his upcoming one-man show, *ReTour de Ned*, before a dress rehearsal on Friday. I wish him luck and we part ways. Nearby, one of the great cross-city cycle routes meets the back-street routes – a satisfying, almost seamless connection of a network, of the kind a national cycle network needs in spades.

20

THIS PATH GOES ALL THE WAY
TO LIVERPOOL

The sun is out, but there's a keen wind in the open spaces. It's early April and Sustrans' CEO Xavier Brice and I cycle from the hotel we were billeted at overnight to the station at Penistone, near Barnsley, South Yorkshire. We're here to meet two of the NCN's stars – one is a route, the other a person.

Xavier is glad to get away from the desk and get out on the bike, though his Brompton, with its tiny wheels, is possibly not the best machine for riding the NCN. With all the bike spaces on the train booked, a folding bike was his only option. Luckily, he's a pretty serious long-distance cyclist in his spare time, so a few mud paths are no big deal.

Xavier is sometimes described as the Laurence Llewelyn-Bowen of the cycling world, for his wavy, often jaw-length, brown hair. This, with his pastel suit jackets, gives him a boyish, almost posh look. In fact, his dad was a teacher and his mum was a worker at the port of Dover. Xavier was, like me, the first person in his family to attend university. He's softly spoken and compassionate, and honest about the challenges and flaws of the NCN. The network is something he cares deeply about and there's a continuity about his work.

Xavier was one of the people behind London's cycling transformation under Boris Johnson. When he wasn't acting as Boris' personal mechanic, in 2007-08 Xavier led the development of London's new walking and cycling strategy under Ken Livingstone and then Boris, which included the precursor to the outer London town centre transformations, initially known as Mini-Hollands, and cycle super-highway routes – though Boris added the 'super' to the name. Xavier also proposed a navigation system, now known as Legible London, which, like the other elements, was implemented in the form of street corner totems featuring maps with walking distances to nearby attractions.

In 2016, after 10 years at TfL, he joined Sustrans. For Xavier, physical movement is a core value, an essential ingredient for a good life, and he wants the NCN to offer all of us opportunities to move, no matter our ability. He may ride long-distance Audax events on weekends, cycling multiple hundreds of miles over fairly short timeframes with diverse groups of often eccentric riders, snatching sleep in bus stops – Audax hotels as they're jokingly called – but he keeps that side of his life firmly away from his day job. The NCN, as Xavier sees it, is not only a way to help people move, regardless of their ability, but it's something with the power to connect us in what is a polarised era. It's a chance to encounter someone on a shared path that you might not normally interact with. He believes it's a great leveller.

While users of our road network enjoy standardised signs, widths and markings, and countless teams of workers funded by billions of taxpayers' pounds to improve and maintain them, NCN users get tens of thousands of blue stickers plastered on street furniture beside anything from rocky farm tracks to main roads, supported by a patchwork of mostly retired volunteers, using a similarly patch-work arrangement of government funds and charitable donations. I've experienced this fiddly Where's Wally signage up and down the UK. Some local authorities do put up their own NCN signs and maintain them as part of their road networks, but there are no hard and fast rules.

Sustrans' Volunteer Rangers programme was founded in 1998 with the aim of maintaining a growing network of routes at little to no cost. Funding for route construction didn't include their ongoing maintenance, so Sustrans had to be creative. Luckily, people love their local paths and were more than happy to help. Drawing once again from its dedicated and generous followers, in 1998 the charity initially recruited 700 willing souls to manage its 10,000 miles of NCN for free. Their main task was ensuring route signage was in place and visible, that signs hadn't been turned or removed, and clearing foliage and litter from paths.

What started as an experiment became a movement: by 2018, volunteer ranger numbers had grown by almost five times to 3200, together committing a quarter of a million hours per year to maintaining the network – roughly six hours per month per volunteer. Astonishingly, after a quarter of a century, many of the same dedicated souls are still managing the same stretches of network. In fact, 83% of them are aged over 55 – and just 5% are under 44. It may reflect the voluntary sector, but Sustrans is trying to encourage younger demographics, via things like the Duke of Edinburgh award and via colleges and universities. The challenge is that clearing paths and maintaining signs are less career-relevant skills than, say, working with schools or community groups. Either way, this army of volunteers ensures the network ticks over, to a large degree, with very little funding and no maintenance budget.

The volunteer ranger we're meeting at Penistone Station is the embodiment of this. In just over three months Kate and the team she leads have spent an eye-popping 422 hours caring for the Trans-Pennine Trail (TPT) around Penistone – more than any other Sustrans volunteer group. January and February were too inclement in the Peak District for outdoor work, so even more astonishingly most of those hours of work took place in March and the first week of April.

Somehow, I have brought, for one night, two full panniers containing three different jackets, a full washbag, a D-lock and a pair of boots, while Xavier has a small bag in his bike basket containing very little. I'm getting a photo of our different setups outside Penistone Station when Kate appears with her bike. A soft-spoken woman, diminutive and silver-haired with a playful smile, Kate explains she started volunteering on the TPT in 2011, when she returned to the area after a period of study. Since then, she has come to lead the local group of rangers and transformed the trail. Kate, it soon becomes apparent, is a powerhouse. One of her volunteers, half joking, calls her 'She who must be obeyed'. It seems people start off doing a bit of volunteering then, thanks to Kate, the commitment grows. She works quietly, without any fuss, almost under the radar, but between the group a lot gets done.

Two more men meet us at the station, one of whom sounds like the comedian John Bishop. This man runs a bicycle recycling charity, giving refurbished bikes to refugees confined in local hotels. He says security at the hotels is stifling and he takes these displaced people, who come from all over the world, out for rides on the TPT to offer some respite from what must feel like imprisonment. These are kind people, trying to make the world a bit of a better place.

Every Wednesday Kate's group gets together, weather permitting, to maintain the path. As a result, the tarmac is neat up to its edges, and Kate and her team regularly clear overgrown foliage to maintain the spectacular views from the path out to the Pennines. This week they removed branches brought down by a dump of snow months earlier.

East–west the TPT runs 215 miles from Southport, via Liverpool, to Hornsea. There's also a north–south route between Leeds and Chesterfield, a spur to York and another to Kirkburton. Together it's 343 miles of trail, much of it on former railway lines. It was also voted the network's most popular route. At the time of construction in the 1990s the TPT was a separate entity from the NCN, with its own Millennium lottery bid. Its founders wanted a path that allowed horse riders too – and John Grimshaw is less keen on cyclists sharing with horses, a belief I share. The TPT still has its own organisation, with a head office and permanent staff, but it's also part of the NCN, stitching together bits of numbers 1, 6, 56 and 62.

Spring arrives at the Peaks three weeks after the south of England and the leaves are only just showing as the subtlest pinkish-brown buds on trees; primulas on grassy banks emerge as tiny leaves and the hint of buttery yellow petals, ready to unfurl. Kate's volunteers plant wildflowers on open grass spaces and banks, and rake the dead grass at the end of each summer to keep conditions right for the flowers the following year – if the soil is too rich, they won't grow.

One railway cutting has bare rock faces, dripping with water, the recent rain on its journey downward. Small species of tree have been planted here. Someone, encouraged by Kate, has made a series of animal carvings from felled tree stumps, for free: an eagle perched on a bank, looking out towards the Peak District; a fox's head on a heavily leaning stump, its inquisitive long nose peering up the path, its tall ears held high. There's a whimsical cartoon rabbit with an expression of slight dismay, always slightly out of reach of a bright orange carrot further along.

We reach a diversion. The Bullhouse Bridge, crossing a main road on the old rail line, is closed. It was also installed using the TPT's millennium funds, but water got under the crossing surface and no-one realised how bad it was until a horse put a hoof through. It will cost the entirety of Barnsley's annual footpath budget – a measly £30,000 – to repair it.

We've gathered up more of Kate's band of volunteers as we go, culminating in a posse of around 10 people, riding the flat, smooth trail. Cath, a retired teacher, remembers the last freight trains coming along this line in the early 1980s. She's a cautious cyclist: when we cycle down and around the closed bridge to cross the main road, she dismounts and pushes. She says she wouldn't cycle if the TPT weren't here and, like many people, women especially, she won't cycle in traffic. Just 35% of women consider local cycling safety good, according to Sustrans research, a figure that's not much better among men, at 40%.

Kate and Xavier are chatting as they ride. Kate sees the path as a way to help children explore, among other things. She and the team have created a 'magic wood' near Hazlehead, to encourage kids from Penistone to travel further afield. Eventually, she hopes, those children will realise the path goes all the way to Liverpool. Who knows, one day they might ride the whole thing – the start of a lifelong love of adventure.

It is also a place of respite. During the pandemic the path, like its counterparts across the UK, was heaving. It's a sports facility. Marathon runners use it for training – a rare flat, smooth surface in a hilly part of the country. Children cycle, people walk dogs and it's busy even on a weekday: we are constantly saying hello, good morning and ringing our bells as we go.

Andy is a chatty man who worked at a local clay pipe factory and, when he was made redundant, bought a local pub. As a result, he knows most people along the path. 'Gee out o' t' way,' he says to them; Northern pub landlord banter.

We stop at a broad clearing near Hazlehead, where yet more volunteers are gathered to welcome Xavier and me. There is a trestle table with large Tupperware boxes of home-made cakes. One man is boiling water for tea and coffee in storm kettles. Xavier says a few words, thanking everyone for all they do.

Andy and Cath walk me to the magic wood, while I finish a mug of rapidly cooling coffee. In a grove of trees beside the main tarmac trail, a dirt path meanders between hand-built fencing, woven from thin branches. Tiny chicks bedeck the trees at Easter, ghosts and plastic spiders at Halloween, and snowmen and angels at Christmas – though they haven't had time to put figurines in for today. Kate says someone removes the figures because they worry the plastic will harm wild animals, but they persevere.

Sunlight streams down over the brow of the railway cutting, through the bare trees and entwined arches of living wood. Andy notices a broken tree stump, holding part of a woven fence around a seating area, and he and Cath move it so no-one trips, and make a note to replace it. There's so much love and care for this place and the people who come here.

The group is also a social club. There's Si, who went backpacking with his partner after they retired, finding themselves after two years in Argentina, just as the pandemic hit. They got the last flight out with a national cricket team. 'We went from being the freest we've ever been to the most constricted,' he says. He'd used the path for years and, back from his travels, when restrictions allowed, he joined Kate's band of volunteers.

Eating some of Cath's delicious cakes, one man tells me he'd wanted to join the volunteers for years, and regularly watched them out and about on a Wednesday with envy. The very first week after retiring, he joined in. He said he came back exhausted after clearing tree branches up and down the path for eight-odd hours. His wife says she could really see the difference in his mood. 'He hasn't been himself for a while,' she says quietly. This is a common story and Sustrans has documented how volunteering on the NCN has transformed the mental and physical health of its now 3500 rangers up and down the country.

While the NCN offers its volunteers life-affirming work and community, they in turn prop up this people-powered wonder for everyone else. The fact we can navigate any NCN routes without a map is largely thanks to volunteers like Kate and her team. They deserve an enormous amount of credit for their quiet dedication, and Sustrans for inspiring and keeping them on board for so long. If these people were paid for their work, annual maintenance would run into multiple millions of pounds.

Wonderful as they are, I'm torn on the issue of leaving path maintenance to volunteers. While the TPT is undoubtedly exemplary, for every path like it there are others left to become overgrown, their signage obscured, making them ever harder to navigate. It seems too much like a lottery to me for something so crucial.

It's true that good volunteer rangers know their local routes better than anyone, riding them regularly and spotting things like broken signs and overgrown foliage. Like Kate, many create communities around them. Neil Hutson is a very fit 78-year-old ranger I met in Exeter, who joined when the ranger programme was in its infancy. He cycles about 100 miles a week, checking on his patch of NCN around Bodmin and 'keeping the Alzheimer's at bay,' as he puts it. With his partner Wendy, Neil leads regular cycle rides for retirees like him, which they jokingly call the 'geriatric group'.

'Everyone's just so chatty and so happy when they're cycling,' he says. 'I don't know what it is. I've had people in the group who had such serious Parkinson's they couldn't walk, but they could cycle.' Some members had bikes they didn't use until joining Neil's group and now they're out regularly. It's empowering: once they know the local routes, he says, they go out for rides by themselves.

Every week around Bodmin, Wendy and Neil say they spot and repair a damaged or turned sign. Without maintenance budgets for much of the NCN it falls to community-spirited, often retired volunteers like Neil to keep the network serviceable. He sums it up as 'a lot of lopping and that sort of thing'. Neil says one sleuth-like volunteer discovered a local contractor had stockpiled metal NCN signs in a depot, having removed them for some reason over a period of time. They managed to commandeer the signs and reinstate them.

One council won't permit signs on posts up on the moors, because of a perverse-seeming sense of aesthetics, instead using white paint on the tarmac. The last time the paint wore out, Neil and Wendy say there was a two-year wait for the budget to replenish the signage. Some councils award funding to sign their local NCN – if it's an important tourist route, for example – but these are the exception rather than the rule.

One downside of this system is, with 3500 volunteers comes as many ideas and opinions about how to manage their stretch, based on their experiences of cycling. Well-meaning as they are, some resist 'cluttering' the roads with signs, even if it makes a route hard to navigate for first-timers, while elderly volunteers might struggle with technological parts of the work. Much of the volunteer training is online, as is the means of logging work. Neil emails his local Sustrans contact instead, to get around the fact he doesn't have a smartphone.

Astonishingly, despite the patchiness and voluntary nature of their workforce, the charity managed to audit the entire network's 16,000 barriers, predominantly using volunteers, in just a year. However, the original audit didn't take into account certain details, such as barriers installed off the NCN that stop people accessing the routes, so it needed doing again. This was no small task: I completed Sustrans' online barrier audit training, an hour-long recorded webinar, and went out with Sustrans' Ed Plowden to do the work in Bristol. It's an in-depth process, ideally requiring two people, a tape measure, a working smart phone with a camera, and not inconsiderable amounts of time.

Someone needs to corral all of these fiefdoms, and each volunteer lead, a Sustrans staff member tasked with managing volunteers, is responsible for supporting 200 volunteers like Neil, which is a lot if they all need tech support. It's also a lot to keep tabs on. In some parts of the country, particularly the harder-to-reach routes, there are no volunteers at all. It's not uncommon for someone to stop volunteering and forget to tell anyone, or to keep going without mentioning it. It's all slightly mind-boggling.

According to Sustrans, in the south west of England for example, of 169 NCN sections, 40 are without a volunteer – about a fifth. Volunteers from adjacent sections will come and help off their beat, when asked, but it's an ask. It's not for a lack of interest, necessarily, but because of capacity issues within Sustrans – they can only properly train and support so many people to become rangers with the resources they have, and they have to be strategic about it.

Back on the TPT Xavier, two Sustrans staff and I say farewell to Kate and her A-team, and head for Penistone. The TPT leaves the level railway track in places and we perform a stiff climb on-road, before descending again along a farm track, half mud, half stream. 'This isn't "for everyone"', notes Xavier, referencing the charity's vision for an accessible network. His Brompton, a bike where everything is close to the ground, is quickly spattered with mud.

We follow the brow of a deep cutting down to the level rail path again at Silkstone Tunnels. An underground fire in a coal seam means the tunnel is regularly filled with smoke. Periodically the fire service comes out to douse it, but it makes the section unsafe for cycling and walking, and it's permanently fenced off.

Two Sarahs meet us on the path: Sarah Ford, Barnsley's rights of way manager and TPT officer, and Sarah Bradbury, who organises a huge geographic area of volunteers for Sustrans. Bradbury spends her life travelling with huge bags of stuff for volunteer activity days, dragging anything from graffiti-cleaning materials to brooms and loppers, covering all of the north west of England, in projects that might be as geographically splayed as Barnsley and Chester, 75 miles apart. True to her car-free ethos, she does this all by train and bike. It clearly takes over your life: her family home serves as a storage facility for some of the time.

Sarah Ford is on foot and wearing a hi-vis jacket. A calm doer and passionate about her work, she and her team manage 50 miles of the TPT, plus another 435 miles of footpaths and bridleways, with just £30,000 a year and four rangers. As a result, they have to use some of their staff and expertise on commercial work, building paths for commercial construction companies. The section we are standing on, beside the rail tunnel entrance, was recently surfaced, paid for by Westminster's post-Covid active travel funds. Like the rest of the NCN, funding is never guaranteed: each year the TPT goes, cap in hand, to the 27 local authorities whose boundaries it crosses, for cash.

It seems a good investment. After they resurfaced the first stretch, Penistone to Thurgoland, back in 2012, usage increased 700%. Sarah Ford couldn't believe it: she kept checking the count data for errors. There were, it turned out, so many people for whom the path was suddenly accessible, year-round. The ground is visibly waterlogged at the sides of the path; you can imagine only mountain bikers could have previously used it in winter. We visit a seating area where yet more volunteers, also DfT-funded, recently cleared tangles of head-height brambles. Now a seating area previously populated by drinkers is surrounded by planters with bulbs, creating a welcoming space to stop and rest.

The TPT conducts annual user surveys. For a lot of the NCN this kind of qualitative and quantitative data isn't available, because it costs money and money is in short supply. The surveys, done in person in previous years and more recently online, show the value of these spaces. For the first time, in 2022 more than half of TPT users were women, though these were often horse riding or walking. For every two men cycling there was one woman – the same ratio we see all over the UK because you have to cycle on the roads to reach paths like this and, as we've seen before, women are less keen about sharing space with fast-moving vehicles.

People use trails for a number of reasons, but the TPT surveys found most of its visitors come for enjoyment, health and wellbeing. The top purpose in 2022, for 27% of people, was to 'get fit/stay healthy' and a further 10% used it for their mental wellbeing. Enjoying the countryside and peace and quiet was the reason 15% of visitors came. This isn't a commuting route – things like 'shopping', 'money saved' and 'journey efficiency' were 1% of reported journeys – but in monetary terms, for the local tourist industry as well as for health, its value is clearly immense.

While some of the automatic counters no longer work, the TPT charity calculated the TPT brings in £34 million cash, annually. This is based on 2.4 million users – 1.6 million walkers and 585,000 cyclists, as well as 91,000 horse riders spending, on average, £44 each. Cafés and businesses that were seasonal before the various trail upgrades now operate year-round. There's still a lot to do to make the path accessible: narrow bits, muddy bits, sections that are too steep or rough, missing signs and barriers. As with the rest of the NCN, it's a long and slow process making it fully accessible to everyone.

Leaving the trail and cycling back to the station we see roadsides strewn with litter – astonishing volumes of it, carpeting the woodland far beyond the tarmac. After the well-tended TPT, it's a stark contrast between a space well-loved by a community and one people simply drive through.

Until I'd met Kate and her team, I was cynical about leaving trails like this to volunteers. Meeting them helped me understand their crucial role not only in the NCN's success but for the people in their communities. I was genuinely touched by the love and care they give the TPT. I was also blown away by the huge impact that committed individuals in local councils and the TPT had in getting hold of funding and improving the path; how much they were able to do with very little.

The trail wouldn't exist in anywhere near its current form without these people, going beyond the call of duty for something they believe in. However, their care doesn't change the fact that something as important to our mental and physical health, affording us access to the outdoors without a car, shouldn't rely on such kindness and dedication. It needs to be embedded into how we manage our land.

———

At this stage, I have a confession: I put off and put off travelling across the Irish sea until it became too late. I suffer horrific sea- and car-sickness, and don't like to fly for environmental reasons. I probably should have taken a ferry while I was in Glasgow, but the realisation only dawned once I was home. In the end, I didn't make it to Northern Ireland. The country, as it transpires, is in cycling limbo, having cut most of its on-road NCN in 2020, and suffering endless political gridlock that leaves any cycling plans in go-slow mode. I can only apologise for my omission, plead for forgiveness and hope for Northern Ireland that transport improvements happen for the better, very soon.

21

GOING FULL CIRCLE

When the alarm goes off, I feel like I've been travelling forever. By September, 2022's violently hot summer is on the wane and I cycle across London once more to catch a train from Paddington to Castle Cary. I navigate the predictably stressful cycle space booking system, wheeling the 25kg ebike, upright, through two moving carriages full of people, to change trains via the short platform at Westbury, managing somehow not to bash anyone's elbows or legs on the way.

I cycle, via some of Somerset's more excitable main roads, to a disused quarry outside Shepton Mallet. At the rear of a farmyard, tents, shepherd huts and campervans are nestled in a grassy amphitheatre, with an audience of little trees on the surrounding rock faces. It looks like a festival site, complete with a marquee and portaloos. A handful of men and women in their 60s and above mill about the site. John Grimshaw is off somewhere shouting at a civil servant about permissions to run a cycle path under a publicly owned bridge, while Caroline Levett is conducting the Greenways and Cycleroutes AGM in the marquee. Even camping she looks glamorous: heeled espadrilles, a skirt and earrings.

This is their annual work camp, the echo of voluntary efforts stretching all the way back to the Bristol and Bath railway path in the early 1980s. Every year since 2016, a path somewhere in the UK gets the work camp treatment, with volunteers descending to spend 10 days performing manual labour for fun. Many of them return each year and each one gets a job. One volunteer, Andy, is in charge of digging holes; a charming Welshman in his 80s, David Judd, runs the concrete mixer; and others prepare meals and tidy up camp. One year they installed a prefabricated bridge on the Waddesdon Greenway in a heat wave. Another involved a week working, like moles, in a dark railway tunnel, installing 132 lights. This year it's the turn of a section of former railway track and a new field-margin path near Shepton Mallet. John tells me: 'At each camp we try something new. We start not knowing how to do it and then by the end we get quite good.'

In a rather neat piece of circularity, literally and figuratively, I'm here to contribute to the Somerset Circle, a 76-mile, traffic-free route rounding the county from Clevedon on the coast to Shepton Mallet inland, which will one day link in with the Bristol and Bath railway path. It will also connect the Bath Two Tunnels Way, the Colliers Way from Radstock (almost) to Frome and the Strawberry Line.

I spend a day and a half helping rebuild a collapsed dry-stone wall and clearing tree stumps, either side of Shepton Mallet. John teases me that I'm on the 'sink' project for less capable workers. The sun shines and sandwiches are delivered from camp at lunchtime as curious cows come to scratch themselves on the wall and inspect the work. At night we sleep in the quarry under a cloudless sky, a new moon hanging over the rockface. There's a campfire and communal meals, and John presents one of his slide shows commemorating former work camps.

He's spent two hours preparing it. Inside the gazebo the cable for the projector is highly precarious and John instructs us not to go near it. An excellent raconteur, he recounts the searing hot year working at Waddesdon Greenway, installing the kit bridge without the right tools for the job. When they finally procured the tools, someone managed to drop them in the river, along with the car keys. Caroline never seems to stop. If anyone goes near her she asks if they want tea or coffee, and she occasionally corrects John. When he says next year they'll dig a tunnel under a road to connect bits of route up, Caroline calls out from the kitchen, 'We'll aim to.' 'That's no good,' replies John.

Mendip District Council, the local authority, is soon to be absorbed into a new, unitary, county-wide authority and Mendip's leader, Ros Wyke, wants as much of their section of the Somerset Circle completed as possible before the end. A determined-looking person with short hair, Ros has been trying to get Mendip's section of the circle built for more than 25 years. She would cycle herself, if there were safe routes. 'The country lanes around here are narrow, with stone walls, and there's no room to duck into a hedge if a driver comes along. There aren't many options other than to drive,' she says. According to the council, 61% of car journeys stay within the district, an area of just 458 square miles and less than 30 miles in length.

'The trouble is it takes the council 30 years to do anything, and then you get John Grimshaw involved and things happen,' she says. Now everyone is going all-out to finish the path in a few short weeks. It has taken considerable ingenuity. Kelly Knight, Mendip's star council officer, managed, after enormous amounts of trial and error, to navigate the council's own planning system to get the path built. While the Bristol and Bath path's planning application took four pages of A4 paper, today, I'm told, it takes more like 500 pages.

Mendip ended up tangled in regulations designed to limit the environmental impact of out-of-town shopping centres, dictating that changes to the countryside must be offset by mitigations like tree planting. John and Caroline say these rules make field margins or overgrown railway paths almost impossible to convert for cycling, because you can't chop down trees for the path, even if you replant more than you remove.

The council spent £20,000 applying to itself for planning permission, only to be set undeliverable conditions by its own cautious planning department. In the end, they administratively separated different parts of the path's construction into its constituent parts and, unsure whether they were breaking planning laws – they weren't as it turned out – decided to take a risk and press ahead, building two and a half miles in the council's final months. It had previously taken two years to build half a mile.

Ros has learned to be patient. As well as navigating planning she, John and Caroline, and the dynamite council officer, Kelly, played the usual intractable landowner chess game, every field seemingly owned by someone else.

Finally, after months of scratching their heads, they realised a solution was staring them in the face. If a farmer builds a path on their land they can do it without planning permission, under what's known as 'permitted development' rights. Mendip District Council agreed with John and Caroline, project managing the route, that paths on the old railway alignment could be restored using permitted development rights, shifting the timescales required, substantially. The ecological surveys, the bat surveys in the railway tunnels, would still take place, and any protected trees would stay protected, but this meant something that took years under planning permission process could be done in months. Separately Mendip Council decided it would, if necessary, use compulsory purchase. While it hasn't to date, this gave the council clout in land negotiations. Stubborn landowners now knew if they refused the path, land could be bought under compulsory purchase powers. In other words, the path was being treated as a strategic piece of infrastructure, and afforded the powers that fitted that status. The flexibility of the permitted development method, an element John is particularly keen on, also allows a route to be tweaked during construction and, he says 'made even better than the original proposals'.

Ros and her team also convinced NH's rail structures' managing body, Historic Railway Estates (HRE), to permit a cycle path under one of their many former rail bridges in Shepton Mallet for the very first time. This will save local people having to cross a dangerous road to get between new homes and schools, and the town centre.

HRE had a poor reputation for infilling bridges, but their new chief, Helene Rossiter, tells me those days are mostly behind us – unless the bridge is genuinely considered a liability. With volunteers helping and a local contractor finishing the job it cost peanuts in infrastructure terms: £160,000 per mile. Months later, two new path sections complete, Kelly receives an impromptu standing ovation from grateful residents at a bus stop.

Ros, Caroline and I walk from the quarry, through a wood, to a railway viaduct, on our host Gavin's land, where volunteers are clearing dead elm stumps. There's a railway tunnel, now disused like the rest of the line. John emerges from the darkness of the tunnel, on foot, and joins us.

Once completed the Somerset Circle will, Ros believes, become a rare and valuable local resource. Another route they built 15 years ago, between Draycott and Rodney Stoke, a 20-minute ride from end to end, is regularly filled with families walking and cycling, and people on horses and wheelchairs. The demand is there, she believes, if you build it.

'What people don't realise about the countryside,' she explains, 'is access is really difficult. Flat tarmac is almost non-existent.' This means there are limited places to do things like learn to cycle and few places for children to ride safely, away from traffic. This route, she says, will change that, for now linking up to a nearby skate and play park, and a football pitch, and in future, to Wells and beyond. In the end, short of cash, they surface the field path in fine grit and hope the funding for tarmac comes along later.

Ros also sees it as a significant tourism resource, a potentially substantial boost for the local economy, but in cost-benefit analyses of cycle paths tourism is, for some reason, worth half of what commuting trips are worth per hour. The decarbonisation value of infrastructure is worth 5–10% of its value, while any health benefits aren't included, except in proxy form. If it's not a commuting path, the odds are stacked against it.

John believes such criteria are selective. 'The government have always been totally dishonest on this, because you get major roads like the north Wales highway through Conway, which are fundamentally about tourist business. And tourism is the major industry in places like Brean and so on. And yet cycling for leisure is denigrated as not as important as cycling for work.' The Brean Down Way, opened in 2017 between coastal towns in west Somerset, is another of John's many paths.

The Somerset Circle, like the NCN, is totemic; it's something people can get behind. We're working on part of the Wells to Shepton Mallet portion, but, John believes, 'People see it as part of a bigger thing. They're only four and a half miles apart, those significant rural towns, and you would expect people to happily cycle four and a half miles if there were a high-quality route, but it wouldn't have been funded if it hadn't been seen as part of this wider project.'

It's not an NCN route, per se, and Sustrans isn't supporting it financially, but it may or may not be incorporated into the network later. In a way, it doesn't matter, but the two serve similar purposes, and here we get into the philosophical heart of what cycle routes are for and what a national network means.

John says, 'The National Cycle Network, fundamentally, is about raising the status of how cycling is seen in the country. I mean, if all you do for cyclists is minuscule little bits of paintwork in a town, why should the population as a whole think cycling is important? If you could create a high-profile national network, you stand a chance of winning people's hearts and minds over to the idea that cycling is a proper way of travelling.

'We have terribly low levels of cycling in Britain and it's because cycling is not seen as of strategic importance in the map of transport. Nobody in their right mind is going to cycle from London to Birmingham or Edinburgh, but the point is, you will cycle from Amersham to Aylesbury and it's much, much easier to build a difficult route like Amersham to Aylesbury if it's part of a national network.'

The vision is what gave the NCN its power during the Millennium lottery bid, when being a part of something big appealed to councils, most of whom had never heard of Sustrans or the concept of a National Cycle Network. 'The original network delivered lots of local routes, which were intensely valuable, which councils wouldn't have countenanced otherwise,' he says. 'Obviously there were some areas we failed completely,' says John, while others, like the eventual blossoming of routes in the South Wales valleys, succeeded. 'There was scarcely a single route before we started and now there's almost one in every valley.'

The momentum and, really, the branding of the NCN allowed councils and varied landowners to put their trust in a small charity, contributing their own resources to something that is at the same time of hyper-local, national and international significance.

That said, part of the Somerset Circle on the NCN in Clevedon, a rare town-centre bike lane installed in late 2022, became the subject of a bizarre string of negative news headlines. Local reporters, seemingly unquestioningly, reported various hysterical claims, including that the seafront route's new roundabout would somehow force people to crash, as if they had no control over their vehicles. The reconfiguring of road space from parking to cycling was reported as a threat that would 'ruin Christmas' for local businesses, while the bike lane's wavy line, presumably intended to be artistic, was the subject of several snide articles, along with the reporting of a 'parking protest' by drivers, straight out of the school playground. By May 2023 the council announced it was reviewing the lane. I can just imagine local councillors deciding the aggro probably wasn't worth it. This is what politicians are up against.

I started my journey believing commuting journeys were the important ones; that the NCN had to be about transport. But I had just been carried along with conventional thinking that only trips that make someone money are worthwhile for investment. Of course, the leisure industry is crucial, particularly for rural economies, but cycling and walking, indeed every journey, is important. We need to move to stay well; to withstand the challenges of life; and to connect with others and with the world around us. I enter a philosophical debate about what the NCN is for with Xavier Brice, Sustrans' CEO. To him it's not just a transport network, but a way of connecting people. It's a strategic network, though, and it needs a legal status reflecting that – which it doesn't currently have.

The founding notion of the NCN was that it would become a national network, going where people needed it to go, and connecting the country with walking, cycling and wheeling paths. The bad bits would be finished and, potentially, the charity building it would be working themselves out of a job. That hasn't happened and, unlike in other countries, the UK government never did step in to finish delivering it and in many cases nor did local authorities. That leaves various disparate groups trying to navigate a byzantine system designed with cycling as an afterthought, if it's considered at all. Meanwhile, local councils take very different approaches to delivering routes.

I've met people working against this system, using all their powers and charm to solve what are in effect political problems; battling to do something that makes eminent sense, and that touches every part of our lives – our health, our finances, our communities, the environment – positively. I'm in awe of their tenacity and resourcefulness, but ultimately no amount of gumption is going to get us a proper national network of routes. Its success, or otherwise, boils down to money and power – or lack, thereof.

22

THEY TAKE US BECAUSE WE NEED TO GO

I've spent a year travelling the NCN, peering over my handlebars to take a closer look at weird bits of pavement, paint and mud paths, attempting to navigate fiddly signs that might send you anywhere, and enjoying gorgeous, but all too brief, stretches of wonderful paths, but I think we need to zoom out. What is the NCN for? What is a cycle route for? It's a question that puzzled me as I scaled rocky paths, shoved my bicycle along sandy beaches and cursed routes that went 'the long way round' because there was just no other safe option with the tiny funds available.

In a way it doesn't matter. It's not a question we necessarily ask of our roads: they are because we are. They take us because we need to go from here to there – for a myriad of reasons: to see a friend or relative, to go to school or work, to the shops, to blow off steam or because we've had a good or bad day, week or year and we want to celebrate or commiserate with someone, or reflect alone. Because there's a cool view, café, river, bench, or place we scattered someone's ashes at the end of it. For many of these journeys a motor vehicle, with all the expense and inconvenience of parking, isn't the tool we need, it's just the only one we happen to have. It wouldn't take a lot to give ourselves other options; it's actually very simple, even if it's not necessarily easy.

In early 2023 I had a glimpse of the future: a 10km brand-new cycle track from Glynde to Polegate in East Sussex. A Lewes resident interested in developing cycle paths tells me about it and invites me along to see it. We see the South Downs, lumpen and picturesque in the early spring sun, but our path, following the line of the road, offers level and easy pedalling. Freshly dug earth sprouts a line of tiny saplings and somewhere, still dormant, there are wildflowers. Occasionally the path runs beside the road to avoid ploughing through someone's garden, but mostly we're tucked away behind a hedge – it's glorious.

National Highways has only gone and built quite possibly the best rural cycling and walking route in the country to date, from scratch. On land tucked away from the A27, beyond the hedgerow, is a billiard table-smooth, 3m wide path, with bridges and proper drainage, just like a road. It's delightfully and unusually uneventful actually, for a UK cycle path, which means we can relax and enjoy the view. I imagine Isabelle Clement, in her handcycle, could ride this without the constant vigilance she usually needs on our cycle routes and roads. It's for people in motorised wheelchairs with the tiny wheels, elderly couples who can't carry their bikes up and down stairs or negotiate rutted gravel, and it's certainly the kind of place you could safely let kids loose.

NH credits volumes of cyclists for making it happen. They were, it seems, slowing down traffic so much on the adjacent main road that NH finally provided an alternative cycle route. Using its considerable expertise and clout, NH apparently breezed through all of the usual problems that can, in other less powerful hands, tie up a cycle path for decades: it acquired field margins through compulsory purchase order (CPO), just like it does for roads; it obtained the necessary permissions and funding; and then put its engineers to work.

Paths like this should happen everywhere there's a cycleable distance between settlements. This could be done via a national 'beyond the hedgerows' plan, to use land beside transport corridors' hedges, to develop a greenways programme. The A27 path glimpses at the results of such a plan: you can cycle as fast as you want for most of the way, although for some reason it gives way to turning traffic at albeit quiet side roads, despite the design standards recommending against it. This is no measly pavement path, though. This is a bicycle road: something that offers a genuine and rather lovely alternative to driving.

A man stands at a gap in the hedge, connecting the path with a pub garden. As a joke I ask if he wants a lift. Peering both ways, he enquires whether we've seen a woman walking. We did – she must be a mile away by this point. I wonder if the path called to her, promising adventure, and her feet answered. How far will she get? I wonder. Will she ever return?

You could use such a route for exercise. I would. You could cycle between Eastbourne and Lewes, for work, to shop, to go swimming or visit friends. You could access the popular South Downs Way. At the Polegate end, the route ends abruptly at a parade of shops nowhere near the town centre; almost as if one of the UK's best cycle paths was built solely to connect rural communities with purveyors of wood flooring, vaping products and takeaway curries. It carries a certain surreal charm. Obviously it needs connecting to the town centre – that's the local council's job – but it certainly shows what's possible.

Midway along we pass the link to the Cuckoo Trail that Claire and I found blocked during construction almost a year ago. The two now connect, even if the bit that East Sussex Council dug up the verge of and closed the road for an entire Bank Holiday weekend to build is just six feet wide, so footpath, not cycle path, spec.

Ultimately, building a cycle network needs two simple things: money and power. Nations around the world have done this quickly thanks to sustained, decent levels of funding and support from politicians, and their officials. Cities around the world, including Cardiff, London and Leicester, built routes in weeks in response to a health emergency – the pandemic – and then they kept on going. With continuing climate and health emergencies, there's still a case for building at pace.

Sustrans, the charitable custodian of the network, does a great job designing routes with communities and local authorities, and running programmes that help people use those routes. What it can't do is adequately fund the network we need or ensure one landowner doesn't put the kibosh on someone's safe cycle route to school. It simply doesn't have the money or power.

We need a national cycle network as a spine of direct, strategic routes that sets the bar for connections nationwide; a national piece of infrastructure with the necessary funding and planning that regional and local officials can get behind and connect their own routes to. While most of our trips won't be from Edinburgh to London, along the way are thousands of connections between homes, businesses and outdoor spaces. The way we're doing it, we're not moving nearly fast enough to harness the power of cycling to reduce transport emissions, improve our health and provide affordable transport. In 2020 2% of all journeys were by bike – which is around the same as in 2012, 2002, 1992 and 1982. While cycling trips grew 11% after the pandemic, it's still 11% of 2% – and then they returned to pre-pandemic levels again. At the same time, more than a quarter of all trips in the Netherlands are cycled.

If we want to ramp up our efforts, we need only look to other European countries for inspiration, and in every successful case local and national government lent its finance and legislative heft to proceedings. Across Europe in 2020, in response to the pandemic, €1 billion went into cycling measures, creating 600 miles of new lanes, traffic-calming measures and car-free streets in a year. Paris led the way, rapidly expanding its network and slowly rebalancing public space in favour of walking and cycling. It heralded a total transformation of the city.

In 2021 the Flemish government set a target and budget for the 'Copenhagen plan', a 620-mile network of new cycle paths as part of its Covid recovery. The aim of the *fietssnelwegen* – fast cycle routes – was to provide alternatives to driving for everyday trips. The routes would be direct and separate from traffic, enabling riders to maintain a constant speed (15mph) with little to no stopping – just like roads. Ambitious as this was, the government underestimated regional enthusiasm for this transformation. Municipalities invested more than their agreed half of the funds and by the end of 2022 Flanders had exceeded its original target, before more than doubling it to 1250 miles. In the process the biggest cycling investment in the history of Belgium, a €32 million bridge, went in. Meanwhile, in 2022–23, Wales' active travel budget was £60 million; in Scotland it was £150 million and in Northern Ireland £12m (capital spend only).

Sustrans' CEO Xavier Brice would argue the NCN needs to stay in Sustrans' hands; it escapes some of the 'culture wars' narrative if it's a charity delivering on its charitable goals; it's not the council or the government snatching land away. However, wonderful as Sustrans' work is, it doesn't have the powers or the funding to manage and grow a national network of cycle routes – and its 'masterplan' ambitions to re-grow the NCN to just 17,000 miles in length reflects this. The government, using an agency with the necessary powers and funding, needs to treat it as crucial infrastructure, for anything from tourism to everyday trips – the same as road or rail, say. That means it needs the funding and the political backing enjoyed by other pieces of transport infrastructure – and a relevant body to manage it. Arguably, Active Travel England already manages England's NCN by funding it, bit by bit, and setting standards and conditions for that funding, but it doesn't set strategic targets or protections for it. We need to go further, faster.

Different departments want different things. Health departments want people to be more physically active. Environment departments to meet air quality and carbon reduction targets. Education wants kids arriving at school alert and happy, which active school journeys do. Business wants people healthy and productive, taking fewer sick days, which active commutes do. Local councils want thriving high streets. Cycling and walking policies tick all these boxes and more.

Active Travel England is working to update its Propensity to Cycle Tool – the one that calculated 10% of Cornish commutes could be cycled – to include all journeys, not just commutes. This will reveal how many more rural trips are possible by bike than we first suspected and will help develop even more understanding of routes. This is important work, but it's a technical solution to a political problem. In cycle-friendly nations cycling and walking is just something that's delivered as part of a nation's transport networks, because it makes obvious sense.

We need a cycling prime minister to bring these things together, but until then, we need politicians at the local and national level to understand that people want to cycle. In every representative poll, between two thirds and four fifths of us say we do, and that we support the investment and the reallocation of road space to achieve this. In Scotland, Wales and in our city regions, leaders are waking up to cycling's potential. Every year a million cyclists go by the Palace of Westminster in London, on a big, protected bike lane; regular people who happen to be travelling on bikes, not just cyclists in Lycra. Our MPs see these people when they go to work and there will be someone in their department who cycles in. However, none of our nations are moving anywhere near fast enough to meet carbon reduction targets – the UK needs to cut motor traffic by at least 20% if we hope to fend off the worst of global heating.

We already have organisations with the power, expertise and funds to deliver a substantial cycling network in the UK rapidly – only our national trunk roads bodies have been busy building us roads we don't need, and can't afford, financially or environmentally. We could deliver the NCN to a decent quality within a handful of years if we refocused their power and funds to the task. A taxpayer-funded organisation whose sole purpose it is to lobby for and build roads, apparently regardless of whether we need them, has no place in modern Britain.

Five of England's biggest road projects, worth £16 billion, represent 'poor' or 'low' value for taxpayers' money, equivalent to most of the £18 billion needed for routes so people across England could walk or cycle for half of all short trips. As well as the power, money and engineering expertise, they own considerable swathes of land and are well-resourced and well-practised at acquiring more. They have shown they can do it, when motivated. Let's follow Wales' example: if a road doesn't improve cycling, walking and public transport provision, we shouldn't be building it. Let's transfer our highways body to our active travel body, ATE, led by people who can deliver cycling, walking and wheeling routes at pace. Let's use National Highways to repair our badly crumbling existing roads with their billions' worth of repair backlog instead.

Much of this isn't that controversial. Bottom line, we can all agree on a few things: that we want safer, quieter streets, cleaner air, cheaper transport options, places children can be independent, and ways for older people to keep their mobility and health for longer by staying active. So how do we get there? Happily, it's not super-complicated, but that's not to say it's easy.

1   **Fund it.** Stop expanding road capacity until we have delivered a comprehensive network of cycling and walking routes, a working public transport network, and an efficient freight system. We're way behind and we need to catch up. Funds for this are already there, they're just being frittered away on new and wider roads. Reallocate that money, as Wales is doing: fix potholes but halt climate-busting road projects.

2   **Be strategic.** We are at the crunch point of a climate and health crisis, and we need to act quickly. We need a four-year strategy, as we do for road and rail, to expand and deliver existing plans for national, regional and local networks of protected cycle paths, quiet lanes and neighbourhoods. Tackling road, rail and river crossings goes a long way towards this. Start in areas of highest demand, in each area. These networks need to be safe, convenient and direct.

3   **Work together.** If every national and local road authority were incentivised to work together we could roll out this network, in rough, in four years. When we resurface roads or dig them up, add in walking and cycling improvements. Nationally, a 'behind the hedgerow act' would allow highways and rail bodies to use land beside transport corridors for direct, rural cycle routes. Active Travel England staff could deliver this. Regional and local highways bodies can deliver the rest.

4   **Integration.** Into wider public transport networks. Cycle routes expand public transport catchment areas substantially, but they have to be consistent and continuous. Improving

and expanding the public transport services our cycleways link to, and vice versa, should be a transport priority.

5 **Empower it.** Cycle routes need legal status so they can't be randomly closed without warning or adequate diversions, blocked or built over. We need to treat them like any other piece of strategic infrastructure, so they are protected and prioritised, and things like compulsory purchase powers are used, where needed. Planning policy needs to work for cycleways, not against them.

6 **Accessibility.** No-one should be locked out of outdoor spaces; paths need to be accessible, which means a decent surface, camber and routing – and no barriers. Wheels for Wellbeing regularly updates its excellent *Guide to Inclusive Cycling*. Disabled people need to be part of the design process.

7 **Maintainance.** Unsexy but crucial. We have a long and inglorious history of failing to maintain our paths, slowly rendering them inaccessible. Maintenance is essential for people to feel confident using these paths. Sustrans' volunteers do an incredible job, but we can't leave upkeep of a crucial piece of infrastructure solely to dedicated retirees.

8 **Protection for users.** While most of us are careful behind the wheel, plenty aren't – with devastating consequences. A good network will design out most of the danger, but not all. Take the worst drivers off the road for good; introduce graded licensing for young drivers and use lifetime bans where appropriate. Speed limiting technology exists – we just need to deploy it and remove the 'exceptional hardship' clause that lets so many dangerous drivers off the hook.

9 **Ebike-fication.** Electric bikes make cycling more accessible, with substantial health benefits. Every other electric vehicle has enjoyed purchase subsidies in the UK, bar ebikes. They're cheaper than cars and cost very little to run, but up-front cost puts them out of reach for too many people and leaves us behind the rest of Europe on cycling. Purchase subsidies

substantially increase ebike uptake and with it the distances people can and will cycle.

10 **People power.** This is a clarion call to you. If we want to be able to cycle and walk more, to not have to rely on a car for so many journeys, we need to show our support for change, in our communities and beyond. Talk to your neighbours, local councillors, media outlets and your MPs. Changing the status quo is never easy, but if there is clamour, if there are votes, politicians will do it. If we don't speak up, the minority who want the status quo will win the argument simply by being loud enough.

The benefits of a proper network of nationwide routes would be many and wide-reaching. Physical inactivity is responsible for one in six UK deaths, equal to smoking; 20 minutes of exercise per day cuts the risk of developing depression by 31% and helps us do our jobs better. Unmitigated climate change costs 5–20% of GDP a year and growing, and increasingly it's costing lives and the ecosystems we depend on. The carbon benefits of switching just one trip per week to walking and cycling could cut our transport emissions substantially, and by up to a quarter.

I saw wonderful things across the NCN: the North Wales Coast Path, mile upon mile of seafront promenade. To avoid a busy road tunnel, east of Llanfairfechan, a metal structure carries the path along a cliff, linking promenade and country lane to make a beautiful, and rightfully revered, tourist route running along almost the entire coast. I rode beside Cambridge's guided busway, on the closest thing I've seen to a Dutch cycle path, where I saw the oldest woman I've seen cycling in the UK, in her eighties, riding as she probably has for decades. I saw city routes taking shape across Britain; new routes in Bristol, Glasgow, Cardiff and London, part of a slowly growing network. Exeter's Exe Estuary Trail is an absolute model of an excellent path that links the city with the countryside: smooth, wide and well signposted, with stunning views, it truly is cycling heaven.

Buckinghamshire is developing a county-wide network of greenways, for everyday journeys and tourism. A rural path John Grimshaw led on, the Waddesdon Greenway, inspired local politicians who saw the route's potential and persuaded their Buckinghamshire colleagues they all need greenways. Within a couple of years, Waddesdon was carrying 160,000 users annually, for leisure and practical trips. Staffordshire is now doing the same. Oxfordshire closed a country lane to through traffic near Didcot, making a formerly dangerous road safe for cycling.

I also saw terrible routes. In Bristol NCN 'improvements' through the city centre were astonishingly bad. Cyclists arriving by train in the hometown of the NCN, are greeted with an incredibly inconvenient series of road crossings on shared pavements and must even cross uneven tree pits, with intermittent cycle lanes that give way at every side road – a decade behind current standards, and infuriating and time-consuming to use.

Wales and Scotland are genuinely moving forward, although progress is patchy and they could do more, and faster. Cities like London, Manchester, Leicester and Coventry, as part of devolved metro mayor regions, are investing in cycling and walking networks. These are places with a vision, political leadership and funding. Plans for a cycleway around HS2, the best value element of the entire project and the only benefit local communities will see, are being revitalised. This could become a true, high-quality national spine of cycle routes, linking communities via bridleways and haul roads, and providing crossings of the railway for local trips and longer adventures.

We've seen what consistent, sustained investment for cycling has done for a decade in London – it's made cycling an option for normal people. We can no longer say, we're not the Netherlands. We are no different from any other cycle-friendly nation, we just need to believe the overwhelming evidence before us and the sheer possibility it offers.

———

My second bout of Covid is closely followed by bacterial tonsillitis; six weeks of annoying illness and exhaustion, and a lot of time stuck indoors. The first place I go to rebuild my strength, without really thinking about it, is my closest stretch of NCN. I take the ebike gingerly to a path that runs along the River Lea and north through a strip of wood to Hackney Marshes, and I only notice I've found my way back to it, as if by homing instinct, when a blue NCN sticker, stuck to a noticeboard, catches my eye. Over the river and underneath a main road, the marshes open up beside me. It's a place I return to regularly now, before work or after work, just for a ride and to see the bramble flowers turn to green berries that ripen over the summer and turn red in autumn. The trains rattle by, the river smoothly passes and the odd kestrel flutters industriously overhead.

Weeks later, still weak, on a whim I take the pink ebike to ride the Devon Coast to Coast. After a year's exploration I realise I see things differently. It starts with the little blue and red signs. At the beginning I saw them as an irritant – they were too small, too erratic, too unreliable – but in the past year I've learned to see in them the love that goes into these routes, in an almost total absence of government support.

I've seen how important these routes are, and how well used they are, albeit too often squashed and compromised just when we need them. Imagine what they could do if we cared for them properly. For me, after more than a decade of regular cycling, and too many scary experiences on the roads, my tolerance of traffic danger is pretty low. Today I'm cycling on genuinely quiet country lanes alongside sparrows, dancing in the air at 20mph beside me. I spot three buzzards on the edge of Dartmoor, floating in circular formation, riding upward on the same thermal current. A large rabbit looks me in the eye from a verge. Nonchalant Dartmoor ponies studiously ignore passing humans, standing marvellously aloof on the moor as one couple tries to get a selfie. Birdsong accompanies my ride as spring unfurls about me, leaving behind the long, grey, dark months of winter. In my exhausted state it brings tears to my eyes.

CODA

In early 2023 Richard Ackroyd and his team constructed the next 1.3km of their missing link in Frome, from the Radstock end. They finally got permission from Network Rail to build alongside the live track, separated by a new fence. In freezing winds, Geoff Pell, an early Sustrans man, hoisted large hunks of metal from a dismantled footbridge off a trailer to support an earth bank. By June they had finished clearing and laying 800 tonnes of ballast on the path, and were trying to find the money to surface it. They've put a bench up at the end of the new stretch with a penny farthing-shaped bike rack. In summer 2023 they finished another stretch: a 450m extension at the Frome end, following the river. It is now even more tantalisingly close to completion!

Richard drives me to Shepton Mallet to meet John Grimshaw and Caroline Levett one last time, for the opening of the two new paths from last year's work camp. We stand with officials as an emotional Ros Wyke and Kelly Knight celebrate their work: 400 new native trees planted, the stone wall and grit path completed by professionals, and the new link under the rail bridge freshly tarmacked. The next sections of the Somerset Circle are already under discussion with the new county-wide local authority and I returned for another work camp there in September 2023.

Claire is still daydreaming. We continue to take cycle trips together, sometimes with her partner too.

Andy Cox moved back to the Metropolitan Police, but his work on road safety continues, and the annual Andy Cox Challenge goes from strength to strength.

Ned Boulting is writing more books, cycling around London and commentating on the Tour de France as usual. Our podcast, *Streets Ahead*, continues.

Chris Boardman is still leading Active Travel England and riding away from the traffic…

Gravesend's atmospheric alley has since been unblocked and is once again open for business.

Isabelle Clement continues her work making cycling accessible to more disabled people nationwide. By the following summer Merton Council, with Transport for London funding, had upgraded a section of Isabelle's beloved Wandle Trail in south London to a wide, sealed, wheelchair-friendly surface, and replaced the wonky railway sleepers with a proper walking and cycling bridge. A second bridge was also replaced and signage on the National Trust property improved by Sustrans.

In Scotland, Mahnoor got a new bike to replace the stolen one, and continues to cycle and lead women's rides in and around Glasgow.

By April 2024, Sustrans still didn't have its UK government grant for the NCN in England confirmed for the closing financial year, but they were busily finishing projects from the previous financial year and, one imagines, crossing their fingers…

Sustrans is working on a new signage strategy, Xavier tells me.

In early 2024 a report by the Institute for Public Policy Research (IPPR) concluded that the NCN needs a ten-year investment plan. The next government, it noted, has an opportunity to correct the historic underfunding of active travel, creating a fairer society with affordable active transport as well as reaping substantial rewards for public investment. For £100m per year, rising to £300m per year by 2030, the NCN could meet its potential for our health, the economy and the environment. That amounts to just £3 per person per year over a decade – part of a £35 per capita investment in active travel infrastructure the NPPR recommended for England by 2029, with a further £15 on supporting measures. This would bring England up to Scotland's investment levels. The report noted money spent on cycling and walking returns on average £5.62 per £1 spent, more than double the average £2.50 for road building.

APPENDIX:
THE FOUNDERS OF A NETWORK

Culture war players would have you believe cycle campaigners are well-heeled individuals secretly funded by wealthy, shadowy forces, apparently intent on making us get on our bikes. Hopefully this book illustrates that the reality is far from it. Over the years countless individuals and groups have worked together, many as volunteers, to achieve something as simple and innocent as a safe cycle route – possibly even one near to where you live. There are so many of these unsung heroes, who sit through endless meetings year after year, witnessing glacial progress, if there's any at all. People who go out on cold, wet days to dig, drag, chop and improve something that will, one day, become a cycle path. Who use all of their skills and strength, without thanks or, often, much recognition. When John Grimshaw, concerned this narrative made him seem too much of a hero, suggested mentioning some of them, a shared list started to grow. It still worries me as I know there will be people who are not on it who should be. Writing this book gave me a glimpse of some of this number and the sheer determination of their efforts. I raise my mug of tea to these people, and the many in the UK and around the world who are not on it, who perhaps should be.

As John Grimshaw put it: 'Beyond the Sustrans team there were numerous other crucial and committed parties including local authorities the length and breadth of the country, the Forestry Commission, and British Waterways Board. It simply cannot be emphasised enough that the whole NCN was the product of numerous players, funders and developers where Sustrans was privileged to play a coordinating role.' Some of the wording below is John's.

People involved in Cyclebag, from 1977 onwards: Secretary and Treasurer: Bill Clarke. Deputy Chairmen of Cyclebag: George Platts, Tony Geeson. Treasurers: George Poole; Chris Eker, who was an also area agent along with: Will Adams; Pat Blundell; Andrew Nicholls; Sharon Mills; David Leeks; Roger Levett; Geoff Perrett; Ginny Duggan (who also did publicity); Ed Raw; Gerry Brooke. Schools officer: Robin Sleeman. Research: Pete Terry. Legal Advisors: Andrew Webb, Roger Hicks. Printers: Digby Norton; Edwin Robson. Rally Secretary: John Barnes. Social Secretary: Peter Featherstone. Artists: Adrian Shaw; Rod Nelson; James Bruges; Richard Childs.

Volunteers: Nick Andrews, Anne Beyer, Hugh Barton; John Brown; Nick Bachellor; Chris Bocci; Wilf Burton; Bob Cable; Georgina Carless; Paul Constable; Marcus Cleaver; Bob Dark; Rennie Dickens; George Easton; Nick Fox; Dave Fernley; Nick Fife; Richard Fowler; Bob Green; Roger Hall; John Howard; Sue and Trevor Habershaw; Sue Jones; Axel Knutson; Cath Leendertz; Louise Naylor; Nick Otty; John Potter; Pete Standing; George Ferguson; Alastair Sawday; Mark Turner; Amanda Theunnissen; Nick Watts; Cathy Woodhead; Les Wilkins; Richard Walker.

Also involved in early Cyclebag years were Cycling UK (then CTC), the Bristol Pedestrian Association, Friends of the Earth, Bishopston Residents Association, Filmacs Cycle Shop, Cymo Cycles, Overbury's Cycles and the Metropole Cinema.

Sustainable Transport, from 1979 onwards: Julia Green; Nick Colling; Julia Colling; Sue Learner; Andrew Nicholson; Chris Hutt; George Platts (director); John Grimshaw (honorary engineer). Photography: David Sproxton; Ben Searle; Marco Hnutiak.

The Board included: Anne Billingham who built the Swindon Old Town routes with men from the Probation Service; Ron Healey in York who took routes through to the York and Selby Line; Pam Ashton who piloted the Liverpool Loop Line through and went on to deliver the Trans Pennine Trail; Chris Curling who was the solicitor; Sandy Scotland who handled accounts.

The 1984 *Study of Disused Railways in England and Wales* relied on many volunteers to carry out the surveys. Richard Biddulph drew up the document, which Peggy Foxwell typed. The early Manpower Services Schemes provided for supervisors, some of whom went on to become core staff, as well as funding some office staff. David Parkes managed the construction of the Pill Tow Path route; John Hughes oversaw the reconstruction of the Kennet and Avon Towpath all the way from Bath to Devises; David Gray first built the Derby and Melbourne Project before moving to Consett to build the Consett and Sunderland path, which he developed into the C2C route; Peter Foster supervised Derby and York before moving over to deal with the Liverpool Loop Line. Dave Jackson supervised the York and Selby construction and then continued to lead the practical construction works all over Yorkshire. Tony Grant ran the Edinburgh and Glasgow offices and went on to be Regional Manager for Scotland. Dave Holliday was the Engineer for all the Scottish projects. Mike Chown built up a considerable portfolio of projects in Wales. Lewis Semple built the Strawberry Line project from Axbridge to Cheddar, and then assisted in the administration of Sustrans for many years. Andrew Combes led early work camp projects.

Sustrans Board members included a number of dedicated trustees including: Jeff Vintner, an expert of Railway Paths; Caroline Levett who led the way to regular quarterly site inspections; Andy Haynes looked after Stratford-upon-Avon and kept a cool head in times of crisis; Richard Farrant who served as Chairman in the Millennium years.

Key team members in the period building up to the 1995 Millennium award: Don Mathew, an invaluable link to the cycling campaign world; Patrick Davis managed the East Midlands; John Palmer covered South Wales; Phil Insall focused on health and active travel; John Naylor worked for Groundwork to drive through the West Cumbria network; Mark Tucker led on land negotiation; Sue Otty as in-house solicitor completing land transactions; Simon Ballantine as bridge engineer; Simon Talbot Ponsonby who coordinated the whole programme; Carol Freeman who developed the membership scheme ahead of the Millennium bid; Malcolm Shepherd the financial director; Katy Hallett led the public arts and sculpture programme;

Michael Woods was the ecologist; Andy Whitehead early route surveyor on safe routes to schools; Paul Osbourne developed the Schools programme. David Hall, route negotiator in Yorkshire and later Regional Manager for the area. Mike Thornborough looked after railway lands. Greg Beecroft led the British Rail Property Board and was a crucial player. Isobel Stoddart organised the key mass rides from Inverness to Dover and Belfast to Land's End which drove forward the Millennium bid.

The Millennium years required a great deal more support, including new regional managers who had to hit the ground running. Simon Pratt took on Berkshire, Buckinghamshire and Oxfordshire; Nigel Brigham covered east Anglia along with Nicola Jones for Lincolnshire; Mark Strong took on the South East; Jeremy Isles managed London; Ben Hamilton-Baillie looked after the South West and Wales; Steven Patterson was Northern Ireland; David Judd developed the routes in west Wales; Graham Cornish made the routes in Devon. The GIS mapping team were critical and included: Chris Sherrington, Andy Wighthead, Adam Hillman and Richard Sanders. The engineers who were tasked with building routes not supplied by local authorities or others included: Jane Ogilvy, Tony Russel, Glyn Evans and Ryland Jones. Volunteers and the new route ranger teams were coordinated by Aunna Elm and Tony Ambrose. Andy Small, ranger for the West Cumbria network, started at this time and continues today. Lucy Thorpe managed the press; Andy Cope coordinated statistical analysis of route usage and public attitudes; Gill Walker looked after staff. Rae Heading was John's PA and Nicola Stinchcombe volunteered on records and filing. Jane Debney produced all the maps for the trailblazing rides. Sue Bergin, like many contemporaries, is still campaigning for the National Cycle Network in Norwich and beyond. Sibylle Riesen was fundraising. The National Cycling Network Steering Group was led by Sir Donald Miller.

REFERENCES

All references accessed between May 2022 and February 2024

INTRODUCTION: FLIGHT

1. '...in England 71% of all trips we made were less than five miles.' Department for Transport National Travel Survey (2022): https://www .gov.uk/government/statistics/national-travel-survey-2022/national -travel-survey-2022-mode-share-journey-lengths-and-trends-in -public-transport-use
2. '...we use a motor vehicle for 67% of trips of less than five miles.' Ibid.
3. '...only 26% of us have ever heard of the NCN.' Sustrans (2018). *Paths for everyone; Sustrans' review of the National Cycle Network 2018*: https://www.sustrans.org.uk/media/2804/paths_for_everyone_ncn _review_report_2018.pdf
4. 'We spend, on average, 13% of our gross income on them...' Walker, P., 'Entrenched car culture' leaves millions of Britons in transport poverty. *Guardian* (2023): https://www.theguardian.com/uk-news/2023/jan /09/entrenched-car-culture-leaves-millions-of-britons-in-transport -poverty
5. 'Taxpayers have forked out roughly £80 billion...' *Office for Budget Responsibility Economic and Fiscal Outlook.* OBR (March 2023): https:// obr.uk/docs/dlm_uploads/OBR-EFO-March-2023_Web_Accessible .pdf
6. '...research found increased our carbon emissions by 7%.' Evans, S., Analysis: Fuel-duty freezes have increased UK CO_2 emissions by up to 7%. *Carbon Brief* (2023): https://www.carbonbrief.org/analysis-fuel -duty-freezes-have-increased-uk-co2-emissions-by-up-to-7
7. 'Transport is the single biggest contributor to our carbon emissions – 34% of our total...' *Provisional UK greenhouse gas emissions national statistics 2022.* Department for Energy Security and Net Zero (2023):

https://www.gov.uk/government/statistics/provisional-uk-greenhouse
-gas-emissions-national-statistics-2022

8. '...physical inactivity is responsible for one in six deaths in the UK, a toll equal to smoking... this costs the UK £7.4 billion annually and the NHS almost £1 billion.' *Physical Activity: Applying All Our Health*. Office for Health Improvement and Disparities (2022): https://www .gov.uk/government/publications/physical-activity-applying-all-our -health/physical-activity-applying-all-our-health

9. 'Getting active can help prevent colon cancer...' *Gear Change: A bold vision for cycling and walking*. Department for Transport (July 2020): https://assets.publishing.service.gov.uk/government/uploads/system/ uploads/attachment_data/file/904146/gear-change-a-bold-vision-for -cycling-and-walking.pdf

10. 'Even if we cycled just once a week...' Brand, C. et al. The climate change mitigation impacts of active travel: Evidence from a longitudinal panel study in seven European cities. *Global Environmental Change*, 67 (2021): https://www.sciencedirect.com/science/article/abs /pii/S0959378021000030?via%3Dihub

11. 'The pandemic saw a cycling renaissance...' Official Statistics. The impact of the coronavirus pandemic on walking and cycling statistics, England: 2020. Department for Transport (September 2021): https:// www.gov.uk/government/statistics/walking-and-cycling-statistics -england-2020/the-impact-of-the-coronavirus-pandemic-on-walking -and-cycling-statistics-england-2020

12. '...visitor numbers on the NCN rose by 19%.' Sustrans. *Paths for Everyone: 3 Years On. 2018-2021 Progress Update* (2022): https://www.sustrans.org .uk/media/9991/sustrans-p4e-three-years-on-eng-digital.pdf

13. 'In Leicester, one of the many cities to embrace the challenge, a mile per week of new main-road bike lanes were rolled out at their peak, at just over £29,000 per mile – a bargain basement price when you consider a trunk road comes in somewhere at around £1 billion per mile': https:// news.leicester.gov.uk/news-articles/2020/may/city-s-covid-19-trans- port-recovery-plan-published/; https://www.whatdotheyknow.com/ request/emergency_active_travel_fund_9

14. '...the charity in charge of the NCN, would cut 25% of the network, or de-designate it...' Laker, L. National Cycle Network cuts a quarter of its routes on safety grounds. *Guardian* (19 July 2020): https://www

.theguardian.com/travel/2020/jul/19/national-cycle-network-sustrans
-cuts-quarter-uk-routes-safety-grounds

15. 'more than 16,000 barriers on its traffic-free routes.' Sustrans. *Paths for everyone: Sustrans' review of the National Cycle Network 2018* (2018): https://www.sustrans.org.uk/media/2804/paths_for_everyone_ncn _review_report_2018.pdf

16. '…Sustrans' CEO, Xavier Brice, admitted to me…' Hookham, M. and Laker, L. Sustrans charity wants £2.8bn revamp for 'crap' cycle trails. *Times* (11 November 2018): https://www.thetimes.co.uk/article/char- ity-wants-2-8bn-revamp-for-crap-cycle-trails-to-get-britain-on-its -bike-rrmqm63f3

17. '…by 2020 4.9 million people took 75 million trips on it…' Sustrans. *Paths for Everyone: 3 Years On. 2018-2021 Progress Update* (2022): https://www.sustrans.org.uk/media/9991/sustrans-p4e-three-years -on-eng-digital.pdf

18. '…it actually carries more walking trips…' Sustrans. *Paths for everyone: Sustrans' review of the National Cycle Network 2018* (2018): https:// www.sustrans.org.uk/media/2804/paths_for_everyone_ncn_review _report_2018.pdf

19. 'By May 2021 the huge growth in cycling on the quiet roads of 2020 were subsiding…'. Official Statistics. Cycling index, England. Department for Transport (2023): https://www.gov.uk/government/ statistics/cycling-index-england/cycling-index-england#chart-1

20. '…amid resurgent traffic levels.' Grant, A. UK road traffic back at pre-Covid levels. *Fleet World* (2021): https://fleetworld.co.uk/uk-road -traffic-back-at-pre-covid-levels/

21. '…the NCN totals more than 12,000 miles.' Sustrans. *Paths for Everyone: 3 Years On. 2018-2021 Progress Update* (2022): https://www.sustrans .org.uk/media/9991/sustrans-p4e-three-years-on-eng-digital.pdf

1: FALLING OUT

1. '…research shows people on foot and bikes spend more in shops than those who arrive by car'. *Walking & Cycling: the economic bene- fits.* Transport for London (2018): https://content.tfl.gov.uk/walking -cycling-economic-benefits-summary-pack.pdf

2. '…polls found more than three quarters of people supported reducing traffic in their local area, and more than two thirds the reallocation

of road space for walking and cycling'. *Gear Change: One Year On.* Department for Transport (2021). https://assets.publishing.service .gov.uk/government/uploads/system/uploads/attachment_data/file /1007815/gear-change-one-year-on.pdf

3. '…the Ordnance Survey map's NCN layer…' Ordnance Survey online map: https://osmaps.ordnancesurvey.co.uk/ncn

2: FOUNDING A NETWORK

1. 'In the 1950s, cycling was a very normal means of transport in the UK…' Hembrow, D. A View From the Cycle Path: The myth of the 'tipping point' and the fragility of cycling. (12 June 2014): http://www .aviewfromthecyclepath.com/2014/06/the-myth-of-tipping-point -and-fragility.html

2. 'In 1961, partially cannibalised by the growth in motor transport and air travel…' Beeching, R., (1963). *The Reshaping of British Railways, Part 1: Report.* London. Her Majesty's Stationery Office (1963): https:// www.railwaysarchive.co.uk/documents/BRB_Beech001a.pdf

3. 'In 1966, as traffic volumes had grown, so had road casualties,' and 'By the late 1970s and early 1980s the situation had improved slightly…' *Reported road casualties Great Britain: 2015 annual report.* Factors affecting reported road casualties. Department for Transport (2016): https://assets.publishing.service.gov.uk/government/uploads/system/ uploads/attachment_data/file/556406/rrcgb2015-02.pdf

4. 'Even as the population increased by two million in two decades and vehicle miles tripled…' *Overview of the UK population.* Office for National Statistics (2022): https://www.ons.gov.uk/peoplepopulatio nandcommunity/populationandmigration/populationestimates/arti- cles/overviewoftheukpopulation/2020

5. '…per mile travelled, road users back then…' Annual distance trav- elled by cars, vans and taxis in Great Britain (UK) from 1960 to 2017. Statista: https://www.statista.com/statistics/467964/total-distance -travelled-by-cars-vans-or-taxis-great-britain/

6. 'Public transport was on the decline, too…' Gunn, S. *The History of Transport Systems in the UK.* Government Office for Science. Centre for Urban History, University of Leicester (2018): https://assets .publishing.service.gov.uk/government/uploads/system/uploads/ attachment_data/file/761929/Historyoftransport.pdf

7. 'The Green Cross Code was relaunched in 1978...' The history of the Green Cross Code. Rhondda Cynon Taf council website: https://www.rctcbc.gov.uk/EN/Council/Performancebudgetsandspending/Councilperformance/RelatedDocuments/CPR181920/PLACELinks/GreenCrossCode.pdf

8. 'Cyclists weren't always on board with cycling improvements...' and 'As cycling historian Carlton Reid put it...' Reid, C. *Roads Were Not Built for Cars*. Front Page Creations (2015).

9. 'In 1977 the Bristol branch of the environmental campaign group Friends of the Earth...' Wickers, D. *Millennium Miles: The Story of the National Cycle Network*. GB Publications Ltd (2000).

10. 'In 1974 John had written a 22-page report...' Grimshaw, J. *Cycling in Bristol* (1974).

11. '...on top of the flat ballast they poured 1600 tonnes of limestone dust.' *The Railway Path & Cycle Route Project*. Railway Path Project (1986) (John Grimshaw copy).

12. '...the government, seeing the potential for other traffic-free paths, commissioned John Grimshaw & Associates...' *Study of Disused Railways in England and Wales: Potential Cycle Routes: A Study for the Department of Transport*. John Grimshaw & Associates. H.M Stationery Office (1982).

13. 'On the job "conditions were fairly rudimentary," a report from the time reads...' *The Railway Path & Cycle Route Project*. Railway Path Project (1986) (John Grimshaw copy).

14. 'Around 500 volunteers finished the final quarter of a mile of the route in four days over the spring bank holiday of 1985, during a break in railway operations.' *The Railway Path & Cycle Route Project*. Railway Path Project (1986) (John Grimshaw copy).

15. 'In 1978, the then Labour government launched a youth training scheme...' Youth Opportunities Programme. Wikipedia: https://en.wikipedia.org/wiki/Youth_Opportunities_Programme

16. 'YOP, and similar employment schemes that followed it...' Youth Policies in the UK: A Chronological Map. School of Sociology and Criminology, Keele University: https://web.archive.org/web/20081006195150/http://www.keele.ac.uk/depts/so/youthchron/Education/8090educ.htm

17. 'Their first commission outside the Bristol area...' The Birth of the National Cycle Network – an interview with John Grimshaw. Railway to Greenway (2008): https://railwaytogreenway.org/archive/the-birth-of-the-national-cycle-network-an-interview-with-john-grimshaw/

18. 'That year Margaret Thatcher launched "roads for prosperity". Roads for Prosperity. Wikipedia: https://en.wikipedia.org/wiki/Roads_for_Prosperity

19. 'In 1991 the charity proposed a 1000-mile route...' Wickers, D. *Millennium Miles: The Story of the National Cycle Network*. GB Publications Ltd (2000).

20. 'Sustrans also produced a map comparing the Dutch and UK national cycle networks at the time.' Sustrans. *Paths for People 15 Year Review, Incorporating Annual Report 1992-3* (1993).

21. '...helping grow the charity's supporters from 178 friends of Sustrans to 9000 by 1995.' Rocco, F. The Great Millennium Lottery. *Independent* (1 January 1995): https://www.independent.co.uk/arts-entertainment/the-great-millennium-lottery-1566247.html

22. 'In 1993, the Danish national cycle route network opened...' Eurovelo for Professionals: History of EuroVelo: https://pro.eurovelo.com/organisation/history

23. '...as the charity later described it in its book, *Millennium Miles*' and 're-us[ing] redundant railway lines, neglected tow-paths and derelict land, transforming urban and rural wasteland into popular and attractive public space.' Wickers, D. *Millennium Miles: The Story of the National Cycle Network*. GB Publications Ltd (2000).

24. 'The appendix to the bid...' Sustrans. The National Cycle Network bid document: Appendix (1995).

25. 'Sustrans' account of the plans, in *Millennium Miles*, claimed it was "the most extensive transport construction since the motorways".' Wickers, D. *Millennium Miles: The Story of the National Cycle Network*. GB Publications Ltd (2000).

26. 'Thanks in part to "very enthusiastic local authorities", as John recalls in *Millennium Miles*.' Wickers, D. *Millennium Miles: The Story of the National Cycle Network*. GB Publications Ltd (2000).

4: BACK TO THE BEGINNING ON THE BRISTOL
AND BATH PATH

1. 'Caroline mentions that Bennerley Viaduct...' The Friends of Bennerley Viaduct. Bennerley Viaduct Official Opening Ceremony Takes Place (8 August 2022): https://www.bennerleyviaduct.org.uk/?p=2963

2. 'Owned by Railway Paths...' Railway Paths website: https://www.rail-waypaths.org.uk/

5: MAPS, A MURDERER AND MUD ON THE KENT
AND SUSSEX COASTS

1. 'This goes for both driving, where just 15% of journeys are commutes...' *National Travel Survey 2021. Household car availability and trends in car trips.* Department for Transport (31 August 2022): https://www.gov.uk/government/statistics/national-travel-survey-2021/national-travel-survey-2021-household-car-availability-and-trends-in-car-trips

2. '...and cycling, where 27% of trips are commutes.' *National Travel Survey 2021. Active Travel.* Department for Transport (31 August 2022): https://www.gov.uk/government/statistics/national-travel-survey-2021/national-travel-survey-2021-active-travel#trends-in-cycling-trips

3. 'In fact, just under a quarter of our trips (23%) are for leisure.' *Transport Statistics Great Britain: 2022 Domestic Travel.* Department for Transport (15 December 2022): https://www.gov.uk/government/statistics/transport-statistics-great-britain-2022/transport-statistics-great-britain-2022-domestic-travel

4. '...56% of journeys on the network are for "functional reasons".' Sustrans. *Paths for everyone: Sustrans' review of the National Cycle Network 2018.* (2018): https://www.sustrans.org.uk/media/2804/paths_for_everyone_ncn_review_report_2018.pdf

5. 'With 26% of people inactive between 2021-22...' *Sport England Active Lives Adult Survey November 2021-22 Report* (2023): https://sportengland-production-files.s3.eu-west-2.amazonaws.com/s3fs-public/2023-04/Active%20Lives%20Adult%20Survey%20November%202021-22%20Report.pdf?VersionId=ln4PN2X02DZ1LF18btg aj5KFHxoMio90

6. '...on the busy Kent coast anywhere between 15% to above 30% of commutes...' Lovelace, R., Goodman, A., Aldred, R., Berkoff, N., Abbas, A. and Woodcock, J. The Propensity to Cycle Tool: An open source online system for sustainable transport planning. *Journal of Transport and Land Use*, 10(1) (2017): https://doi.org/10.5198/jtlu.2016.862

7. 'With 43% of all urban and town journeys in England shorter than two miles...' *Decarbonising Transport: A Better, Greener Britain.*

Department for Transport (2021): https://assets.publishing.service
.gov.uk/government/uploads/system/uploads/attachment_data/file
/1009448/decarbonising-transport-a-better-greener-britain.pdf

8.   '…funded with more than half a million pounds from the trunk roads
     body, National Highways.' Sustrans. More than £500,000 to improve
     National Cycle Network in Dover. Sustrans (20 October 2019): https://
     www.sustrans.org.uk/our-blog/news/2019/november/more-than-500
     -000-to-improve-national-cycle-network-in-dover

6: MILLENNIUM MILES, MOSS AND AN OMERTA

1.   'At its launch, Sustrans believed the NCN had three purposes…'
     Cotton, N. and Grimshaw, J. *The Official Guide to the National Cycle
     Network*. Sustrans (2002).

2.   'Sustrans estimated the 30-year return on these bridges to be up to
     £8 for every £1 invested.' Sustrans. Dr Adrian Davis, Living Streets
     and The TAS Partnership. *Active Travel and Economic Performance:
     A 'what works' review of evidence from cycling and walking schemes.*
     (2017): https://www.sustrans.org.uk/media/4472/4472.pdf

3.   '…much of this in health benefits.' iConnect and Sustrans. *Fit for Life:
     Independent research into the public health benefits of new walking
     and cycling routes* (2016): https://www.sustrans.org.uk/media/3691/
     sustrans-fit-for-life.pdf

4.   'Office staff would jokingly pin a *Bike Mag* article on the noticeboard…'
     Curry, L. Champion of the Cause. *The Bike Mag* (1995). Spring 1995
     issue, pp 17-19

5.   '…by 2014 Sustrans had gained a place on the UK's top 100 charities
     list…' Mason, T. Sustrans takes its place among UK's top 100 charities.
     Civil Society News (3 April 2014): https://www.civilsociety.co.uk/news
     /sustrans-takes-its-place-among-uk-s-top-100-charities.html

6.   'There wasn't a huge amount of quantity, though, either.' Brice, X. The
     United Kingdom's National Cycle Network: Paths for Everyone, Past,
     Present and Future. In: Pileri, P. and Moscarelli, R. (eds). *Cycling &
     Walking for Regional Development*. Research for Development series.
     Springer, Cham (2021): https://doi.org/10.1007/978-3-030-44003-9
     _14

7.   'The money Westminster did spend on cycling had an impact…'
     Sloman, L., Dennis, S., Hopkinson, L., Goodman, A., Farla, K., Hiblin, B.

and Turner, J. (2019). *Summary and Synthesis of Evidence: Cycle City Ambition Programme 2013-2018*. Department for Transport (2019): https://assets.publishing.service.gov.uk/government/uploads/system /uploads/attachment_data/file/1007473/summary-and-synthesis-of -evidence-cycle-city-ambition-programme-2013-to-2018.pdf

8. '...many roads, by then 67% of the network...' Sustrans. *Paths for everyone: Sustrans' review of the National Cycle Network 2018* (2018): https://www.sustrans.org.uk/media/2804/paths_for_everyone_ncn _review_report_2018.pdf

9. 'The vision behind the 'For Everyone' approach...' Ibid.

10. 'While the review characterised more than half of the network (53%) as "good"...' Ibid.

11. '...6000 NCN users, surveyed online as part of this reckoning...' Coded user survey responses with counts for each grouping. Sustrans (2018).

12. 'in 2018 he [Xavier Brice] told me ... people had had enough of the crap bits of the NCN, and they needed fixing.' Hookham, M. and Laker, L. Sustrans charity wants £2.8bn revamp for 'crap' cycle trails. *Times* (11 November 2018): https://www.thetimes.co.uk/article/charity -wants-2-8bn-revamp-for-crap-cycle-trails-to-get-britain-on-its-bike -rrmqm63f3

13. 'In 2020 the charity removed its branding from the worst quarter of the network...' Laker, L. National Cycle Network cuts a quarter of its routes on safety grounds. *Guardian* (19 July 2020): https://www .theguardian.com/travel/2020/jul/19/national-cycle-network-sustrans -cuts-quarter-uk-routes-safety-grounds

14. 'The charity's ambitions ramped up again.' Laker, L. Cycling charity launches ambitious plan to boost UK-wide path network. *Guardian* (16 February 2022): https://www.theguardian.com/lifeandstyle/2022 /feb/16/cycling-charity-launches-ambitious-plan-to-boost-uk-wide -path-network

15. 'The Dutch national cycle network started in the 1920s and 1930s.' Dekker, H-J. *Cycling Pathways: The Politics and Governance of Dutch Cycling Infrastructure, 1920-2020*. Amsterdam University Press (2021).

16. '...a group of French activists began lobbying...' Velo & Territoires, National Cycle Route Plan. (Updated 4 March 2023): https://www.velo -territoires.org/schemas-itineraires/schema-national/

17. '…the French government claimed there were now 50,000km of cycle routes…' Ibid.
18. 'supporting measures over the following four years, with €250 million a year for bike routes alone…' De Clercq, G. France to spend 2 billion euros to boost bicycle usage. Reuters (5 May 2023): https://www.reuters.com/world/europe/france-spend-2-billion-euros-boost-bicycle-usage-2023-05-05/

7: CRIME AND ACCIDENTAL PUNISHMENT ON THE ISLE OF WIGHT

1. '…his strategy to target lawbreaking drivers…' Laker, L. Speeding or using phone at wheel should be as socially unacceptable as drink-driving, says roads police chief. inews (15 November 2021): https://inews.co.uk/news/cars-road-accidents-deaths-speeding-phone-drink-driving-police-andy-cox-roadpeace-1298162
2. 'In 2022, 85 people were killed cycling in Great Britain and 376 people were killed while walking.' Department for Transport. *Reported road casualties, Great Britain, provisional results: 2022* (2023): https://www.gov.uk/government/statistics/reported-road-casualties-great-britain-provisional-results-2022/reported-road-casualties-great-britain-provisional-results-2022
3. '…updated collision reports increased the proportion of crashes in which speeding was a factor by three to four times.' Hellen, N. Speeding causes three times as many road deaths as previously thought. *Times* (15 May 2022): https://www.thetimes.co.uk/article/speeding-causes-three-times-as-many-road-deaths-as-previously-thought-8xbvp6doq
4. 'In 2021, with the University of Westminster's Active Travel Academy…' Laker, L. Road Collision Reporting Guidelines (2021): https://www.rc-rg.com/_files/ugd/c05c10_3f73627e43894c8496f379a2b9e84fd3.pdf

8: CYCLING ACROSS CORNWALL WITH A SHRUB

1. '…in perhaps the hardest cycling territory in the UK, 10% of people could commute by bike.' . Lovelace, R., Goodman, A., Aldred, R., Berkoff, N., Abbas, A., & Woodcock, J. The Propensity to Cycle Tool: An open source online system for sustainable transport planning.

Journal of Transport and Land Use, 10(1) (2017): https://doi.org/10
.5198/jtlu.2016.862

2. 'Tourist spend in Cornwall was £970 million in the three years 2016
   to 2018...' *English local authorities ranked by spending of domestic
   holiday tourists from Great Britain between 2016 and 2018, in million
   GBP*. Statista (2020): https://www.statista.com/statistics/582549/most
   -spend-english-cities-by-residents-great-britain-on-holiday/

3. '...the famous Camel Trail, one of the jewels in the NCN's crown,
   quickly became Cornwall's second most popular attraction...'
   Partnership improves the Camel Trail. North Cornwall Matters (12
   June 2003): https://web.archive.org/web/20071023090841/http://www
   .ncdc.gov.uk/media/adobe/north_cornwall_matters.pdf

4. 'It is trumped only by the Eden Project.' Cornwall's 20 most popular
   attractions revealed by visitor figures. Cornwall Live (23 February
   2020): https://www.cornwalllive.com/whats-on/whats-on-news/corn-
   walls-20-most-popular-attractions-3848639

5. 'Each year visitors swell motor traffic by 12%...' The Cornwall Transport
   Plan; Local Transport Plan to 2030 Evidence Base. Cornwall Council
   (2016): https://www.cornwall.gov.uk/planning-and-building-control/
   planning-policy/adopted-plans/

6. '...has begun widening the A30...' A30 Chiverton to Carland Cross.
   National Highways (2020). https://nationalhighways.co.uk/our-roads
   /south-west/a30-chiverton-to-carland-cross/

7. 'In an NH review of evaluations of 80 of its own road projects...'
   Sloman, L., Hopkinson, L. and Taylor, I. *The Impact of Road Projects
   in England*. Campaign to Protect Rural England (2017): https://www
   .cpre.org.uk/wp-content/uploads/2019/11/TfQLZ-ZTheZImpactZofZ
   RoadZProjectsZinZEnglandZ2017.pdf

8. '...boasts it's the biggest builder of cycle routes in Britain.' National
   Highways. *Net zero highways. Our 2030 / 2040 / 2050 plan.* (No date)
   https://nationalhighways.co.uk/netzerohighways/

9. '...confirmed National Highways not only hadn't assessed its own
   existing cycling provision...' Laker, L. National Highways accused
   of 'systemic failure' on cycling provision in England. *Guardian* (27
   July 2023): https://www.theguardian.com/news/2023/jul/27/national
   -highways-accused-of-systemic-failure-on-cycling-provision-in
   -england

10. 'On 11 March 2020, Westminster announced £27.4 billion settlement for NH…' *Road Investment Strategy 2 (RIS2): 2020 to 2025*. Department for Transport (2020): https://www.gov.uk/government/publications/road-investment-strategy-2-ris2-2020-to-2025

11. 'That same year the NCN got *nothing* from the DfT…' Figures from Sustrans (2022).

12. 'Cornwall Council had big plans for their cycle network'. Whitehouse, R. Saints Trails review: Only half new cycle paths in Cornwall to happen. *The Falmouth Packet* (8 January 2023): https://www.falmouth-packet.co.uk/news/23235492.saints-trails-review-half-new-cycle-paths-cornwall-happen/

13. 'An independent review identified…' Whitehouse, R. Review finds that Cornwall Council's Saints Trails project was 'undeliverable'. Cornwall Live (5 January 2023): https://www.cornwalllive.com/news/cornwall-news/review-finds-cornwall-councils-saints-7994631

14. '…in early 2023 the second two years of the NCN's funding settlement were cut…' Sustrans responds to active travel funding cuts in England. Sustrans (10 March 2023): https://www.sustrans.org.uk/our-blog/news/2023/march/sustrans-responds-to-active-travel-funding-cuts-in-england.

15. '…in a footnote to a money-saving announcement about HS2…' Walker, P. Cuts to cycling and walking budget in England 'will cost £2bn in long term'. *Guardian* (20 March 2023): https://www.theguardian.com/news/2023/mar/20/cuts-cycling-walking-budget-england-cost-more-long-term-labour

16. '…ignore the negative climate impact of road-building…' Horton, H. Road-building spree will derail UK's net zero targets, warn campaigners. *Guardian* (12 April 2023): https://www.theguardian.com/environment/2023/apr/12/road-building-spree-will-derail-uks-net-zero-targets-warn-campaigners

17. '…half a million trees, planted by NH…' Heap, T. Half a million trees have died next to one 21-mile stretch of road, National Highways admits. Sky News (18 March 2023) https://news.sky.com/story/half-a-million-trees-have-died-next-to-one-21-mile-stretch-of-road-national-highways-admits-12836768

18. '…new badger setts and tunnels and animal crossing points…' Cornwall road upgrade's crossing off milestones as new A30 route takes shape.

National Highways (2 December 2021): https://nationalhighways.co
.uk/our-roads/south-west-news/cornwall-road-upgrade-s-crossing
-off-milestones-as-new-a30-route-takes-shape/

10: LAKER CLOSE, AND A REUNION OF SORTS, IN SOMERSET

1. 'A few months earlier I'd written an article for the *Guardian*...' Laker, L. New greenfield housing forcing people to use cars, report finds. *Guardian* (7 February 2022): https://www.theguardian.com/society /2022/feb/07/new-greenfield-housing-forcing-people-to-use-cars -report-finds

2. 'An investigation by the campaign group Transport for New Homes (TfNH)...' Transport for New Homes. Building Car Dependency: The tarmac suburbs of the future (2022): https://www.transportfo rnewhomes.org.uk/wp-content/uploads/2022/02/Building-Car -Dependency-2022.pdf

3. 'One role of the government's new cycling and walking delivery body, Active Travel England...' Active Travel England to be consulted on all large planning applications. Active Travel England (2023): https:// www.gov.uk/government/news/active-travel-england-to-be-consulted -on-all-large-planning-applications

4. 'Sometimes councils have tried to intervene without upsetting traffic...' *Local Highway Panels Members' Guide: 11 Quiet Lanes*. Essex Highways (2021): https://www.essexhighways.org/uploads/lhp/mg/11 _ecclhpmembersguidequietlanesb.pdf

5. 'In south-east England, Surrey Council is trialling long-overdue 20mph speed limits' Browne, D. UK first as Surrey plans speed reduction trials on 60mph roads. Local Gov (9 August 2022): https://www .localgov.co.uk/UK-first-as-Surrey-plans-speed-reduction-trials-on -60mph-roads/54651

6. 'In Oxfordshire Sustrans "filtered" a dangerous rural road to through traffic...' Sustrans. Oxfordshire road repurposed to put walking, wheeling and cycling first. (19 June 2023): https://www.sustrans.org.uk/our -blog/news/2023/june/oxfordshire-road-repurposed-to-put-walking -wheeling-and-cycling-first

7. '...there are historical examples of traffic reduction going back to the 1970s and beyond...' Walker, P. Critics of UK low-traffic schemes told

that 25,000 filters already existed. *Guardian* (16 May 2021): https://
www.theguardian.com/environment/2021/may/16/critics-of-uk-low
-traffic-schemes-told-that-25000-filters-already-existed

8. 'With 90% of our landmass rural...' House of Lords Library. Fact file:
Rural economy (27 January 2020): https://lordslibrary.parliament.uk/
fact-file-rural-economy/

9. 'The Active Lives Survey found 11% of people cycled at least once a
week in 2021, up from 10.7% in 2020...' Sport England. *Proportion of
adults who cycle, by purpose, frequency, and local authority, England,
November 2015 to November 2021* (2023): https://assets.publishing
.service.gov.uk/government/uploads/system/uploads/attachment
_data/file/1100942/cw0302.ods

11: PROGRESS AND FLIPPING BORIS THE BIRD

1. 'This was the first of almost a billion pounds of new cycle routes...'
Mayor of London and London Assembly. 'Crossrail for the bike' in
Mayor's £913m cycling plan (2013): https://www.london.gov.uk/press
-releases-4996

2. 'Approximately 13% of Londoners were driving into the centre every
day. Possible. Frequent drivers: who is driving down London's streets?
(2022): https://www.wearepossible.org/latest-news/frequent-drivers
-who-is-driving-down-londons-streets

3. 'At the time 17% of traffic was delivery vehicles...' Mayor of London.
Proportion of London Traffic Made Up Of Deliveries, Mayor's
Question Time (24 February 2022): https://www.london.gov.uk/
who-we-are/what-london-assembly-does/questions-mayor/find-an
-answer/proportion-london-traffic-made-deliveries

4. '...of a whopping 21,000 respondents, 84% supported the schemes.'
Mayor of London and London Assembly. Mayor joins the diggers on
'Crossrail' Cycle Superhighways (10 March 2015): https://www.london
.gov.uk/press-releases/mayoral/mayor-joins-the-diggers-on-cycle
-superhighways

5. 'Soon they were moving 46% of people in just 30% of the road space...'
Transport for London. Update on the implementation of the Quietways
and Cycle Superhighways programmes (2016): https://content.tfl.gov
.uk/pic-161130-07-cycle-quietways.pdf

6. 'Within five years it had carried an estimated 11 million cycle journeys...' London Cycleway C3/CS3's Crowdsourced Count (April
2023): https://twitter.com/CS3Count/status/1644029731900104728

7. '26% of staff working in Westminster now cycle, walk or jog to work...'
Laker, L. A quarter of Parliamentary staff plan to travel actively, survey
finds. Cycling Industry News (8 September 2023): https://cyclingin-
dustry.news/a-quarter-of-parliamentary-staff-plan-to-travel-actively
-survey-finds/

8. 'changed the face of London.' Laker, L. Audio. We've changed the
face of the city. Road.cc (2016): https://road.cc/content/news/188966
-audio-weve-changed-face-city

9. '....cycling in outer London areas that received investment increased
by 18% and walking 13%...' Transport for London. Getting more people
walking and cycling could help save our high streets (2018): https://tfl
.gov.uk/info-for/media/press-releases/2018/november/getting-more
-people-walking-and-cycling-could-help-save-our-high-streets

10. 'London's subsequent mayor, Sadiq Khan, expanded that early
network...' Mayor of London and London Assembly. Record-breaking
growth in London's cycle network continues (2021): https://www
.london.gov.uk/press-releases/mayoral/mayor-and-tfl-announce
-work-on-four-new-routes

11. '...and the Bow Roundabout part-way along it...' BBC. Bow roundabout 'cannot be made safe' – TfL (2 April 2012): https://www.bbc.co.uk
/news/uk-england-london-17618659

12. '...certified death traps for cycling...' BBC. Mayor urged to prevent
more cycle superhighway deaths (22 October 2013): https://www.bbc
.co.uk/news/uk-england-london-24625018

13. '...funded emergency pop-up lanes and LTNs...' Department for
Transport, Office for Zero Emission Vehicles, Office for Low Emission
Vehicles and Shapps, G. £2 billion package to create new era for cycling
and walking (2020): https://www.gov.uk/government/news/2-billion
-package-to-create-new-era-for-cycling-and-walking

14. '...the proportion of children driven to school had trebled in 40 years...'
Department for Transport. Gear Change: A bold vision for cycling and
walking. (July 2020): https://assets.publishing.service.gov.uk/govern-
ment/uploads/system/uploads/attachment_data/file/904146/gear
-change-a-bold-vision-for-cycling-and-walking.pdf

12: CHRIS BOARDMAN, CHESTER AND THE 'LEAST SHIT OPTION'

1. '...Chester's first 'home zone', installed in 2004...' Cheshire Live. City's homes are in the zone (2004): https://www.cheshire-live.co.uk/news/chester-cheshire-news/citys-homes-zone-5291329

2. 'In 2020, cycling rose 46%...' Department for Transport. *Impact of the coronavirus pandemic on walking and cycling statistics, England: 2020* (2021): https://www.gov.uk/government/statistics/walking-and-cycling-statistics-england-2020/the-impact-of-the-coronavirus-pandemic-on-walking-and-cycling-statistics-england-2020

3. '...some were pulled out at the first whiff of dissent...' Wall, T. Get on your bike? Not if some Tory councils have their way. *Guardian* (27 March 2022): https://www.theguardian.com/politics/2022/mar/27/get-on-your-bike-not-if-some-tory-councils-have-their-way

4. '...sometimes after complaints from MPs themselves.' McIntyre, N. English councils backpedal on cycling schemes after Tory backlash. *Guardian* (15 July 2020): https://www.theguardian.com/world/2020/jul/15/english-councils-backpedal-on-cycling-schemes-after-tory-backlash

5. '...vandalised and even set alight...' Pal, A. LTN planters overturned and set on fire by vandals on the first day of trial. Road.cc (2023): https://road.cc/content/news/planters-overturned-and-set-fire-300165

6. 'Between two thirds...' IPSOS. New survey shows public back action to encourage cycling and public transport but remain attached to their cars (2020): https://www.ipsos.com/en-uk/new-survey-shows-public-back-action-encourage-cycling-and-public-transport-remain-attached-their

7. '...and four fifths of people support this agenda...' Department for Transport. *£175 million more for cycling and walking as research shows public support* (2020): https://www.gov.uk/government/news/175-million-more-for-cycling-and-walking-as-research-shows-public-support

8. '...the city had reached its target of 35% of all journeys being cycled – 13 years ahead of time...' Reid, C. How a Belgian port city inspired Birmingham's car-free ambitions. *Guardian* (20 January 2020): https://www.theguardian.com/environment/2020/jan/20/how-a-belgian-port-city-inspired-birminghams-car-free-ambitions

9. '...saw a 200% increase in cycling in one year...' Greater Manchester Combined Authority. Greater Manchester Walking and Cycling Progress Report (2020): https://democracy.manchester.gov.uk/mgConvert2PDF.aspx?ID=20371

13: GUNG-HO HAND-CYCLING

1. 'According to Lambeth council...' Lambeth Council. Streatham Hill Low Traffic Neighbourhood (2021): https://www.lambeth.gov.uk/streets-roads-transport/low-traffic-neighbourhoods-o/streatham-hill -low-traffic-neighbourhood
2. 'Analysis of 50 boundary roads across 12 LTNs installed between 2020 and 2022...' Department for Transport. *Gear Change: One Year On* (2021). https://assets.publishing.service.gov.uk/government/uploads/system/uploads/attachment_data/file/1007815/gear-change-one-year -on.pdf
3. 'Concerns about traffic being displaced onto other roads are under-standable...' Thomas, A. and Aldred, R. Changes in motor traffic inside London's LTNs and on boundary roads. Possible (2023): https://smarttransportpub.blob.core.windows.net/web/1/root/changes-in-motor-traffic-inside-londons-ltns-and-on-boundary -roads.pdf
4. '...reports and research with national and international reach...' Wheels for Wellbeing. Guide to Inclusive Cycling (2020): https://wheelsforwellbeing.org.uk/campaigning/guide/
5. 'The charity's national survey, published in 2021...' Wheels for Wellbeing. *Disability & Cycling, Report of 2021*. National Survey Results (2021): https://wheelsforwellbeing.org.uk/wp-content/uploads/2022/05/Disability-and-Cycling-Report-of-2021-national -survey-results.pdf
6. '...Sustrans identified 831 miles of routes that were unsuitable for a narrow-tyred hybrid bike to pass comfortably.' Sustrans. *Paths for everyone: Sustrans' review of the National Cycle Network 2018* (2018): https://www.sustrans.org.uk/media/2804/paths_for_everyone_ncn _review_report_2018.pdf
7. '...research shows physical activity can cut depression rates by 30%.' Wolf S., Seiffer B., Zeibig J.M., Welkerling J., Brokmeier L., Atrott

B., Ehring T. and Schuch F.B. Is Physical Activity Associated with Less Depression and Anxiety During the COVID-19 Pandemic? A Rapid Systematic Review. *Sports Medicine*, 51(8), 1771-1783 (2021): doi:10.1007/s40279-021-01468-z

8. 'The design standards for most of the above already exist...' Department for Transport. Cycle infrastructure design (LTN 1/20) (2020): https://www.gov.uk/government/publications/cycle-infrastructure-design-ltn-120

15: THANK GOODNESS FOR WALES

1. '...tarmacked thanks to lobbying from cyclists.' Reid, C., *Roads Were Not Built for Cars*. (Front Page Creations, 2015).

2. '...abruptly replacing three lanes of almost constant traffic with 240 al fresco dining spaces.' BBC. Cardiff's Castle Street has been turned into an al fresco dining area (30 July 2020): https://www.bbc.co.uk/news/av/uk-wales-53583018

3. 'However, in a consultation 53.8% of people wanted it reopened to traffic.' BBC. Covid: Castle Street, Cardiff, reopens after pandemic closure (31 October 2021): https://www.bbc.co.uk/news/uk-wales-59090663

4. 'They weathered cries it would ruin trade...' Wales Online. Latest plans to change Wellfield Road in Cardiff unveiled – and here's how local businesses reacted (2020): https://www.walesonline.co.uk/news/wales-news/wellfield-road-cardiff-shopping-roath-19025847

5. 'Research from cities like New York and London has shown improving pedestrian and cycle space can boost retail spend'. Transport for London. Walking & Cycling: the economic benefits (2018): https://content.tfl.gov.uk/walking-cycling-economic-benefits-summary-pack.pdf

6. '...research repeatedly shows business owners overestimate the proportion of car-borne visitors...' von Schneidemesser, D. et al. Local Business Perception vs. Mobility Behavior of Shoppers: A Survey from Berlin. Transport Findings (2021): https://findingspress.org/article/24497-local-business-perception-vs-mobility-behavior-of-shoppers-a-survey-from-berlin

7. '...with a safe route every 250m or so in central areas, meeting Welsh legislation requirements...' Welsh Government. Active Travel Act

Guidance (2021): https://www.gov.wales/sites/default/files/publications/2022-01/active-travel-act-guidance.pdf

8. '...continuous and cohesive, linking all key destinations within the locality as a complete journey so that cyclists can travel seamlessly on good quality infrastructure...' Ibid.

9. '...small areas dug out from parking bays, remove an estimated 9.5 cubic miles of surface run-off from Cardiff's combined sewer system.' Susdrain. Greener Grangetown, Cardiff, Case Study (2019): https://www.susdrain.org/case-studies/pdfs/greener_grangetown_case_study_lightv2.pdf

10. 'By 2016 the mapping work was done...' Laker, L. Wales gives cyclists legal right to propose new bike routes. *Guardian* (6 September 2016): https://www.theguardian.com/environment/bike-blog/2016/sep/06/wales-gives-cyclists-legal-right-to-propose-new-bike-routes

11. 'Wales' Active Travel Board (ATB) acknowledged that local authorities had been given a mammoth task...' Welsh Government. Cross Party Group on the Active Travel Act – Review of the Active Travel (Wales) Act 2013 (2022): https://www.dropbox.com/s/xyflnxnr9tsa5x2/Active%20Travel%20Act%20Review%20Report%20Final%20June%202022.pdf?dl=0

12. 'Health was, at the time, 48% of the Welsh government's total budget...' Laker, L. Wales gives cyclists legal right to propose new bike routes. *Guardian* (6 September 2016): https://www.theguardian.com/environment/bike-blog/2016/sep/06/wales-gives-cyclists-legal-right-to-propose-new-bike-routes

13. 'With cars accounting for 55% of Wales' transport emissions...' Welsh Government. Transport: Sector Emission Pathway (2019): https://www.gov.wales/sites/default/files/publications/2019-06/transport-sector-emission-pathway-factsheet.pdf

14. 'Its new appraisal tool includes social and environmental factors...' Welsh Government. Welsh transport appraisal guidance (WelTAG) (2021): https://www.gov.wales/welsh-transport-appraisal-guidance-weltag

15. '...cycling and walking funding ramped up from £12 million in 2016.' Welsh Government. Active Travel Annual Report 2016/17 (2017): https://www.gov.wales/sites/default/files/publications/2017-10/active-travel-annual-report-2017.pdf

16. '...to £70 million in 2022 – an almost 600% increase. This translates to more than £22 per person per year... more than the £1 per head in England...' Welsh Government. Welsh Government celebrates Clean Air Day with £58m boost for active travel (2023): https://www.gov .wales/welsh-government-celebrates-clean-air-day-58m-boost-active -travel

17. '...although less than Scotland's £58 per head.' Transport Scotland. Funding boost for walking, wheeling and cycling (2020): https://www .transport.gov.scot/news/funding-boost-for-walking-wheeling-and -cycling/

18. 'In November 2020 the Welsh government's Burns Commission produced a report...' Senedd Research. 'A network of alternatives' to the M4 relief road? – Burns Commission publishes its final recommendations (2020): https://research.senedd.wales/research-articles/a -network-of-alternatives-to-the-m4-relief-road-burns-commission -publishes-its-final-recommendations

19. '...cycle routes can expand the catchment area of public transport interchanges'. van Mil, J.F.P., Leferink, T.S., Annema, J.A. et al. Insights into factors affecting the combined bicycle-transit mode. *Public Transport*, 13, 649–673 (2021): https://link.springer.com/article/10.1007/s12469 -020-00240-2

20. 'Belgium has developed some of its growing network of cycleways using rail-side land'. Bicycle Highways. Overview bicycle highways (2023): https://fietssnelwegen.be/fietssnelwegen

21. 'Surrounding Copenhagen in Denmark is a network of 120 miles of cycle routes...' Office for Cycle Superhighways. Cycle Superhighway Bicycle Account (2019): https://supercykelstier.dk/wp-content/ uploads/2016/03/Cycle-Superhighway-Bicycle-Account-2020.pdf

22. 'They had become "one of the most profitable infrastructure investments in Denmark" in socioeconomic terms'. Office for Cycle Superhighways, (2019). Cycle Superhighway Bicycle Account 2019, from https://supercykelstier.dk/wp-content/uploads/2016/03/Cycle -Superhighway-Bicycle-Account-2020.pdf

16: LAKER IN THE LAKES

1. '...Wordsworth...was among those who railed against the arrival of steam trains...' Defining Moment: Wordsworth embraces 'Nimby-ism',

October 16 1844. *Financial Times* (2010): https://www.ft.com/content/8f7680ca-3584-11df-963f-00144feabdco

2. 'Today, more than 85% of the roughly 20 million annual visitors bring their own vehicles...' Lake District National Park Partnerships Management Plan 2020-2025 (2021): https://www.lakedistrict.gov.uk/caringfor/lake-district-national-park-partnership/management-plan/sustainable-travel-and-transport

3. 'In Kendal, a key hub for tourism and jobs, 40% of commutes are less than three miles...' Cumbria County Council. Kendal Local Cycling and Walking Infrastructure Plan. (LCWIP) 2022–2037 (2021): https://councilportal.cumbria.gov.uk/documents/s121713/Appendix%201%20SLLC%2022.3.22%20KENDAL%20LOCAL%20CYCLING%20AND%20WALKING%20INFRASTRUCTURE%20PLAN.pdf

4. '...ebikes could solve those problems...' Philips, I., Anable, J. and Chatterton, T. e-bike carbon savings – how much and where? CREDS Policy brief 011. Centre for Research into Energy Demand Solutions: Oxford (2020): https://www.creds.ac.uk/publications/e-bike-carbon-savings-how-much-and-where/

5. 'the debate quickly goes national...' BBC. Hundreds oppose Lake District path asphalt plan (7 August 2019): https://www.bbc.co.uk/news/uk-england-cumbria-49268888

6. '...turning the Lakes into a theme park...' Parveen, N. Lake District authority accused of turning region into 'theme park'. *Guardian* (13 October 2019): https://www.theguardian.com/uk-news/2019/oct/13/lake-district-authority-loses-no-confidence-vote-over-path-decision

7. 'In 2014 it stopped subsidising bus services...' BBC. Cuts to Cumbria bus subsidies and fire engines modified (14 February 2014): https://www.bbc.co.uk/news/uk-england-cumbria-26181881

8. '...the DfT and NH admitted its planned £1.49bn splurge on widening the A66 represented "poor value for money"...' Department for Transport. A66 Northern Trans-Pennine project accounting officer assessment (October 2022) (2023): https://www.gov.uk/government/publications/government-major-projects-portfolio-accounting-officer-assessments/a66-northern-trans-pennine-project-accounting-officer-assessment-october-2022#accounting-officers-conclusion

9. 'In fact, analysis by the Transport Action Network found £16 billion of our roadbuilding projects represented poor or low value for money...'

Transport Action Network. Scrap road schemes to grow the economy (2022): https://transportactionnetwork.org.uk/scrap-road-schemes-to-grow-the-economy/

10. On a topographical map the Lakes are bordered by mountain, marsh and sea – the [Scottish] border hills, the Pennines, the Solway and Morecambe Bay. Nicholson, N. *Lakers, The Adventures of the First Tourists*. Robert Hale Ltd (1955).

11. '…great coaches of travellers would take the short cut, traversing the sands and sometimes getting bogged down under their sheer weight…' Ibid.

12. 'According to a 2019 analysis, an e-bike grant in the UK could be more than twice as effective at cutting CO_2…' Newson, C. and Sloman, L. *The Case for a UK Incentive for E-bikes*. Bicycle Association (2019): https://www.bicycleassociation.org.uk/wp-content/uploads/2019/07/The-Case-for-a-UK-Incentive-for-E-bikes-FINAL.pdf

13. 'Research by the University of Leeds found ebikes could cut England's transport emissions by half.' Philips, I., Anable, J. and Chatterton, T. e-bike carbon savings – how much and where? CREDS Policy brief 011. Centre for Research into Energy Demand Solutions. Oxford (2020): https://www.creds.ac.uk/publications/e-bike-carbon-savings-how-much-and-where/

17: CALEDONIAN PEOPLE POWER

1. 'In 2018 the Scottish government doubled its active travel spending to £80 million.' Transport Scotland. Active Travel Task Force Report (2018): https://www.transport.gov.scot/media/42284/active-travel-task-force-june-2018.pdf

2. '…by 2024 10% of Scotland's devolved transport spend will go to cycling and walking…' Transport Scotland. Funding boost for walking, wheeling and cycling (2023): https://www.transport.gov.scot/news/funding-boost-for-walking-wheeling-and-cycling/

3. There's also, rather boldly, the target to cut car journeys by 20% by 2030.' Transport Scotland. Reducing car use for a healthier, fairer and greener Scotland (2022): https://www.transport.gov.scot/media/50872/a-route-map-to-achieve-a-20-per-cent-reduction-in-car-kms-by-2030.pdf

4. '…the NCN is worth £345m in cycle tourism and leisure cycling alone…' Brophy, M., Kummerer, M. and Wray, E. *The value of cycling*

to the Scottish economy: Report for Cycling Scotland (2018): https://www.cycling.scot/mediaLibrary/other/english/2548.pdf

5. '...part of a wider £8.8m project with Sustrans, Scottish Canals and Glasgow City Council, connecting the Panmure Gate and Woodside communities'. Scott Lamand. Glasgow's new nature reserve opens its doors (2021): https://www.scottishcanals.co.uk/news/glasgows-new-nature-reserve-opens-its-doors

6. 'MP Fabian Hamilton put it in a meeting of the All-Party Parliamentary Group for Walking and Cycling...' Norman, J. All Party Parliamentary Group for Walking and Cycling (2023): https://allpartycycling.org/2023/02/02/jesse-norman/

7. 'Tourist spots in Europe saw up to 200% increases in cycle tourism during the pandemic...' *Cycling Industry News*. Economies benefit as cycle tourism sets records in European countries (2020): https://cyclingindustry.news/economies-benefit-as-cycle-tourism-sets-records-in-european-countries/

8. '32% of holidaying cyclists use trains...' European Cyclists' Federation. Cycle-tourism combined with train: How did it go this Summer? (2020): https://ecf.com/news-and-events/news/cycle-tourism-combined-train-how-did-it-go-summer

18: THE DREAM TEAM

1. The people currently cycling on Britain's roads only give the impression you do, because they're the sporty, confident, often wealthier ones...' Steinbach, R., Green, J., Datta, J., Edwards, P. Cycling and the city: A case study of how gendered, ethnic and class identities can shape healthy transport choices. *Social Science & Medicine*, Volume 72, Issue 7. (2011): https://www.sciencedirect.com/science/article/pii/S0277953611000785

2. 'Active travel academic, Professor Rachel Aldred, points out women are less willing to share with traffic...' Aldred, R. Culture, equity and cycle infrastructure (2015): http://rachelaldred.org/writing/culture-equity-and-cycle-infrastructure/

4. '...around the world the proportions of women cycling grew in response to a drop in traffic and billions of pounds' investment in cycling.' Laker, L. Europe doubles down on cycling in post-Covid recovery plans. *Guardian* (12 March 2021): https://www.theguardian.com/lifeandstyle/2021/mar/12/europe-cycling-post-covid-recovery-plans

5. 'In 2018 women's sport was 4–10% of coverage...' Women in Sport. Research Report: *Where are all the Women? Shining a light on the visibility of women's sport in the media* (2018): https://womeninsport.org/resource/where-are-all-the-women/

6. '...though by 2022 it had risen to 15%, according to one analysis' Women's Sport Trust. Record-breaking figures for women's sport viewership in 2022 (2022): https://www.womenssporttrust.com/record-breaking-figures-for-womens-sport-viewership-in-2022/

7. 'There was a plan back in 2017 for a protected cycle route along the main road through Aviemore...' Merrit, M., Strathspey and Badenoch Herald. Bill could be £17m for bike-friendly Aviemore (2018): https://www.strathspey-herald.co.uk/news/bill-could-be-17m-for-bike-friendly-aviemore-133010/

20: THIS PATH GOES ALL THE WAY TO LIVERPOOL

1. 'Just 35% of women consider local cycling safety good, according to Sustrans research...' Sustrans. Walking and Cycling Index 2021 (2022): https://www.sustrans.org.uk/media/10527/sustrans-2021-walking-and-cycling-index-aggregated-report.pdf

2. 'For the first time, in 2022 more than half of TPT users were women...' TPT National Team. TPT visitor survey (2022): https://www.transpenninetrail.org.uk/wp-content/uploads/2022/10/TPT-Visitor-Survey-2022-Report.pdf

21: Going full circle

1. 'According to the council, 61% of car journeys stay within the district, an area of just 458 square miles and less than 30 miles in length.' Mumby, D. 14 cycle routes in Mendip could be upgraded. Somerset Live (2020): https://www.somersetlive.co.uk/news/somerset-news/14-cycle-routes-mendip-could-4190036

2. '...part of the Somerset Circle on the NCN in Clevedon, a rare town-centre bike lane installed in late 2022, became the subject of a bizarre string of negative news headlines.' Sanders, T. Town's new road markings look like they've been painted for drink drivers. *Metro* (2023): https://metro.co.uk/2023/01/10/somerset-wiggly-road-lines-make-clevedon-like-balamory-from-hell-18072626/

22: THEY TAKE US BECAUSE WE NEED TO GO

1. 'Across Europe in 2020, in response to the pandemic, €1 billion went into cycling measures...' Laker, L. Europe doubles down on cycling in post-Covid recovery plans, *Guardian* (12 March 2021): https://www.theguardian.com/lifeandstyle/2021/mar/12/europe-cycling-post-covid-recovery-plans

2. '...by the end of 2022 Flanders had exceeded its original target, before more than doubling it to 1250 miles.' Van der Merwe, D. Flanders surpasses target of 1000km of new cycle paths, *Brussels Times* (2022): https://www.brusselstimes.com/339994/flanders-target-of-1000-kilometres-of-additional-cycle-paths-reached

3. 'In the process the biggest cycling investment in the history of Belgium...': https://www.facebook.com/watch/?v=494829682356620

4. '...20 minutes of exercise per day cuts the risk of developing depression by 31%...' *Gear Change: A bold vision for cycling and walking.* Department for Transport (July 2020): https://assets.publishing.service.gov.uk/government/uploads/system/uploads/attachment_data/file/904146/gear-change-a-bold-vision-for-cycling-and-walking.pdf

5. 'Unmitigated climate change costs 5–20% of GDP a year and growing...' The cost of inaction: Recognising the value at risk from climate change. *The Economist* and AXA (2021): https://www.cisl.cam.ac.uk/system/files/documents/eiu-aviva-economic-cost-of-inaction.pdf

6. 'Plans for a cycleway around HS2, the best value element of the entire project and the only benefit local communities will see...' Laker, L. Scrapped HS2 bike path 'five times better value than HS2 itself'. *Guardian* (1 February 2019): https://www.theguardian.com/environment/bike-blog/2019/feb/01/scrapped-hs2-bike-path-could-have-reaped-five-times-more-than-hs2-itself

CODA

1. 'In early 2024, a report by the Institute for Public Policy Resarch...': Singer Hobbs, M., and Frost, S. Stride and Ride; England's path from laggard to leader in walking, wheeling and cycling. Institute of Public Policy Research (2024): https://www.ippr.org/articles/stride-and-ride

ACKNOWLEDGEMENTS

Thank you to everyone who helped make this book possible – those who joined me on the cycle routes and roads, gave me a place to stay, answered my emails and calls, talked through ideas and sense-checked my work and workings – or simply inspired me along the miles, and the words that came from them. I have borrowed from so many people's expertise, energy and ideas, which were generously given. This includes, but is not limited to: Richard Ackroyd; Professor Rachel Aldred; Shgufta Anwar; Immy Ashby; Hamish Belding; Chris Boardman; Ned Boulting; Adam Bronkhorst; Ben Broomfield; Aleksander Buczyński; Kunal Buxani; Ruth Cadbury; Adrianne Calsy; Mahnoor Campbell; Emily Chappell; Jim Chisholm; Adam Clarke; Isabelle Clement and everyone at Wheels for Wellbeing; Andy, Dave, Douglas and Rosemary Cox; Lee Craigie; Lydia Crimp; Chris Curling; Agathe Daudibon; Roxanne De Beaux; Brian Deegan; Duncan Dollimore; Elizabeth Fielding; Carol Freeman; Peter Frost-Pennington; Steve Gash; Roger Geffen; Sophie Gordon; David Gray; Greg and Norton; John Grimshaw; Peter Huxford; Natasha Hirst; Caspar Hughes; Philip Insall; Phil Jones; Sam Jones; Peter Knowles; Ele Laker; The Jim Laker Fund; Ciara Lee; Caroline Levett; Kirsty McCaskill-Baxter; Aneela McKenna; Emma Moody; Louise Nolan; Mark Philpotts; Jonathan Powell; Rebecca, Tom, Theo and Isabel Ravenscroft; Chris Roberts; Andy Salkeld; Selaine Saxby; Jess Shankleman; Mick Shaw; Malcolm Shepherd; Colin Simpson; Lynn Sloman; Shane Snow; Beccy Smart; Isobel Stoddart; Mark Strong; Izzy Styles; Simon Talbot-Ponsonby; Nick Tebbutt; Tom Tibbits; Chris Tomlin; Adam Tranter; Dafydd Trystan; Sjors van Duren; Szilvia Varnai; Jools Walker; Claire Webb; Nicole Wheatley; Yasmin Yildirim.

Thank you to the wonderful staff and volunteers at Sustrans, Sustrans Cymru, Sustrans Northern Ireland and Sustrans Scotland for making time for me, organising meetups and ride-alongs, answering endless questions and providing me with honest answers, particularly: Alexa Bingham, Sarah Bradbury, Caroline Bloomfield, Christine Boston, Xavier Brice, Paul Bruffell, James Cleeton, Rosslyn Colderley, Sally Copley, Claire Daly, Kate Dobson, Neil and Wendy Hutson, Alex Johnston, Ryland Jones, Sarah Leeming, Michael Melton, Jonah Morris, Simon Murray, Ed Plowden, Simon Pratt, Sarah Roe, Dave Shuttle, Matt Webster and Sam Wood.

Thanks to those who helped me and Lily the mighty pink ebike (and other bikes) out of some sticky situations along the way, including Ben Cooper at Kinetics; BikeSeven cycle shop, Carlisle; Dales Cycles, Glasgow; Rob Howes, formerly of the Green Commute Initiative; Saint Piran Service Course, Redruth; Tower Park Camping, St Buryan, Penzance; the folks at Trainline; and at Wisper bikes, for keeping Lily on the road, even though she was asked to do far more, in rather more challenging circumstances, than she was probably intended for.

Thank you to Charlotte Croft, Megan Jones and everyone at Bloomsbury for helping make this book far better than it might otherwise have been, for patiently challenging and carefully checking my work and for believing in this book from the start; thank you to my agent David Luxton for his encouragement and support along the way.